A HISTORICAL GUIDE TO
Mark Twain

HISTORICAL GUIDES
TO AMERICAN AUTHORS

The Historical Guides to American Authors is an interdisciplinary, historically sensitive series that combines close attention to the United States' most widely read and studied authors with a strong sense of time, place, and history. Placing each writer in the context of the vibrant relationship between literature and society, volumes in this series contain historical essays written on subjects of contemporary social, political, and cultural relevance. Each volume also includes a capsule biography and illustrated chronology detailing important cultural events as they coincided with the author's life and works, while photographs and illustrations dating from the period capture the flavor of the author's time and social milieu. Equally accessible to students of literature and of life, the volumes offer a complete and rounded picture of each author in his or her America.

A Historical Guide to Ernest Hemingway
Edited by Linda Wagner-Martin

A Historical Guide to Walt Whitman
Edited by David S. Reynolds

A Historical Guide to Ralph Waldo Emerson
Edited by Joel Myerson

A Historical Guide to Henry David Thoreau
Edited by William E. Cain

A Historical Guide to Edgar Allan Poe
Edited by J. Gerald Kennedy

A Historical Guide to Nathaniel Hawthorne
Edited by Larry Reynolds

A Historical Guide to Mark Twain
Edited by Shelley Fisher Fishkin

A
Historical Guide
to Mark Twain

EDITED BY
SHELLEY FISHER FISHKIN

OXFORD
UNIVERSITY PRESS
2002

OXFORD
UNIVERSITY PRESS

Oxford   New York

Auckland   Bangkok   Buenos Aires   Cape Town   Chennai
Dar es Salaam   Delhi   Hong Kong   Istanbul   Karachi   Kolkata
Kuala Lumpur   Madrid   Melbourne   Mexico City   Mumbai   Nairobi
Sao Paulo   Shanghai   Singapore   Taipei   Tokyo   Toronto

and an associated company in Berlin

Copyright © 2002 by Oxford University Press, Inc.

Published by Oxford University Press, Inc.
198 Madison Avenue, New York, New York 10016

www.oup.com

Oxford is a registered trademark of Oxford University Press

Library of Congress Cataloging-in-Publication Data
A historical guide to Mark Twain / edited by Shelley Fisher Fishkin.
p.   cm.—(Historical guides to American authors)
Includes bibliographical references and index.
ISBN 0-19-513292-0; ISBN 0-19-513293-9 (pbk.)
1. Twain, Mark, 1835–1910—Knowledge—History.
2. Twain, Mark, 1835–1910—Political and social views.
3. Literature and history—United States—History—19th century.
4. Literature and society—United States—History—19th century
I. Fishkin, Shelley Fisher.   II. Series.
PS1342.H5 H57 2002
818'.409—dc21   2001055962

1 3 5 7 9 8 6 4 2

Printed in the United States of America
on acid-free paper

"Always do right. This will gratify
some people & astonish the rest."
—Mark Twain

*In memory of my father, Milton Fisher,
who gratified and astonished daily*

Contents

A HISTORICAL GUIDE TO
Mark Twain

Introduction

Shelley Fisher Fishkin

On July 3, 1907, George Bernard Shaw wrote Samuel Clemens that "the future historian of America will find your works as indispensable to him as a French historian finds the political tracts of Voltaire."[1] Shaw's insight was remarkably prescient. For more than a century, Twain's work has been quoted, valued, cited, mined, and invoked as much for what it illuminates about the cultural conversation as for what it contributed to that conversation itself.

Why has the work of this imaginative writer provided generations with such rich insight into his country's zeitgeist? Twain himself suggests one answer to this question when he observes that "almost the whole capital of the [native] novelist is the slow accumulation of unconscious observation—absorption."[2] Knowledge of a nation's "soul, its life, its speech, its thought," Twain wrote, ". . . is acquirable only one way . . ." by

> years and years of unconscious *absorption*; years and years of intercourse with the life concerned; of living it, indeed; sharing personally in its shames and prides, its joys and griefs, its loves and hates, its prosperities and reverses, its shows and shabbiness, its deep patriotisms, its whirlwinds of political

passion, its adorations—of flag, and heroic deed, and the glory of the national name.[3]

Twain made these comments in the context of explaining why a French writer named Paul Bourget, who purported to explain America to Americans and the world, would never be able to get it right. Twain's argument might seem to suggest that not only any native novelist, but also any native, period, would have a leg up on any Frenchman when it came to probing what made America tick. But few if any of Twain's contemporaries have come to play the role George Bernard Shaw foresaw for Twain. What makes Twain so special in this regard?

Perhaps it was a lesson he learned on the river. "How easily and comfortably the pilot's memory does its work; how placidly effortless is its way; how *unconsciously* it lays up its vast stores, hour by hour, day by day"[4] On a given trip, the pilot takes part in conversations going on around him while the leadsman drones an endless string of "half twains" into which a lone "quarter twain" call is interjected.

> Two or three weeks later that pilot can describe with precision the boat's position on the river when that quarter twain was uttered, and give you such a lot of head-marks, stern-marks, and side-marks to guide you, that you ought to be able to take the boat there and put her in that same spot again yourself! The cry of "quarter twain" did not really take his mind from the talk, but his trained faculties instantly photographed the bearings, noted the change in depth, and laid up the important details for future reference without requiring any assistance from him in the matter.[5]

"Astonishing things can be done with the human memory," Twain wrote, "if you will devote it faithfully to one particular line of business."[6]

There are clear resonances between the native novelist laying up capital through "unconscious observation—absorption" and the riverboat pilot's memory "*unconsciously* laying up its vast stores," "[laying] up the important details for future reference."

The "particular line of business" to which the pilot's memory is devoted is, of course, piloting, while the "particular line of business" of the writer is writing. But to be successful both pilot and writer must train their memories to "instantly [photograph]" the subtle tints and textures and timbres of their world. Twain learned to master the art of unconscious absorption on the river and later transferred that art to the printed page. Genius aside, his works are remarkable windows on his world, as a result.

But what was Twain unconsciously absorbing during all those years? What were the big pictures, whose "details" his memory subliminally "laid up," whose "bearings" his "trained faculties" unconsciously "photographed . . . for further reference"? What, in short, were some of the historical contexts that inform Mark Twain's work? These questions are the focus of *A Historical Guide to Mark Twain*.

During Twain's lifetime, from 1835 to 1910, the nation underwent a series of tumultuous social, cultural, political, and technological transformations, as the dual chronology in this volume reminds us. Born three years before transatlantic steamship service between America and Europe began and two years before Queen Victoria ascended to the throne, Sam Clemens would eventually immortalize perhaps the most famous transatlantic steamship journey from the New World to the Old (in *The Innocents Abroad*) and would build one of the most celebrated Victorian homes in the country in Hartford. Born into a slave-holding family, he would live to see slavery abolished and former slaves guaranteed citizenship and equal protection under the law; he would also watch (with "unconscious absorption," as well as a fair measure of conscious anger) as the nation incrementally reneged on its promises of post-war freedom and justice for African Americans. Twain began writing *Huckleberry Finn* during the summer of the centennial of the Declaration of Independence, and he published *Pudd'nhead Wilson*, a complex satire on the meaning of race, the year before W.E.B. Du Bois became the first African American to receive a Harvard Ph.D. The typewriter and dynamite were invented the year Twain published his first book. During his lifetime, great fortunes were made, great business enterprises were consolidated, and great poverty and exploitation led armies of exhausted industrial workers to call a record number of strikes. There were major changes in widely held attitudes toward religion, commerce, race, gender, class, and America's role in the world. Virtually every upheaval in his world touched Twain's life, and much of what touched his life made it into his work. *A Historical Guide to Mark Twain* explores the ways in which his writing reflected, challenged, revised, endorsed, assented to, or rejected trends in his society during this intriguing and complex period in American history. The historical essays in this volume are designed to give the reader a sense of the social and cultural milieu that helped make Sam Clemens—and Mark Twain—who he was.

Sam Clemens/Mark Twain. What do we call him? And who was he? A human being who piloted riverboats and prospected for silver and married and had children and laughed and smoked and ate and drank and hosted parties? Or a fictitious creation of that living, breathing human being who purportedly wrote books? When one interviewed the living-breathing-human being, was it the fictive persona who was giving the answers or the man behind it? Or were they ultimately the same—or possibly too close to disentangle? Such questions make writing a "biographical sketch" of "Mark Twain" a balancing act requiring intrepid ingenuity—which is precisely what Forrest Robinson offers us in his essay, "Mark Twain: A Brief Biography."

The basic facts of Sam Clemens's life are well known. Born in 1835 in the small town of Florida, Missouri, he moved to Hannibal, Missouri, in 1839 and began school there the following year. Declining fortunes forced the family to give up their home and move in with a local pharmacist, supplying meals in exchange for rent in 1846. In 1847, his father died, and twelve-year-old Sam began taking odd jobs in local stores and newspaper offices. He continued working for newspapers for the next several years, occasionally publishing short squibs under his own name and various inventive pseudonyms. He left Hannibal in 1853 to work as a journeyman printer for the next two years in St. Louis, New York, Philadelphia, Washington, D.C., and other cities. He spent two years learning the river and becoming a riverboat pilot, but his career on the river was ended by the Civil War. He spent two weeks as an irregular in the Missouri State Guard, and then set out for the Nevada Territory with his brother. Although he failed as a prospector, he succeeded as a journalist, adopting the pen name of "Mark Twain" in 1863. He left Nevada for San Francisco in 1864, where he worked on several newspapers and got his first taste of national fame when his "Jumping Frog" story was published. He visited Hawaii as a newspaper correspondent, enjoyed some success as a lecturer, and traveled to Europe on the *Quaker City*, paying his way with articles about the trip published in papers back home. He courted Olivia Langdon of Elmira, New York, and published *Innocents Abroad* in 1869, to great popular acclaim. He married, started a family, and began writing the books for which he is best known today. He built the family a mansion in Hartford, where he entertained lavishly, and invested in a range of promising new technologies, most notably, the Paige typesetter. Financial problems forced him to close the house and relocate the family to Europe in the early 1890s. Later in that decade, he would pull himself out of bankruptcy by embarking on a world lecture tour that took him to Africa and Asia. As the nineteenth century ended and the twentieth century began, he condemned his country—and several European powers—for the imperialist adventures they had pursued around the world. The accolades and honors bestowed upon him in his later years— honorary degrees, birthday celebrations—did little to fill the hole in his heart created by the death of his wife and two of his daughters. He died in 1910.

"Biographies," he once wrote, "are but the clothes and buttons of the man—the biography of the man himself cannot be written."[7] And if the "man" is simultaneously the living-breathing-human being, whose comings and goings were chronicled above, *and* a timeless, enduring fictive persona, who sometimes resembles his creator, sometimes seems to compete with him, and sometimes displaces him entirely, the challenge of biography is all the more daunting. As early as 1869, Sam Clemens observed that his private character "has been mixed up with my public one." Forrest Robinson's "Brief Biography" tackles this complex private-public mix-up head-on, exploring the range of possibilities that confront us as we try to understand the multiple valences and significations attached to "Sam Clemens" and "Mark Twain." Robinson probes the ways in which Clemens's failure to reach any closure on the subject himself may have helped fuel his imaginative inventiveness. "Always his own best subject," Robinson writes, he was "half-consciously driven by the riddle of identity to endless experiments in self-construction." The question "Who was he?" turns out to be as puzzling to the author and the man as to his future biographers. In Robinson's hands this confusion transforms the perfunctory genre of "capsule biography" into an illuminating meditation on the elusiveness of identity.

Noting that "Twain's own spiritual evolution mirrored many of the major trends and developments in American religion" during his lifetime, Harold Bush's "'A Moralist in Disguise': Mark Twain and American Religion" provides a context for understanding some of the religious transformations of the nineteenth and early twentieth centuries and their impact on Twain. Twain's "movement from a rather primitivistic form of Protestant Christianity, through deism, and later into more scientific and psychological forms of belief," Bush writes, "roughly squares with the general movement of the nation as a whole." Bush ranges from discussions of the frontier Protestantism of Clemens's childhood to the sources of his anti-Catholic strain to the impact on him of the rise of liberal theology and modern biblical criticism. He always keeps in mind the complexity of Twain's iconoclastic response to religion, a response that vacillated between attraction and repulsion, fascination and disgust, a response as hard for critics to chart as it was for Twain to explain to himself.

Gregg Camfield's "A Republican Artisan in the Court of King Capital: Mark Twain and Commerce" sets Mark Twain's responses to America's love affair with money, from his earliest work to his latest, in the context of the massive economic changes taking place in the second half of the nineteenth century. Although the era may have been best known for the creation of unparalleled wealth and high expectations, Camfield notes that "failure was more common than the colossal successes for which America became known." Camfield places Twain's misadventures as a "venture capitalist" against the backdrop of the economic transformations his society was undergoing. At the same time, he examines Twain's efforts to grapple with the place of the worker in the new economy (an issue central to Robert Weir's essay in this volume). With Camfield as our guide, we come to view Twain's jarringly inconsistent attitudes toward the world of commerce as understandable responses to a world transforming itself under his feet, even as he wrote.

My essay, "Mark Twain and Race," sets Twain's work on this subject in the context of the ideologies that dominated American society's discourse on race over the course of his life. From the religious and pseudoscientific rationales for slavery during Twain's childhood to the ersatz-empirical justifications for segregation that surfaced in the 1890s, the nation never ran short of fiendishly inventive excuses for racism. Set against the backdrop of assumptions that the majority of his peers widely accepted, Twain's efforts to negotiate (in published work and unpublished fragments) the social, political, and moral complexities of living in a "civilized" society that was built upon, and that still tolerated, racism, are all the more striking. The fact that a number of the issues that Twain tried to address would become some of the central themes animating African-American writing in the twentieth century suggests that Twain was on the right track, even if he was often destined to be derailed.

Born when the "cult of true womanhood" was ascendant, Mark Twain died when the "New Woman" was coming into her own. In her essay "Mark Twain and Gender," Susan K. Harris suggests that "Twain's noted ambivalences about women's behavior and his fraught relationships with powerful men, his adulation of prepubescent girls and his cross-dressing characters, are signs of his engagement in a society that was disturbed about changing behaviors and looking for ways to talk about the differences between sex and gender." Harris places Twain's sexual conservatism within the context of the code of propriety that pervaded the world in which he grew up, nineteenth-century health reformers' focus on the importance of regulating the body (their views ubiquitous in the popular press), and the definitions of femininity that were most prized in his social milieu. She also addresses the fact that "at the same time that he played the sexual conservative Twain was writing clandestine pieces revealing his fascination with the sexuality, both male and female, that public representations of acceptable behavior sought to deny." Her insightful analysis helps us see Twain as he "struggles, largely unsuccessfully, to free himself from the sex/gender assumptions of his age" by "investigating gender much as he investigated other social categories that most people took for granted."

In his essay "Mark Twain and Social Class," Robert E. Weir examines Twain's attitudes toward class privilege, labor, and exploitation against the backdrop of the tumultuous labor movement of his day. Mark Twain shared the workers' ambivalence about civilization and progress, Weir tells us, and voiced opinions close to those of Knights of Labor organizer Terrence Powderly. Yet for all his professed sympathy toward labor and for all his acerbic critiques of the powerful, Twain's "conspicuous consumption, his placement in well-defined social networks, his preference for non-manual labor, and his concern for social order" help us see him as firmly rooted in "a rising middle class in the process of defining itself." "Twain saw himself," Weir tells us, "as a man in the middle, sandwiched between the potentially corrupting influences of unfettered power and privilege from above and debilitating poverty from below." As he limns the social values of the middle class that Twain and his peers articulated and elevated into ideals, Weir helps us understand how Twain could praise labor unions while lambasting mass democracy or heap scorn on financier Jay Gould while sharing cigars and quips with Standard Oil's Henry Huttleston Rogers.

As Jim Zwick notes in "Mark Twain and Imperialism," Americans accustomed to Twain's being honored with public celebrations typically featuring jumping frogs, river rafts, and white-washed fences may be surprised by the fact that outside the United States it is sometimes Twain's opposition to imperialism that is most honored and celebrated. Twain's anti-imperialism is most often associated with the impassioned writings of his later years, when he served as an officer of the Anti-Imperialist League, the country's first national anti-imperialist organization. But, as Zwick demonstrates, one can find portents of Twain's acidic attacks on the "Blessings-of-Civilization Trust" in some of his Sandwich Island lectures and letters from the 1860s and 1870s.

And while the Anti-Imperialist League itself did not come into being until close to the end of the century, its emergence was facilitated by the development of a national network of reform organizations that responded to the era's widespread concern about social, political and economic problems—most notably, Henry George's single tax movement. Zwick's astute portrait of the Anti-Imperialist League and the men and women who supported it gives us new insight into the dynamics of Twain's engagement with the issue of imperialism and new understanding of the roots of his growing disillusionment with his country.

For readers stimulated by these seven essays to read more of Twain's work and to delve more deeply into critical responses to it and historical contexts that inform it, the bibliographical essay at the end of this volume provides a roadmap.

I want to thank Hal Bush, Gregg Camfield, Susan Harris, Forrest Robinson, Rob Weir, and Jim Zwick for the care and effort that went into their essays, and I'd like to thank Jim Zwick additionally for his generous assistance in securing the illustrations in the "Illustrated Chronology." I am grateful to the Mark Twain House for allowing us to include so many prints from their collection, and I appreciate the gracious help and support of R. Kent Rasmussen, Kevin Bochynski, and Randall Knoper. I'd also like to thank T. Susan Chang for developing this series and commissioning this volume, Elissa Morris for bringing the project to completion, and Niko Pfund and Laura Brown for steering Oxford University Press past reefs and sand bars. I am grateful to Cynthia Frese, Janice Bradley, Jeremy Lewis, and Jennifer Kowing for their help in preparing the final manuscript, and to my family, as always, for their patience, encouragement, and love. Finally, thanks are due to the riverboat pilot whose "trained faculties instantly photographed the bearings" of his ship and preserved them, across time, for us: Mark Twain.

NOTES

1. George Bernard Shaw to Samuel L. Clemens, July 3, 1907, quoted in Albert Bigelow Paine, *Mark Twain: A Biography*, 3 vols. (New York: Harper & Brothers, 1912), 3:1398.

2. Mark Twain, "What Paul Bourget Thinks of Us," in Mark Twain, *How to Tell a Story and Other Essays* [1897], ed. Shelley Fisher Fishkin (New York: Oxford University Press, 1996), p. 187.

3. Ibid., p. 186.

4. Mark Twain, *Life On The Mississippi* [1883], ed. Shelley Fisher Fishkin (New York: Oxford University Press, 1996), p. 154.

5. Ibid., p. 154.

6. Ibid., p. 155.

7. Mark Twain, *Mark Twain's Autobiography*, ed. Albert Bigelow Paine, 2 vols. (New York: Harper & Brothers, 1924), 1:2.

Mark Twain
1835–1910

A Brief Biography

Forrest G. Robinson

"How many of us feel that we know Mark Twain? That what he wrote was written for us, with the intimate frankness of a friend talking over a cigar?" These questions were addressed to readers of the *Wilmington* (N. C.) *Morning Star* on the occasion of the great writer's death in April 1910.[1] The questions bore with them the confident assumption that virtually all readers would acknowledge a sense of close familiarity with Mark Twain and his major works. This was taken for granted.

Today, nearly a century later, many Americans, perhaps even most, feel the same way. The name Mark Twain gives rise to the image of a well-dressed gentlemen in late middle age. He has a wide moustache, bushy brows, a mane of white hair, a cigar in hand, and a puckish expression on his face. It is an image redolent of warmth and good humor. This is a man in whom, we feel, "the boy" still lives. Indeed, the meaning of Mark Twain may seem incomplete to us until the figures of Tom Sawyer and Huckleberry Finn have been brought into the picture. The boys complete the man by making explicit the themes of youth, freedom, imagination, and the great out-of-doors. Many who have never read the novels think they have, for the stories, and the values that attach to them, are everywhere at large in our midst. Now as then, if you take Mark and Tom and Huck out of the

American cultural equation, you are left with a mightily diminished thing.

But the figure so warmly and confidently embraced as the real Mark Twain is, in fact, a fiction created by Samuel Langhorne Clemens, who was a twenty-seven-year-old journalist living in the Nevada Territory when he first adopted the now famous nom de plume in 1863. The matter is complicated by the fact that the humorist used both names when addressing family and friends. For years, in hundreds of letters to his most intimate and enduring friend, William Dean Howells, he referred to himself as "Mark." Howells, meanwhile, addressed his letters to "My dear Clemens," thus avoiding his friend's pseudonym because, as he complains in *My Mark Twain*, it "seemed always somehow to mask him from my personal sense."[2] Late in their lives, Howells encouraged his friend—"poor fellow"—to "get rid of Mark Twain."[3]

A kindred brand of confusion surfaces in the works, where the nom de plume refers to a variety of quite different personae. The Mark Twain of "The Celebrated Jumping Frog of Calaveras County" is an effete if rather myopic and humorless Eastern lawyer, who succumbs without knowing it to the wiles of garrulous Simon Wheeler. He is distantly related to the avuncular, mildly condescending Mark Twain who presides over *The Adventures of Tom Sawyer*, but altogether remote from the complexly "innocent" traveler in *Roughing It*, the ironist in *Pudd'nhead Wilson*, and the sober witness to imperialism who narrates *Following the Equator*. The fictional Mark Twain is thus no singular thing but rather a varied cast of characters.

Not surprisingly, confusion in the matter of names and identities has spread to the biographies and critical writing. For example, the title figure in Henry Nash Smith's classic study, *Mark Twain: The Development of a Writer*, is a living, breathing historical personality who was born in 1835, died in 1910, and wrote books such as *Huckleberry Finn* and *The Prince and the Pauper*. What then of Samuel Langhorne Clemens? Smith generally steers clear of him, as if to suggest that his identity has been subsumed into Mark Twain's. This may help to explain why Samuel Langhorne Clemens is omitted from Smith's copious index (though, rather

weirdly, several members of the Clemens family turn up there).
But is there more to be made of this curious omission? Is it an
oblique concession that Mark Twain is a fictional nonentity or,
more probably, the expression of an impulse to wish a vexed
question out of sight and mind? The confusion is compounded
on those very few occasions when Smith refers to his subject as
"Clemens." This undercuts the admittedly problematical clarity
resulting from the subsumption of Samuel Clemens in Mark
Twain; for it asserts a distinction between the two that is not sustained over the course of the book. When the question arises, for
example, "what Mark Twain's attitude . . . actually was" about
a textual detail, Smith insists that "the question is ultimately
unanswerable insofar as it concerns the mental processes of
Samuel L. Clemens."[4] What then of those quite numerous
points in his narrative when Smith confidently describes Mark
Twain's attitudes, but without reference to "the mental processes
of Samuel L. Clemens"? Is Mark Twain an independent historical
writer with a mind of his own or is he the fictional alter ego of
Samuel L. Clemens? Smith has it both ways on this key question.

Cognate questions attach to Andrew Hoffman's recent *Inventing Mark Twain: The Lives of Samuel Langhorne Clemens*. Hoffman
insists at the outset on a rigid distinction between the historical
Samuel Langhorne Clemens, on the one side, and the fictional
Mark Twain, a carefully constructed "public image, not a flesh-
and-blood man," on the other. He adds that Clemens was himself
aware of a "sharp separation between image and identity," an
awareness that gave rise to his "nearly seamless presentation of
an invented self named Mark Twain."[5] As we have seen, however, the line separating Clemens from Twain was far from clear
to the man who bore those names. It is not altogether surprising,
therefore, that Hoffman has problems of his own in maintaining
the distinction. His confident assumption that Clemens and
Twain—he describes them as "two people occupying the same
body"—can be kept separate rests on an essentialist conception
of human identity, manifest in his notion that humans possess a
"fundamental self," a "true self," an "essential identity." Hoffman
appears to believe that such terms are transparent and thus deploys them in an entirely unexamined way, never pausing to

elaborate on what "the essential person—the man or woman within" might be expected to look like. Thus, even as he faults Justin Kaplan—whose celebrated *Mr. Clemens and Mark Twain* won the Pulitzer Prize for biography in 1966—for having failed to capture "the essence of Samuel Langhorne Clemens," Hoffman lacks utterly the theoretical foundation on which one might begin to fill the putative lack.[6]

Hoffman fares no better with the second panel of his dyptich, the "nearly Seamless" image of Mark Twain that Clemens presented to the world. In fact, there is little in the record to suggest that Clemens was self-conscious or systematic in shaping his public persona. The best evidence on this score, as we have already observed, is the large gallery of fictional figures that answer to the name Mark Twain. John C. Gerber long ago identified seven such "poses"; more recently, Michael J. Kiskis has added four more.[7] Doubtless the exact count will vary from survey to survey, but it is nonetheless irresistibly clear that the lineaments of what Hoffman describes as Clemens's "false" self are just as elusive as those of his "real" or "essential" self. It is telling in this regard that the comically garrulous old-timer featured in "How to Tell a Story"—the humorist's brief primer on his "art"—bears scant resemblance to Hoffman's portrait of "the brilliant, though acerbic, public man of letters known as Mark Twain."[8] And neither of these personae prepares the reader for the complexly mingled tone of the speaker in "The Private History of a Campaign That Failed," or for the restrained horror and rage in the voice that presides over "The United States of Lyncherdom." If Hoffman's "essential" Clemens is too broadly and vaguely defined, then his Mark Twain is too narrowly precise.

Seeking to avoid such pitfalls, I will use the name Samuel Langhorne Clemens to refer to the historical figure and noted American novelist. For my purposes, Clemens, who was born and died and had a wife and children, was also the man who wrote *Tom Sawyer, Huckleberry Finn,* and all the other works frequently attributed to Mark Twain. I am thus quite literal in assigning fictional status to Mark Twain and in declining, therefore, to confer authorship on him. I understand John C. Gerber's distinction between the "essential" Mark Twain and the Mark

Twain of "the comic pose,"[9] but find it impossible to sustain. For the same reason, I avoid what has been described as "the usual convention of using 'Clemens' to refer to Samuel L. Clemens in his extra-authorial identity and 'Twain' to refer to the authorial self."[10] Just as I resist the temptation to make Mark Twain "real" that frequently accompanies the decision to make Samuel Clemens into two people or "selves." Samuel Clemens was a historical person of many and complex dimensions, but there was only one of him. Mark Twain was a fiction of many and complex dimensions—not the least of them his relationship to his maker—but he was a fiction, nonetheless. In what follows, I will attempt to keep clear the important difference between them.

To name the historical Clemens is not, of course, to settle the question of his identity. Herman Melville's *Pierre*, an autobiographical novel subtitled *The Ambiguities*, opens an especially apt perspective on this issue. Likening the search for human identity to an attempt to unearth an ancient, entombed mummy, Melville leads the reader deep into a tomb, where "by horrible gropings we come to the central room; with joy we espy the sarcophagus; but we lift the lid—no body is there!—appallingly vacant as vast," he concludes, "is the soul of a man!"[11] Toward the end of his life, in *The Mysterious Stranger*, Samuel Clemens arrived at a similarly blank perspective on the human condition. "It is all a Dream, a grotesque and foolish dream," he wrote, the self included, which is described as "a *Thought*—a vagrant Thought, a useless Thought, a homeless Thought, wandering forlorn among the empty eternities!"[12] Identity so construed is inessential, ephemeral, arbitrary; there is no self, only rootless, nameless fictions adrift and unobserved in boundless space and time.

But unlike Melville, who, according to his friend Hawthorne, was prone to brooding on "everything that lies beyond human ken,"[13] Clemens was intuitive and unsystematic in his approach to philosophical issues. There is no evidence, for example, that the decision to adopt a nom de plume in 1863 gave rise to serious reflection on the complexities of human identity. True, there is anecdotal attention to divided identities in "Personal Habits of the Siamese Twins," a brief essay on the famous Chang and Eng, published in 1869, but Clemens makes nothing of the oft-noted, analogous twinning in his own identity. Rather, he approaches the subject as a humorous curiosity, closing with the suggestion that "there is a moral" in the example of the twins, but then retreating in comical fashion from declaring what that moral might be. The piece is a kind of thematic trial run for *Pudd'nhead Wilson,* published twenty-five years later, in which twinning is again invoked, though with similarly ambiguous implications. Variations on the same theme turn up in "The Recent Carnival of Crime in Connecticut," *Huckleberry Finn, The Prince and the Pauper,* and in a host of late, often fragmentary writings in which, as Susan Gillman has shown, Clemens came back again and again, persistently if inconclusively, to the vexed question of human identity.[14] It was, we suspect, his own complex and elusive nature that propelled his interest. Who am I? he wanted to know; how do the varied and conflicting elements in my nature hang together?

Clemens's failure to penetrate the riddle of his own identity was almost certainly overdetermined. Granted, it was a complex and elusive identity, as his critics and biographers have discovered. "To the end," Justin Kaplan concludes, he was "an enigma and a prodigy to himself."[15] But it seems clear as well that he was unprepared to settle in a final way for any of the solutions that presented themselves during a lifetime of speculation. One part of his divided self sought the truth; another side, like Pilate, would not stay for an answer. Indeed, this interplay between opposed and intersecting impulses to reveal and conceal himself, everywhere at large in his vast literary corpus, is a defining feature of Clemens's interior life. Willy-nilly, he was always his own best subject, half-consciously driven by the riddle of identity to endless experiments in self-construction.

Clemens's impulse to tell stories, most often and most memorably stories that derived from personal experience, was a strong and enduring trait. Clearly enough, he responded to an urgent drive to impose order on a world—not least the mysterious inner world of the self—forever verging on chaos. His humor, dwelling as it does in the absurd and incongruous, bears witness to the authority of disorder in his consciousness. Narrative offered a stay

against confusion, though the relief was almost always temporary, in good part because virtually all stories, rooted as they
were in personal memory, eventually found their way into re-
gions of remorse. Guilt, as we shall see, was dominant in
Clemens's inner experience. He had an infallible nose for guilt. If
there was something to feel guilty about—and of course there
was always something to feel guilty about—he could be relied on
to take full and anguished responsibility for it. "If on any occasion," observed his daughter Clara, "he could manage to trace
the cause of some one's mishap to something he himself had
done or said, no one could persuade him he was mistaken. Self-
condemnation was the natural turn for his mind to take, yet
often he accused himself of having inflicted pain or trouble when
the true cause was far removed from himself."[16] Guilt gave special urgency to Clemens's sense of inner disorder and energized
the alternating currents of his impulse to reveal and conceal that
interior. His narrative drive thus expressed a deep craving for redemption. But as his stories regularly brought him face-to-face
with intimations of his own immorality—his selfishness and
pride and insensitivity—they perversely rekindled the very feelings of guilty disorder from which the narrative impulse initially
took rise. And so the telling recommenced, the ceaseless flood of
words testifying to lifelong, recapitulating cycles of torment and
release, remorse and redemption.

There is evidence that the positive pole of the process grew
more elusive in the humorist's later years. More than ever, he
was unable to finish what he had started, largely because the increasing gravity of his disenchantment with himself and the
world made narrative resolution more difficult to achieve. The
craving for order and redemption was frustrated by a diminished
ability to imagine them. It was the great attraction of the autobiographical dictations he undertook during the final decade of
his life that they offered a narrative path of minimal moral resistance. "Finally in Florence, in 1904, I hit upon the right way to do
an Autobiography," he wrote; "start it at no particular time of
your life; wander at your free will all over your life; talk only
about the thing which interests you for the moment; drop it the
moment its interest threatens to pale, and turn your talk upon

the new and more interesting thing that has intruded itself into your mind meantime."[17] Such easeful modes of composition were associatively linked for Clemens with life on a raft in the midst of a wide river. This is where that troubled child, Huck Finn, finds a modicum of peace; it was the same for his maker. "The motion of a raft," Clemens observes in *A Tramp Abroad*, "is gentle, and gliding, and smooth and noiseless; it calms down all feverish activities, it soothes to sleep all nervous hurry and impatience; under its restful influence all the troubles and vexations and sorrows that harass the mind vanish away, and existence becomes a dream, a charm, a deep and tranquil ecstasy."[18] What better measure of the humorist's inner turmoil that this rapturous account of an interval's relief!

Clemens often complained that he was restrained from truth-telling by the shackles of convention and the herd-mentality of his audience. "Writers of all kinds are manacled servants of the public,"[19] he observes in *Life on the Mississippi*. It was the great advantage of his autobiography, he liked to think, that its posthumous publication would free him from such restraints. "I speak from the grave rather than with my living tongue, for a good reason," he declared: "I can speak thence freely."[20] But he knew better, and more than once admitted that the principal obstacle to truth in his autobiographical reflections was neither convention nor audience, but his own inability to tell it. "When I was young I could remember anything, whether it happened or not," he humorously observed to his biographer, Albert Bigelow Paine; "but I am getting old and soon I shall remember only the latter."[21]

But Clemens shrewdly perceived that while it was himself he was angling to deceive, a vigilant reader might not take the bait. "An Autobiography is the truest of all books," he wrote to William Dean Howells, "for while it inevitably consists mainly of extinctions of the truth, shirkings of the truth, partial revealments of the truth, with hardly an instance of plain straight truth, the remorseless truth *is* there, between the lines, where the author-cat is raking dust upon it which hides from the disinterested spectator neither it nor its smell . . . the result being that the reader knows the author in spite of his wily diligences."[22] He goes even further along this line in a memorable passage from the *Autobiography.* The writer, he observes,

> *will* tell the truth in spite of himself, for his facts and his fictions will work loyally together for the protection of the reader; each fact and each fiction will be a dab of paint, each will fall in its right place, and together they will paint his portrait; not the portrait *he* thinks they are painting, but his real portrait, the inside of him, the soul of him, his character. Without intending to lie, he will lie all the time; not bluntly, consciously, not dully unconsciously, but half-consciously— consciousness in twilight; a soft and gentle and merciful twilight which makes his general form comely, with his virtuous prominences and projections discernible and his ungracious ones in shadow. His truths will be recognizable as truths, his modifications of facts which would tell against him will go for nothing, the reader will see the fact through the film and know his man. There is a subtle devilish something or other about autobiographical composition that defeats all the writer's attempts to paint his portrait *his* way.[23]

Once again, the urge to conceal is found in close company with a "subtle devilish" urge to reveal. The writer is not so much compelled as seduced by a half-conscious impulse to magnify and mitigate with subtle highlights and half-tones; he surrenders without resistance to his own blandishments. By contrast, the undistracted reader readily penetrates the ruse. Detection is partly the result of audience perspicacity; but even more decisive is the mysteriously self-subversive strain inherent in the autobiographical enterprise. The lie cannot hide its true face. In the broader view, then, the ordering energy of the autobiographical narrative is colored on one side by a "half-conscious" impulse to redeem the subject by portraying him in a "merciful twilight," and on the other by a "subtle devilish" drive to betray the guilty truth. The needs to order, to judge, and to redeem work simultaneously but at cross purposes to produce the complexly mingled fabric of the autobiographical narrative, a confused, confusing, but, to a discerning observer, a faithful rendering of the writer's "real portrait, the inside of him, the soul of him, his character."

Usually halting and evasive in describing his writing methods, Clemens is in this passage notably direct and yet subtle, insightful and yet willing to acknowledge gaps in his understanding. The discussion centers on autobiography; and yet because so much of what Clemens wrote was autobiographical—indeed, it is arguable that virtually everything he wrote was autobiographical—the approach to his life and work here advanced applies quite broadly to his writing, and not simply to materials narrowly focused on his personal experience.

In the section of the *Autobiography* immediately following the passage just quoted, Clemens sets it down as the basic "law of *narrative*" that it "has no law" at all. Flowing freely, like "a brook that never goes straight for a minute, but *goes*, and goes briskly,"[24] narrative follows the path of least resistance. Yet precisely because it is carefree, chartless, and headlong—because it pursues its own "natural" course without obstruction—this half-conscious narrative stream offers itself as a faithful mirror of the writer's "soul." The most revealing kinds of writing thus commence for Clemens in what are comparatively the most mindless acts of composition. You will find me in such places, Clemens affirms, especially autobiographical places, where, to the discerning observer, my attempts at concealment invariably reveal much more than they hide. Look carefully, with imaginative empathy, and with special attention to the dark side of the ledger—to the "remorseless truth" which I, the "author-cat," have buried—and you will find me.

Autobiographical narrative, then, has its first motive the retrieval of experience from encroaching disorder—the discovery and articulation, or construction, of a coherent self. Its second, no less urgent motive is to redeem the life that it describes, to give it value. The first motive explains the initiating impulse to tell; the second motive explains the impulse to bring the narrative to a satisfactory conclusion. The two motives are doubtless closely linked, for the initiating impulse to tell will arise and proceed confidently only when the prospect of satisfactory closure is good. When the achievement of a satisfactory outcome is in doubt, the impulse to tell may be reduced to desperate but futile repetition, beginning over and over but never ending, producing mere fragments of stories; or, when all hope of achieving closure is lost, the impulse to tell will recede completely, leaving silence. To the extent that disorder is another face of guilt—as it is, for example, in the Old Testament story of the fall—the two motives may be said to be one. They were virtually the same for Samuel Clemens, who knew that "a man must and will have his own approval first of all, in each and every moment and circumstance of his life,"[25] and wrote compulsively to achieve it. A man "will always do the thing which will bring him the *most* mental comfort," he wrote, "for that is *the sole law of his life.*"[26] Clemens wrote to achieve the consummate but utterly elusive "mental comfort" that came with self-approval. His works are the rich yield on a failed quest for personal redemption.

Mark Twain's (Burlesque) Autobiography and First Romance was published in 1871. A strange performance by all estimates, the slender booklet is comprised of three principal elements. The opening section, a transparent send-up of conventional autobiography, traces the Twain surname through a copious rogues gallery of felons and frauds, beginning in the Middle Ages and ending at the time of the American Revolution. As for his own life, the putative subject of the work, the narrator Mark Twain sets it aside, insisting belatedly that "it is simply wisdom to leave it unwritten until I am hanged."[27] The second section, an "Awful, Terrible Medieval Romance," is also unfinished. The lord of Klugenstein forces his daughter to masquerade as a son, Conrad, hoping thereby to seize control from the Duke of Brandenburgh, the lord's older brother, who has a daughter of his own, but no male heir. The plot works well enough until the Duke's daughter gives birth to a child, fathered, she claims, by her cousin, Conrad, the false heir apparent, who now faces an impossible decision. He must dispute the charge or die; but to reveal that he is a woman will also make him subject to the death penalty. In the outcome, Twain concludes, "I have got my hero (or heroine) into such a particularly close place, that I do not see how I am ever going to get him (or her) out of it again—and therefore I will wash my hands of the whole business."[28] Finally, running continuously through the two sections are a series of illustrations satirically attacking the ruthless promoters of the Erie Railroad and featuring cartoon portraits of Jim Fisk, Jay Gould, and Cornelius Vanderbilt.[29]

What are we to make of this motley effort? Critics at the time and since have dismissed the book as a failure, scarcely worthy of comment.[30] Clemens himself promptly adopted this view and even tried to destroy the plates of the ill-fated volume.[31] In the most emphatic way possible, then, there is evidence here of strongly competing impulses to reveal and to conceal the self. At one level, Clemens's chronicle of degenerate forbears makes a jest of the autobiographical enterprise. But few readers have been amused, in good part, as Justin Kaplan observes, because the would-be humorist's "self-hatred" is "so nakedly displayed that what was meant to be a joke ends up being genuinely unpleasant."[32] The impulse to explore personal history is thus no sooner broached than subverted; at the same time, the manner of the subversion betrays an undercurrent of guilty self-abasement which takes the fun out of the presumptive joke. "My parents were neither very poor nor conspicuously honest," the humorist confesses.[33] He might have added that their name was Clemens, not Twain, and that he was as uncomfortable in the latter, pseudonymous role of disreputable Western funny man as he was in the new and contrasting role of respectable Eastern paterfamilias that came with his recent marriage.

Samuel Clemens wanted to tell the story of himself, but neither of the stories available seemed true. In one, he felt foolish and degraded; in the other, he was an outlander fallen on fabulous but contemptible wealth. Uncertainty in the matter of identity had grown more acute since his marriage to Olivia ("Livy") Langdon in February 1870. Fragile and fine in the best Victorian manner, his new wife was the absolute quintessence of Eastern respectability. Her father, Jervis Langdon, was a wealthy coal magnate and first citizen of Buffalo, New York. For the notorious bohemian humorist from the Far West, marriage to the rare jewel of this lofty family represented a dazzling leap into wealth and social status. None of this was lost on Clemens. His family background was proud but comparatively quite modest; meanwhile, the stories that followed him from California and Nevada, solicited as character references by the Langdons, were nothing short of scandalous. And his professional reputation as "the wild humorist of the Pacific Slope" conformed perfectly to the ragged personal profile. "Poor girl," Clemens wrote of Livy to his friend, Mary Fairbanks, "anybody who could convince her that I was not a humorist would secure her eternal gratitude! She thinks a humorist is something perfectly awful."[34] Magnanimously, but somewhat mysteriously as well, Jervis Langdon looked with compassion on his daughter's suitor and finally welcomed him into the family.

Clemens openly admitted the errors of his past and just as openly committed himself to reform. "I shall do no act which you or Livy might be pained to hear of," he wrote to Mary Fairbanks; "I shall seek the society of the good—I shall be a *Christian*. I shall climb—climb—climb—toward this bright sun that is shining in the heaven of my happiness until all that is gross & unworthy is hidden in the mists & the darkness of that lower earth whence *you* first lifted my aspiring feet."[35] But climb as he might, Clemens was slow to find his ease in the role of a rich man. He bristled at the suggestion that Livy's chief attraction was her wealth and protested to her mother that he wanted nothing of the family fortune. His "Open Letter to Commodore Vanderbilt," which heaps scorn on its subject's predatory greed and moral bankruptcy, was published during his courtship with Livy in March 1869 and may be read as a compensatory assault on the culture of fabulous new money into which he was about to rise. Such sentiments notwithstanding, however, the new bridegroom acquiesced without complaint in the opulent material rewards that came with his marriage. In fact, Clemens's contempt for money was matched by his craving for it. "The code he detested," Justin Kaplan observes, "was also, in part, the one he lived by."[36] The contradiction, as conspicuous as the ambivalence from which it sprang, was hardly resolved when *Mark Twain's (Burlesque) Autobiography and First Romance* appeared in March 1871.

As we have observed, Clemens's impulse to narrate his life story surrenders almost at once to humorous distraction. But the evasive maneuver is itself telling, bearing witness as it does to guilt-laden misgivings about his background, personal reputation, profession, and recent rise in the social and economic order. If he knows full well what to reject in his past and future, he has nothing of substance to set in its place. Identity, like the autobiography itself, is thus vexed, evasive, a poor and empty jest. Kindred thematics surface in the masquerade plot of the "Awful, Terrible Medieval Romance," and in the fraudulent maneuverings of the promoters of the Erie Railroad. Self-concealment is in both instances selfishly motivated, though with rather different implications. The robber barons are shameless in their greed and deceit, but readily exposed and held comfortably at arm's length. Here, as in the "Open Letter to Commodore Vanderbilt," Clemens's preoccupation with errant capitalism resonates in an obvious way with his recent personal experience but betrays no suggestion of moral threat. He was the ambivalent beneficiary of a vast new American fortune and felt the need to distance himself from the excesses of such wealth; that done, he felt relatively free of contamination.

It is a different matter with Conrad, the false heir, who complains remorsefully to his (her) father, "my life hath been a lie."[37] Rationalizing material advantage was one thing, but coming to terms with the damning sense of personal falsehood was quite another. Like Conrad, Clemens felt like a fake; he needed look no further than his famous nom de plume for a reminder. He was one thing for his family, another for his audience, and another still for Livy and the rest of the Langdons. In all these masquerades he sought comfort and personal advantage, but in none, he felt, was he true. His uneasiness on this score, as the (*Burlesque*) *Autobiography* clearly suggests, surfaced in fits and starts, in painful feelings and intimations, rather than in a settled conviction. His sentiments were vague and evanescent, in part, because of a marked tendency to recoil almost reflexively from emotional discord, but in even greater part because his identity was itself so unformed and free-floating that it provided no anchor from which various roles and masks might be perceived to depart. Because it had no center, his sense of self was vague, almost boundless. Susan Gillman very usefully deploys the term "imposture" to describe this condition of "indeterminate identity" and to set it apart from merely "confused, switched, or mistaken identities," in which the existence of a true self is taken for granted. "Imposture," she writes, "is the pose of a pose, the fake of a fake; the word implies no possible return to any point of origin." The self, so defined, and—more to the point—so experienced, is vague and fleeting, the elusive locus for the kinds of oblique moral maneuverings on display in *Mark Twain's (Burlesque) Biography and First Romance.* It is precisely this elusive sense of unease that Gillman points to in observing that "imposture raises but does not resolve complex connections between morality and intentionality."[38] Whose guilt is finally on display in the confessed "lie" that is Conrad's life or in the ill-gotten gains of Cornelius Vanderbilt and company? Mark Twain's, clearly, though the case he brings against himself is tellingly indirect and equivocal.

So much, then, for the ordering impulse to tell a story of the self, and the answering, guilty retreat into concealment. What now of redemption? On this question we can move more quickly to clarify. For if family history, false Conrad, and predatory Cornelius Vanderbilt obliquely incriminate Samuel Clemens, they extenuate the charges against him in much the same way. Yes, the humorist seems to concede, I am lowborn, false and greedy; but so, he insists at the same time, are lots of other people. My family tree is no straighter, but neither is it more crooked, than most; and anyway, my ancestors are none of my doing. I am not what I seem, perhaps, but who really is? History is long on pretenders, after all. As for wealth, it is true that I crave it, but who doesn't? It is also true that a little of it came my way just recently, but I didn't stoop to scramble for it. Nobody's perfect.

We are reminded that the strangely paired narratives in *Mark Twain's (Burlesque) Autobiography and First Romance* are incomplete, that the teller cannot find his way to the end of the stories. His failure is meant to be funny; but the joke, a failure of a different kind, and a lie of sorts, collapses under under the weight of heavier intimations. The half-formed plea for understanding gives way to a tide of implied self-accusation, with the result that neither story is permitted to reach completion. Revelation without redemption yields concealment, not closure. But, as Clemens pointedly insists, the concealment is bound to fail; the autobiographer lies half-consciously and without intending to, but in such a way that the truth may be inferred. An important feature of the truth emergent from the self-portrait attempted in *Mark Twain's (Burlesque) Autobiography and First Romance* is its lack of a clear subject. There are several images on display, but they cast only indirect light on what Clemens calls "the inside" and "the soul" of the writer, "his character." For all of his names and roles, then, Samuel Clemens in 1871, Westerner, Southerner, bohemian, humorist, husband, father, nouveau riche, and newcomer to the civilized Northeast, was uncomfortable in some degree with all the selves available to him and baffled as to the nature of the real thing.

As it happened, his true self—or, rather, one of the selves that would come in time to seem truest to him—was a boy from Hannibal, already alive in 1871 in Clemens's shaping memory and imagination, but not yet fully formed. That boy's advent would have to await *The Adventures of Tom Sawyer,* first undertaken in 1874 and published two years later. But the outlines of his character were already clearly discernible in a long letter to Will Bowen—"My First, & Oldest & Dearest Friend"—which Clemens composed on the afternoon of Sunday, February 6, 1870, just four days after his wedding. Livy, "much the most beautiful girl I ever saw . . . & she is the *best* girl," was upstairs napping in their elegant new home as he wrote. It was a setting rich with fresh and exciting possibilities; yet Clemens withdrew from it and surrendered instead to a powerful wave of nostalgia, a strong pull back from the present and future to something earlier, simpler, and more innocent. "The old life has swept before me like a panorama," he exclaims;

> Heavens what eternities have swung their hoary cycles about us since those days were new! Since we tore down Dick Hardy's stable; since you had the measles & I went to your house purposely to catch them. Since Henry Beebe kept that

envied slaughter-house, & Joe Craig sold him cats to kill in it;
. . . since Jimmy Finn was town drunkard & we stole his dinner while he slept in the vat & fed it to the hogs in order to
keep them still till we could mount them and have a ride;
. . . since we used to undress & play Robin Hood in our
shirt-tails, with lath swords, in the woods on Holliday's Hill on
those long summer days,[39]

and on and on at impressive length, the fond, copious memories
of boyhood rising effortlessly into consciousness. Here, set in a
familiar and manageable social order, featuring activities governed by the arcane principles of play, with guilt and redemption
balanced at tolerable levels, all made pliant by memory to the
exigencies of present, adult consciousness, the narrative of a true
self had begun to take form. Livy must have glimpsed this axial
dimension in her husband's makeup, for she soon settled on
"Youth" as his pet name. This seemed to express him best.

Clemens was an utterly fanciful genealogist. His imagined forbears were fabulously rich, fabulously powerful, fabulously rebellious, fabulously malign, but never, never dull. The truth of the
matter was in fact pretty prosaic. On the paternal side, he was
descended from sturdy, slave-owning pioneer farmers. Born in
1798, his father, John Marshall Clemens, named for the future Justice of the Supreme Court, was fragile, proud, ambitious, hard-
working, and by all accounts quite stern. In 1823, having earned a
license to practice law in Kentucky, he married Jane Lampton,
who came from a line of Kentucky hunters, Indian fighters,
and small slave-holders. Esteemed for her beauty and generous
high spirits, she loved parties and dancing and was invariably
contrasted with her dour husband The couple settled for a
while in Jamestown, Tennessee, where John Marshall practiced
law, ran a country store, and bought some 70,000 acres of
local, Fentress County land. In the eyes of its new owner, this
huge wilderness tract was the surest guarantee that his children
would never be poor. In reality, the infamous "Tennessee Land"
proved worse than worthless, for, as Clemens later observed, it

"laid the heavy curse of prospective wealth"[40] on the family and thereby encouraged the habit of speculation.

Declining prospects in Jamestown prompted a move in 1831 to the nearby Three Forks of the Wolf River, and thence four years later to the frontier village of Florida, Missouri. Clemens's parents were lured West by various members of the Lampton family, most notably by Jane's brother-in-law, John Quarles, a friendly, robust optimist who offered John Marshall a partnership in his store. Seeking a livelihood was certainly a first priority, as the family now included four children—Orion, born in 1825, Pamela in 1827, Margaret in 1830, and Benjamin in 1832—and their remaining slave, Jennie. Samuel Langhorne Clemens, premature and physically frail, was born in November 1835 and barely survived his first winter. "I was always told that I was a sickly and precarious and tiresome and uncertain child, and lived mainly on allopathic medicines during the first seven years of my life," Clemens recalled in his old age.[41] The last of the Clemens children, Henry, was born in 1838, about the same time that young Sam, still frail and sickly, had the first of what became recurrent episodes of sleepwalking. There was much in a child's life to be troubled about. Mother was overworked; father, remote in the best of times, was rather desperately trying to make ends meet; and sister Margaret died in 1839, to be followed by brother Benjamin three years later.

Through intervals of prosperity, family fortunes fluctuated, though the long-term trend was discouraging. In addition to storekeeping, John Marshall invested in several plots of government land and purchased a substantial Florida homesite. He was a leader in several ill-fated schemes for the commercial and cultural development of the region and was sworn in as a judge of the Monroe County Court in 1837. A year later he moved his wife and children into a comfortable new house. But their prospects in Florida were not bright. The "Judge" showed little aptitude for farming, the preferred livelihood of "Uncle" John Quarles, and the town lay 30 miles west of the Mississippi, the main artery of commerce. And so, despite increasing signs of poor health, John Marshall decided to make yet another fresh start, this time in nearby Hannibal, Missouri, a rapidly growing village on the Mis-

sissippi. It was not a happy time for young Sam, who later recalled that his parents set off for Hannibal without him. "Toward
night, when they camped and counted up the children, one was
missing. I was the one. I had been left behind. . . . I was well
frightened, and I made all the noise I could, but no one was near
and it did no good. I spent the afternoon in captivity and was not
rescued until the gloaming had fallen and the place was alive
with ghosts."[42] In fact, it was Orion who had been forgotten, not
Sam; but the memory is faithful enough as testimony to the precarious inner life of a fragile child.

Hannibal in 1839 was a prosperous frontier community, a
"white town drowsing in the sunshine of a summer's morning,"
as Clemens recalls it in *Life on the Mississippi*,

> The streets empty, or pretty nearly so; one or two clerks
> sitting in front of the Water Street stores, with their splint-
> bottomed chairs tilted back against the wall, chins on breasts,
> hats slouched over their faces, asleep—with shingle-shavings
> enough around to show what broke them down; a sow and a
> litter of pigs loafing along the sidewalk, doing a good business
> in watermelon rinds and seeds; two or three lonely little
> freight piles scattered about the "levee;" a pile of "skids" on
> the slope of the stone-paved wharf, and the fragrant town
> drunkard asleep in the shadow of them; two or three wood
> flats at the head of the wharf, but nobody to listen to the
> peaceful lapping of the wavelets against them; the great Mis-
> sissippi, the magnificent Mississippi, rolling its mile-wide tide
> along, shining in the sun.

Presently, the scene comes alive as people gather on the wharf to
admire an arriving steamboat. "And the boat *is* rather a handsome sight, too. She is long and sharp and trim and pretty," and
for a few minutes the bustle of activity continues. Then the magnificent boat pulls away, leaving the town "dead again," and the
boy's imagination aflame with the "permanent ambition" to be a
steamboat pilot someday.[43]

Clemens's major fiction returns almost invariably to the scene
and events of his boyhood in Hannibal during the 1840s. "It was,"

as Bernard DeVoto long ago observed, "an idyll and a cosmos,"[44] and it was this image not only for its creator but also for the generations of readers who have warmed in a special, proprietary way to his evocations of frontier America. *The Adventures of Tom Sawyer* is the fullest and most faithful fictional record of Clemens's childhood and a rich repository of culturally resonant images. The setting is composed of a small town, St. Petersburg, with its dirt streets set in grid fashion along the river, and the surrounding forest, Cardiff Hill, Jackson's Island, and McDougal's cave. The community is a representative hierarchy, with the judge and the preacher at the top, teachers and merchants and the mass of respectable citizens in the middle, and drunkards like Pap Finn and Muff Potter joining the slaves at the bottom.

The Clemens family occupied a number of houses in Hannibal, the most famous being the Mark Twain home at 206 Hill Street, the small, two-story frame building visited by thousands annually. Sam attended several different schools and excelled at none of them—except in spelling—but made many friends, including Will Bowen, his best friend, and Tom Blankenship, the model for Huck Finn. In her old age, Laura Hawkins—Becky Thatcher in *Tom Sawyer*—remembered Sam as a "humorous" fellow with "a drawling, appealing voice," who came from a good but "very poor" family. He shared his candy and oranges with her and carried her books to school, but "played hookey" a lot and ran around "with a gang of boys."[45] Sam's pleasures were many and included swimming and boating in the river, picnics, playing Robin Hood in the woods, taking in the circus, the minstrel shows, and other traveling entertainments, and marching in gaudy uniforms with the Cadets of Temperance. Best of all, he loved the annual visits to his uncle John Quarles's farm, which lasted for two months and more each summer. "It was a heavenly place for a boy, that farm of my uncle John's,"[46] he recalled.

But a boy's life was not all fun, even as it is represented in the immortal idyll of *Tom Sawyer*. Injun Joe is the novel's principal figure of darkness, an abused outcast, who lurks along the margins of society, seeking bloody-minded revenge. The real Hannibal had many and similar horrors. Sam witnessed the murder of the drunkard, "poor old Smarr," in the main street of town and

vividly recalled "the great family Bible spread open on the profane old man's breast by some thoughtful idiot."[47] The episode
later served as the source for the Boggs murder in *Huckleberry
Finn.* Equally unforgettable was the corpse of the stabbed emi-
grant that Sam fell upon in his father's office one evening, and
that he describes in detail in *The Innocents Abroad.* "Villagers of
1840–3," a fragmentary manuscript written in 1897, is replete with
kindred memories, ghastly and pathetic. The most indelible of
these features is a drunken tramp who incinerated himself in the
village jail with matches given to him by charitable Sam
Clemens. "I was *not* responsible" for the poor man's death, the
humorist later wrote, "for I had meant him no harm but only
good, when I let him have the matches; but no matter, mine was
a trained Presbyterian conscience and knew but the one duty—to
hunt and harry its slave upon all pretexts and on all occasions, especially when there was no sense nor reason in it. The tramp—
who was to blame—suffered ten minutes; I, who was not to
blame, suffered three months."[48] Clemens notably traces the
strong strain of self-accusation, so evident here and elsewhere in
his work, to his religious training. Church was better than school
only because it met less frequently. The Clemens children attended a Methodist Sunday school until 1843, when their mother
shifted allegiance to the local Presbyterian church. Here Sam
heard and took to heart the standard teachings on inherited sin
and eternal punishment, a message that was vividly reinforced at
the feverish revivals and camp meetings to which his mother was
attracted. Little wonder that the burning tramp, and other similarly accusing figures, continued to haunt his dreams.

There is little of slavery in *Tom Sawyer,* but it dominates *Huckleberry Finn.* That difference is an important key to the dramatic
contrast in the tone and meaning of the two books. Slavery was
certainly a central feature of Clemens's boyhood in Hannibal.
Jennie, the last of his father's slaves, lived with the family for
most of his childhood. Sam once looked on as his father flogged
her for insubordination. He was also friendly with the many
slaves on his uncle John Quarles's farm, and especially remembered superstitious "Aunt" Hannah, an adept in witchcraft, and
"Uncle Dan'l," the model for Jim in *Huckleberry Finn,* "whose

heart was honest and simple and knew no guile."[49] Slavery was accepted without much protest in antebellum Hannibal, though people recoiled inwardly from the inevitable excesses brought on by the institution. "When I was ten years old," Clemens later recalled, while traveling in India, "I saw a man fling a lump of iron-ore at a slave-man in anger, for merely doing something awkwardly—as if it were a crime. It bounded from the man's skull, and the man fell and never spoke again. He was dead in an hour. I knew the man had a right to kill his slave if he wanted to, and yet it seemed a pitiful thing and somehow wrong, though why wrong I was not deep enough to explain if I had been asked to do it. Nobody in the village approved of that murder, but of course no one said much about it."[50]

The brutalities of slavery were as much a part of life in Hannibal as the murders and stabbings and beatings regularly witnessed in the streets and along the river. Indeed, the closer we look at Clemens's childhood, the less idyllic it seems. Domestic life provided some sanctuary, of course, but the deaths of siblings and the gathering weight of poverty doubtless took their toll at home. So, in a more decisive way, did the declining health of his father, who died of pneumonia in March 1847. The shock was compounded for Sam when he witnessed John Marshall's postmortem examination. Jane, meanwhile, seizing on her son's remorseful mood, made him promise to be faithful, industrious, and upright, like his father. Albert Bigelow Paine reports that Sam walked in his sleep on several nights in succession after the funeral.[51]

It is difficult to quarrel with the view that his father's passing marked the end of young Clemens's childhood. The threat of economic hardship that had dogged the family for years, and that gave the edge to Sam's lifelong and insatiable craving for wealth, was now a harsh reality. Orion now provided the main financial support by working as a printer in St. Louis; Pamela gave music lessons; and Jane, after moving her family to a smaller house, took in guests. Sam continued in school for a couple of years but began to work as well, first at odd jobs, and then as an apprentice and "printer's devil" living in the home of Joseph Ament, publisher of the *Missouri Courier*. It was a meager subsistence, to be sure, but the youngster made rapid strides in mastering his new vocation and enjoyed the company of his fellow apprentice, Wales McCormick, who "constantly and persistently and loudly and elaborately" made sexual advances to the mulatto daughter of Ament's slave cook. The girl's evident distress produced little save amusement in the household, where—as the fascinated apprentice later recalled—it was "well understood that by the customs of slaveholding communities it was Wales's right to make love to that girl if he wanted to."[52]

Sam took the next step as a printer-journalist in 1851, when he hired on as a typesetter and editorial assistant with the *Western Union* and later with the Hannibal *Journal*, local newspapers published by his brother, Orion, who had returned from St. Louis. Despite the fact that his weekly wages of $3.50 were rarely paid, Sam continued to make progress in his new trade. His first published writings—brief articles and humorous squibs—soon began to appear in the newspaper, and "The Dandy Frightening the Squatter," a more ambitious sketch, was published over the signature "S.L.C." in the Boston *Carpet-Bag* in 1852. But Hannibal could not hold him. He had felt the pull of adventure and glittering opportunity when the first gold rush enthusiasts poured through town in 1849; and the gorgeous boats passing daily along the Mississippi were a constant reminder of the more exciting places to which they traveled. The inevitable occurred in June 1853, when Sam bid mother and family farewell and took passage first to St. Louis, where he worked for a few weeks as a typesetter, and then, in late August, to New York. Jane Clemens sadly helped her restless son to pack, and then asked him to swear that he would "not throw a card or drink a drop of liquor" while he was gone.[53]

"I should greatly like to re-live my youth, and then get drowned," Clemens wrote in 1900.[54] At a distance in time, boyhood in Hannibal often looked grand; deaths in the family, poverty, and pervasive violence were swept aside in recurrent waves of nostalgia. For the provincial youth newly arrived in New York in August 1853, however, the present and future were brimming with excitement and promise. His letters home are energized by delight in such big city attractions as P. T. Barnum's

Museum and the World's Fair, by the discovery of his ability to support himself working in print shops, and by accounts of his sojourns in Philadelphia and Washington. In the spring of 1854, Sam returned home and worked for the next three years as a printer-journalist in St. Louis and other towns along the Mississippi and Ohio Rivers. In April 1857, en route from Cincinnati to New Orleans, he met Horace Bixby, a veteran steamboat pilot, who agreed to take him on as an apprentice (or "cub") pilot for $500. For the next two years, Clemens studied—virtually memorized—the course of the Mississippi between St. Louis and New Orleans and received his pilot's license in April 1859. For two years more, until 1861, when the outbreak of the Civil War closed the river to commercial traffic, he was steadily employed, very well paid, and evidently quite happy in his work as a pilot. "I loved the profession far better than any I have followed since," he declares in *Life on the Mississippi*. "and I took measureless pride in it."[55]

Clemens's writing during this period (1853–1861) is sparse and reflects the fact that he had not yet settled on his final calling. In addition to his newspaper correspondence, he wrote humorous dialect letters under such pseudonyms as "Thomas Jefferson Snodgrass," and a merciless burlesque of Captain Isaiah Sellers, a venerable if rather long-winded fixture of New Orleans journalism. Clemens's formal education was a thing of the distant past, of course, but he continued nonetheless to read widely and to study French. Perhaps the most revealing of the written records in his letter of June 18, 1858, to his sister-in-law, Mollie Stotts Clemens, reporting the death of his younger brother, Henry, who was mortally injured in an explosion on the steamboat *Pennsylvania* just days before. Sam is overcome with grief; but his grief is, in turn, overrun by a tide of remorse for real and imagined sins against the victim. "O, God!" Clemens cries out, "this is hard to bear. Hardened, hopeless—aye, lost—lost—lost and ruined sinner as I am—I, even I, have humbled myself to the ground and prayed as never man prayed before, that the great God might let this cup pass from me—that he would strike me to the earth, but spare my brother—that he would pour out the fulness of his wrath upon my wicked head, but have mercy, mercy, mercy upon that unoffending boy."[56] This brief passage, like the letter more generally, is floridly rhetorical in tone, detached in its literary allusiveness, and oddly inattentive to its putative subject, the deceased victim. Evidently enough, Henry's death produced an emotional crisis in Sam, a sudden convulsion of conflicted and heavily charged feelings too volatile to contain and yet impossible to face directly. The letter is a kind of failed performance in which the speaker's conspicuous inauthenticity brings attention to rest on the elusive identity of the figure behind the remorseful mask. The lie thus points to a truth. Not surprisingly, Clemens returned again and again to the story of Henry's death, but never succeeded in constructing a narrative of the tragedy that laid his uneasiness to rest.[57]

Left without work at the outbreak of the Civil War, Clemens returned to Hannibal in June 1861 and helped organize the Marion Rangers, a ragtag troop of volunteers, who disbanded after a few weeks without seeing combat. Clemens was highly ambivalent about the war and seized on the opportunity to relocate to the remote Far West as assistant to his brother, Orion, who had been recently appointed secretary of the Nevada Territory. They left in mid-July, and after a month's travel by boat and stagecoach, arrived in Carson City, Nevada. Sam's adventures on the mining frontier are amply chronicled in *Roughing It*, a humorous narrative of initiation into the uncouth customs of the region. "I was young and ignorant," he recalls, and anxious to "see the gold mines and the silver mines, and maybe go about of an afternoon . . . and pick up two or three pailfuls of shining slugs, and nuggets of gold and silver on the hillside."[58] The innocence on display is manifestly simulated, and yet it hints at the truth that Clemens's ambitions often outran opportunity during his years in Nevada and California. Along with many others, he tried his hand at prospecting, and failed; he made timber claims, and failed; he speculated in mining stock, and failed.

What didn't fail him was his pen. His occasional newspaper correspondence caught the eye of Joseph T. Goodman, editor of the Virginia City *Territorial Enterprise*, who in September 1862 hired Clemens as a reporter for $25 per week. In addition to routine journalism, the newcomer began to develop his own brand of freewheeling frontier humor, exemplified in hoaxes such as the "Petrified Man" and "A Bloody Massacre Near Carson," both widely reprinted. In February 1863, he first used the psuedonym "Mark Twain," imagining that it would serve well enough as a temporary nom de plume. His circle of friends seen grew to include other well-known writers, most notably the humorist Artemus Ward, with whom he spent a riotous Christmas holiday in 1863, and Bret Harte, who offered valuable editorial advice when Clemens moved to San Francisco the following June. The move was precipitated by another revealing-because-unresolved episode in our subject's life. In an unsigned editorial, Sam charged that the proceeds from a charity ball were being secretly sent to a Miscegenation Society in the East. Besides betraying the writer's Southern sympathies, the letter outraged James Laird, a rival journalist, with whom Clemens exchanged insults and challenges to a duel. But when push came to shove, Sam thought better of the fight and abruptly left the territory. "First there had been the war," observes James M. Cox; "now there was the duel." In both instances, "Clemens had, by ordinary standards, failed in courage and honor."[59] It was another of those vexed episodes he came back to again and again, trying in vain to find a version of the story he could live with.

During the next two years, spent largely in California, Sam supported himself by writing for the *Golden Era* and the *Californian,* both literary magazines, the latter edited by Bret Harte, and as a reporter for the San Francisco *Morning Call.* His now seasoned nose for trouble led him into conflict with the San Francisco police, who took umbrage when he criticized them in print for corruption and mistreatment of the Chinese. Clemens beat a temporary retreat to the Sierra foothills, where, in the cabin of Jim Gillis on Jackass Hill in Tuolumne County, he first heard the story of the frog that would make him famous. Originally scheduled for publication in a humorous volume patched together by Artemus Ward, "The Celebrated Jumping Frog of Calaveras County" finally made its debut in the New York *Saturday Press* in November 1865. The story was an instant success, and thanks to widespread reprinting, it brought the name Mark Twain to a large national audience.

Back in San Francisco, Sam labored at journalism for a while longer but soon grew restless for change. When the *Sacramento Union* offered to hire him as a roving correspondent to the Sandwich Islands, he accepted with enthusiasm and sailed for Honolulu on March 7, 1866. Horseback tours of the island, the curious customs of the natives, the equally curious behavior of the missionaries, a meeting with King Kamehameha, and a visit to an active volcano are among the featured topics in the chapters on Hawaii toward the end of *Roughing It.* What Clemens does not mention, but later reported to Albert Bigelow Paine, was a formative encounter with Anson Burlingame, the American minister to China, who urged him to "seek companionship among men of superior intellect and character. Refine yourself and your work. Never affiliate with inferiors; always climb."[60] The clarity with which Clemens recalled these words is one indication among many that he took them to heart.

Returning to San Francisco in August, Sam was prompted by the success of his Sandwich Islands letters to try his hand at lecturing. Just a year earlier, as his thirtieth birthday approached, he confessed to Orion his sense that life was passing him by. His piloting career was a thing of the past, and the ambition to be a preacher was blocked by his lack of "the necessary stock in trade—i.e. religion." But, he continued, "I *have* had a call to literature, of a low order—i.e. humorous. It is nothing to be proud of, but it is my strongest suit."[61] Clemens was scarcely reconciled to his vocational fate; and taking his humor on stage may not have satisfied Anson Burlingame's standards of refinement; but it was a step up, nonetheless, and it was an immediate success. The capacity crowd at Maguirre's Academy of Music responded with vigorous laughter and applause to the lecturer's drawling jokes and anecdotes, which were supplemented for "style" with florid descriptions of Sandwich Islands scenery. Encouraged no doubt by very favorable reviews, Sam took his show on the road and lectured with equal success in the larger towns of California and Nevada.[62] Back once again in San Francisco, he was hired on attractive terms as a roving correspondent for the *Alta California.* Burlingame might have been pleased. Sam certainly was. "I am running on preachers,"[63] he crowed to his family in a letter of

December 4, 1866, indicating that as a celebrity he had ascended to an elite social sphere that included famous men of the cloth as its members. Less than two weeks later, armed with letters of introduction to Henry Ward Beecher and other eminent East coast preachers, he left California on the steamship *America*. The most pleasurable feature of the journey was keeping company with the ship's captain, Ned Wakeman, a boisterous, irreverent storyteller and the model for the hero of "Captain Stormfield's Visit to Heaven." A cholera outbreak which took the lives of seven passengers was much less amusing.

Clemens arrived in New York on January 12, 1867 and promptly got his career into high gear. In addition to writing for several newspapers, and delivering lectures both in New York and in various midwestern cities, he persuaded his editors at the *Alta California* to hire him as a correspondent on an excursion to Europe and the Holy Land organized by Henry Ward Beecher's church in Brooklyn. The cruise ship *Quaker City*, whose passengers were generally too old and staid to suit Clemens, sailed on June 10. Still, he made a few friends, among them Moses Sperry Beach, editor of the New York *Sun*, and his daughter Emma; Mary Mason Fairbanks, who was to become a faithful confidante; and Charles Jervis Langdon, the son of a wealthy coal magnate from Elmira, New York, who showed the admiring Clemens a picture of his sister, Olivia. These and a few other kindred spirits provided relief from the rather leaden piety of most of the "pilgrims," as they made their way around the Mediterranean, returning to New York on November 19. Clemens's impressions of his companions and the many places they visited are recorded in *The Innocents Abroad*, his first best-seller, published in 1869. The book's great popularity was undoubtedly rooted in its humorous, vernacular critique of the pretense and hypocrisy on display among the bourgeois American excursionists. "Such was our daily life on board the ship," Clemens groused, "solemnity, decorum, dinner, dominoes, devotions, slander.[64]

Sam's personal and public lives advanced briskly and profitably in the years after his return from Europe. On the personal side, he accompanied Livy Langdon and her family to a New York reading by Charles Dickens in late December 1867. The courtship, involving frequent visits to Elmira and an extensive correspondence, ended with their marriage two years later. Bored after a year in Buffalo, the newlyweds moved to Hartford, Connecticut, where they rented for a while, but then built the large, very striking "Mark Twain House" in Nook Farm, a wealthy suburb. Among their neighbors were Harriet Beecher Stowe, author of *Uncle Tom's Cabin,* Joseph H. Twichell, a Congregational minister and one of Sam's closest friends, and Charles Dudley Warner, a writer with whom he would collaborate on *The Gilded Age* (1873), the novel that gave a name to the period of political scandal and predatory speculation in America just after the Civil War. Langdon Clemens, their first child, was born on November 7, 1870, just three months after the death of his namesake, Livy's father. A premature and sickly child, Langdon succumbed two years later, not long after the birth of Olivia Susan Clemens, the first of three daughters (Clara was born in 1874, Jean in 1880).

On the professional side, Sam resumed work as a newspaper correspondent and at the same time served briefly in Washington as private secretary to Nevada Senator William M. Stewart. He also signed an agreement with Elisha Bliss of the American Publishing Company, who persuaded him to expand his correspondence into a book to be sold by the new and extremely profitable "subscription" method. *The Innocents Abroad,* with sales of nearly 70,000 copies in its first year, was the happy result. It was reviewed enthusiastically by William Dean Howells, who became a very close, lifelong friend. Howells wrote with equal approval of *Roughing It,* a second, very profitable subscription book, when it appeared in 1872. Two years later, he accepted Clemens's moving account of a slave mother's sorrow, "A True Story," for publication in the high-brow *Atlantic Monthly,* which he edited. Gratified by his elevation to the literary elite, and with Howells's encouragement, Clemens next turned to "Old Times on the Mississippi," a series of seven articles on his steamboating experiences which appeared serially in the *Atlantic* in 1875. As a humorist and travel writer, he had clearly arrived.

Clemens was equally successful on the lecture circuit, where his famous drawl and impeccable timing gave a distinctive humorous edge to talks on such subjects as "Our Fellow Savages of

the Sandwich Islands" and "Roughing It on the Silver Frontier."
In 1869, he contracted with James Redpath, the Scottish-born
writer and founder of the Boston Lyceum Bureau, for a tour of
the Northeast and Midwest. The venture was sufficiently profitable that a second tour was scheduled for the winter months of
18771–1872. There were occasional lectures in the years that followed—in the major English cities in 1873–1874, for example—
and a joint tour with George Washington Cable, billed as the
"Twins of Genius," in 1884–1885. Finally, in 1895–1896, the sixty-
year-old humorist undertook a global lecture tour which he describes in *Following the Equator* (1897). Lecturing was sometimes
pleasurable—"he was the most consummate public performer I
ever saw," Howells testifies[65]—but Clemens missed home and
wearied of train travel, hotels, and restaurant food. He undertook the grind principally for the money to meet the increasing
demands that came with a growing family and the lavish lifestyle
of a celebrity.

Indeed, it would be difficult to exaggerate the importance of
money in Clemens's outlook on life. The craving went well beyond practical need; it arose from an insatiable hunger, born
partly of the experience of childhood poverty and as much or
more from the sheer exhilaration of material excess. Justin Kaplan, who is especially insightful on this topic, allows that "it is
hard to think of another writer so obsessed in his life and work
by the lure, the rustle and chink and heft of money." Kaplan goes
on to add that while Clemens "was notoriously reticent about depicting mature sexual and emotional relationships, he did write a
kind of pornography of the dollar."[66] It is commonly observed
that he wrote with an eye principally to profit and came in his
middle years to think of himself as a businessman first, and a
writer only second. His plays—notably *Colonel Sellers* (adapted
from *The Gilded Age*), *Ah Sin* (a collaboration with Bret Harte),
and dramatizations of *Tom Sawyer* and *The Prince and the Pauper*—
were business ventures, pure and simple. "The promise of quick
money from the theater enchanted Sam," observes Andrew
Hoffman.[67]

Clemens's materialism—admittedly incongruous in a man
who raged against the money-getting spirit of post-Civil War

America—was clearly accountable for his incurable, and frequently disastrous, attraction to get-rich-quick schemes of every kind, including inventions and assorted business speculations. He developed a self-pasting scrapbook, owned patents on an adjustable garment strap and a board game, and showed interest in railroad steam brakes, specialized grape scissors, and an outdoor history "course" laid out with pegs, one foot per year, along his driveway. The financial stakes were much higher in Clemens's business affairs, and generally he came out a loser. He lost $10,000, for example, when he sold his interest in the Buffalo *Express* in 1871, and his substantial investments in Kaolatype, an engraving process, and the health food Plasmon also went sour. Things went better, at least for a time, in publishing. Sam founded his own firm, Charles L. Webster and Company, named after his nephew, who ran the operation, and made good initial profits selling his own books. The company's greatest success came with the posthumous publication of Ulysses S. Grant's *Personal Memoirs* in 1885, which brought more than $400,000 in royalties to the former president's family and handsome profits for Clemens as well. But the fate of Webster and Company was bound up with Clemens's most infamous speculative venture, an intricate and finally unworkable typesetting machine designed by James W. Paige. So infatuated was Clemens with the machine, and with the fabulous fortune it seemed to promise, that he vastly overextended himself in promoting its development, and finally went bankrupt in 1894, taking Webster and Company down in the process. He partially righted himself, and certainly enhanced his public image, by fully repaying his creditors with the proceeds from a widely publicized lecture tour that took him around the world. Meanwhile, his new friend, Henry Huttleston Rogers, the predatory director of the Standard Oil Company, restored stability to Clemens's finances and left him in very comfortable circumstances.

As we have seen, Sam was as disenchanted by the national scramble for wealth as he was fatally attracted to it. The negative pole of his ambivalence, already evident in his (*Burlesque*) *Autobiography* of 1871, surfaced fully two years later in *The Gilded Age*, with its biting critique of post-Civil War America. Having de-

scended imaginatively into the fallen world of the present, he recoiled from it into a wave of nostalgia that carried him back to
the idyll of his Hannibal childhood, and that endured, in one
form or another, for the rest of his life. The idealized "Old Times
on the Mississippi" of 1875—reproduced in the opening chapters
of *Life on the Mississippi* (1883)—was followed a year later by
The Adventures of Tom Sawyer, which was no sooner published
than Clemens began work on *Huckleberry Finn,* which finally appeared, after a long gestation, in 1885. The boy and the village figure equally prominently in *The Mysterious Stranger* and the *Autobiography,* both published posthumously, and to a lesser degree
in *The Prince and the Pauper* (1881), *A Connecticut Yankee in King
Arthur's Court* (1889), *Pudd'nhead Wilson* (1894), and assorted
minor works. The more deeply he immersed himself in the realities of modern American life, the more Clemens withdrew imaginatively to an earlier, simpler time. The contradiction is only
slightly more conspicuous in him than in the culture he has done
so much to define.

Clemens's misgivings about America, grounded as they were
in misgivings about himself, were also manifest in his conflicted
attitudes toward two prominent repositories of national pride,
the New England literary establishment and General Grant. Taking an active, well-publicized role in the production of the great
Union hero's *Memoirs* was gratifying to Clemens because it allowed him to approach symbolic parity with a man who had
been heroic in the war from which he, by painful contrast, had
fled. In making a fortune for the dying warrior's family, the publisher earned a kind of reprieve from the embarrassment of his
youthful failure of nerve. A kindred redemptive impulse drives
"The Private History of a Campaign that Failed," Clemens's 1885
contribution to a series on the Civil War published in *Century
Magazine.* A reconstruction in largely humorous terms of the
young soldier's retreat from combat, the essay reveals even as it
attempts to conceal an intractable burden of self-accusation.
Grant read the essay and was apparently amused.[68]

As an unlettered western parvenu and comedian, Clemens
was ambivalent in a rather different way in his response to the
venerable guardians of elite New England literary culture. His

feelings came rather nakedly to view at an 1877 banquet in honor of John Greenleaf Whittier, at which Clemens was invited to speak. He told the story of a hospitable Western miner's unfortunate run-in with three deadbeats, who pass themselves off as Ralph Waldo Emerson, Oliver Wendell Holmes, and Henry Wadsworth Longfellow. Few in the audience were amused. Though Emerson, Holmes, and Longfellow, who were all present, took little offense, the animus of the anecdote was lost on no one. No one, that is, except Clemens who was horrified by the failure of the joke. Only later did he come to recognize the strong current of aggression running through his little tale. "It seems as if I must have been insane when I wrote that speech & saw no harm in it, no disrespect toward those men whom I reverenced so much,"[69] he wrote to Howells. The guilt and humiliation never left him. Nearly thirty years later, going over the speech with Paine, Clemens at first found it "gross, coarse . . . offensive and detestable." Upon rereading it, however, he changed his mind completely, and judged it "just as good as it can be. It is smart; it is saturated with humor. There isn't a suggestion of coarseness or vulgarity in it anywhere."[70] What a striking example of the paired, virtually simultaneous impulses to reveal and to conceal the same thing!

In 1885, the year of his fiftieth birthday, Clemens reached his life's zenith. His health was good, his family was happy (Susy was writing his biography!), and he was rolling in money. *Huckleberry Finn* and Grant's *Memoirs* were both published that year; the lecture tour with Cable ended successfully (profitably); and the Paige typesetter still looked very promising. Money and good will were in such abundance that Clemens wrote to the dean of the Yale Law School on the day before Christmas and offered to pay the board of a black student, Warner T. McGuinn.[71] To be sure, there were successes aplenty still in store—much wealth, several important books (notably *A Connecticut Yankee in King Arthur's Court*, *Pudd'nhead Wilson*, *Following the Equator*, and *The Mysterious Stranger*), and ever-increasing fame and influence. In the years around the turn-of-the-century, Clemens made a bold and effective public stand against injustice at home and abroad. He spoke out both in widely publicized speeches, statements to

the press, and in a series of influential articles. His brilliant indict-
ment of imperialism, "To the Person Sitting in Darkness," was
published in 1901, while "King Leopold's Soliloquy," an attack on
European brutality in the Belgian Congo, appeared four years
later.[72] Meanwhile, there were honors and honorary degrees (notably from Yale, Missouri, and Oxford) in gratifying abundance.

But the dominant theme after 1885 was decline. As we have
seen, a lavish lifestyle, in combination with the failure of the
typesetter and the publishing company, produced humiliating
bankruptcy. Financial troubles were also involved in the decision
to live abroad during most of the 1890s, when the family settled
at intervals in Germany, Italy, France, Switzerland, Austria, and
England. Clemens's mother died in 1890, as did Livy's. He suffered more regularly than ever before with rheumatism and
other ailments; she developed heart trouble. Most crushingly of
all, Susy succumbed to spinal meningitis in August 1896, just as
Clemens was completing this global lecture tour. Jean was diagnosed as epileptic at about the same time. The return to America
in 1900 was cut short three years later when doctors advised that
Livy go back to Europe for her health. But the move brought
scant relief; Livy died in Florence on June 5, 1904. Jean had her
first epileptic seizure in more than a year; Clara collapsed from
shock; their father was stricken with grief and remorse.

Clemens soon returned to the United States, resided for several years in a house on Fifth Avenue in New York, and then took
possession of Stormfield, a newly constructed home in Redding,
Connecticut. His seventieth birthday party at Delmonico's was a
grand social event, with almost 200 guests. Albert Bigelow Paine
sought and received permission to be his official biographer in
1906 and became a permanent member of the household. At
about this time, Clemens's love of display drew him into the habit
of wearing white suits in public. Meanwhile, his circle of friends
expanded to include a number of young girls with whom he liked
to visit and exchange letters. He called them his "angelfish."
Clemens continued to be troubled by a variety of ailments, most
ominously by a heart condition diagnosed late in 1909. A few
weeks later, on Christmas Eve, Jean had a seizure and drowned in
the bathtub at Stormfield. It was a terrible blow. Her grieving fa-

ther went south to Bermuda to recover, but soon began to suffer severe chest pains and hastened home. He died at Stormfield on April 21, 1910.

With just about everything else in his life, Clemens's writing declined during his final years. His published work was frequently inferior—witness *Merry Tales* (1892) and *The American Claimant* (1892)—while his most ambitious projects either languished in fragments or were purposely withheld from publication. His inability to bring works to completion was especially marked, as the dozens of fragments gathered at the Mark Twain Papers in Berkeley, and published in various posthumous collections, surely testify. Bernard DeVoto, a careful student of these late materials, observes that a majority of them "develop and embroider the twinned themes: man's complete helplessness in the grip of the inexorable forces of the universe, and man's essential cowardice, pettiness, and evil."[73] Such is the irresistible thrust of the unfinished manuscripts of *The Mysterious Stranger*, just as it is of *What Is Man?*, Clemens's dialogue on the spiritual poverty of the human condition, published anonymously in a limited edition in 1906. It was as though he had finally conceded the impossibility of writing a satisfactory narrative of his own inner experience, a narrative that at once ordered and redeemed life as he knew it. The older he got, and the more his family and friends and personal powers declined, the more impossible that story seemed. His Olympian relish for the bounty of creation had given way almost completely to determinism, nihilism, despair. Life was base and pointless; people were haplessly selfish and self-deceived. If there was any consolation in this dire outlook, it derived from the thought that the chaos—as Clemens tried to persuade himself—was no longer his responsibility.

NOTES

1. As quoted in Louis J. Budd, *Our Mark Twain: The Making of His Public Personality* (Philadelphia: University of Pennsylvania Press, 1983), p. 4.

2. William Dean Howells, *My Mark Twain*, in *Literary Friends and*

Acquaintance, ed. David F. Hiatt and Edwin H. Cady (Bloomington: Indiana University Press, 1968), p. 257.

3. *Mark Twain-Howells Letters,* ed. Henry Nash Smith and William M. Gibson (Cambridge: Harvard University Press, 1960), p. 838.

4. Henry Nash Smith, *Mark Twain: The Development of a Writer* (Cambridge: Harvard University Press, 1962), p. 18.

5. Andrew Hoffman, *Inventing Mark Twain: The Lives of Samuel Langhorne Clemens* (New York: William Morrow and Company, 1997), x, xiii.

6. Ibid., xiii, xii, xv.

7. John C. Gerber, "Mark Twain's Use of the Comic Pose," *PMLA* 77 (1962): 297–304; Michael J. Kiskis, ed., *Mark Twain's Own Autobiography* (Madison: University of Wisconsin Press, 1990), xxxiii.

8. Hoffman, *Inventing Mark Twain,* xiii.

9. Gerber, "Mark Twain's Use of the Comic Pose," p. 297.

10. Susan Gillman, *Dark Twins: Imposture and Identity in Mark Twain's America* (Chicago: University of Chicago Press, 1989), p. 11. Gillman goes on to observe that "the two selves do not remain fixed in their proper categories, making it difficult to maintain the linguistic distinction consistently."

11. Herman Melville, *Pierre; or the Ambiguities* (Evanston: Northwestern University Press, 1971), p. 285.

12. *The Mysterious Stranger,* ed. William M. Gibson (Berkeley: University of California Press, 1970), p. 405.

13. Nathaniel Hawthorne, *The English Notebooks,* ed. Randall Stewart (New York: Russell & Russell, 1962), p. 432.

14. Gillman, *Dark Twins,* p. 8 and passim.

15. Justin Kaplan, *Mr. Clemens and Mark Twain* (New York: Simon and Schuster, 1966), p. 388.

16. Clara Clemens, *My Father, Mark Twain* (New York: Harper and Brothers, 1931), pp. 6–7.

17. *Mark Twain's Autobiography,* ed. Albert Bigelow Paine, 2 vols. (New York: Harper and Brothers, 1924), 1:193.

18. *A Tramp Abroad* (New York: Oxford University Press, 1996), p. 126. In this and subsequent references to writings published during Clemens's lifetime, I will use the recent, twenty-nine volume Oxford University Press edition of facsimiles of the first American editions of his work, edited by Shelley Fisher Fishkin.

19. *Life on the Mississippi* (New York: Oxford University Press, 1996), p. 166.

20. Paine, ed., *Mark Twain's Autobiography*, 1:xv.

21. Ibid., 1:xii.

22. Smith and Gibson, eds., *Mark Twain-Howells Letters*, p. 782.

23. Paine, ed., *Mark Twain's Autobiography*, 1:235–36.

24. Ibid., 1:237.

25. "Corn-Pone Opinions," in *Mark Twain: Collected Tales, Sketches, Speeches, and Essays 1891–1910*, ed. Louis J. Budd (New York: Library of America, 1992), p. 510. The editor indicates that the essay was written sometime in 1901.

26. *What Is Man?* (New York: Oxford University Press, 1992), p. 22.

27. *Mark Twain's (Burlesque) Autobiography and First Romance* (New York: Sheldon & Company, 1871), p. 18.

28. Ibid., p. 45.

29. On the flagrant greed and corruption that attached to the Erie Railroad, see David Mountfield, *The Railway Barons* (London: Osprey, 1979), ch. 5; and Charles Francis Adams, Jr., "A Chapter of Erie," in *Chapters of Erie* (Ithaca: Cornell University Press, 1956).

30. See *Mark Twain's Letters, Volume 4: 1870–1871*, ed. Victor Fischer and Michael B. Frank (Berkeley: University of California Press, 1995), p. 381n1, for contemporary responses.

31. Kaplan, *Mr. Clemens and Mark Twain*, p. 124.

32. Ibid.

33. *Mark Twain's (Burlesque) Autobiography and First Romance*, p. 18.

34. *Mark Twain's Letters, Volume 3: 1869*, ed. Victor Fischer and Michael B. Frank (Berkeley: University of California Press, 1992), p. 8.

35. *Mark Twain's Letters, Volume 2: 1867–1868*, ed. Harriet Elinor Smith and Richard Bucci (Berkeley: University of California Press, 1990), p. 284.

36. Kaplan, *Mr. Clemens and Mark Twain*, p. 96.

37. *Mark Twain's (Burlesque) Autobiography and First Romance*, p. 27.

38. Gillman, *Dark Twins*, pp. 5–6.

39. Fischer and Frank, eds., *Mark Twain's Letters, Volume 4*, pp. 50–51.

40. Paine, ed., *Mark Twain's Autobiography*, 1:3–4.

41. Ibid., 1:108.

42. *Mark Twain's Own Autobiography*, p. 112.

43. *Life on the Mississippi*, pp. 62–65.

44. Bernard DeVoto, *Mark Twain's America* (Boston: Little, Brown, 1932), p. 52.

45. Newspaper interview of April 21, 1910, and obituary notice in the Hannibal *Courier-Post*, December 26, 1928; as cited in Dixon Wecter, *Sam Clemens of Hannibal* (Boston: Houghton Mifflin, 1952), p. 182.

46. Paine, ed., *Mark Twain's Autobiography*, 1:96.

47. Ibid., 1:131.

48. *The Autobiography of Mark Twain*, ed. Charles Neider (New York: Harper and Brothers, 1959), p. 41.

49. Ibid., pp. 5–6.

50. *Following the Equator* (New York: Oxford University Press. 1996), p. 352.

51. Albert Bigelow Paine, *Mark Twain: A Biography*, 4 vols. (New York: Harper and Brothers, 1912), 1:74–75.

52. Paine, ed., *Mark Twain's Autobiography*, 2:276–77.

53. Paine, *Mark Twain: A Biography*, 1:93.

54. *Mark Twain's Letters to Will Bowen*, ed. Theodore Hornbrger (Austin: University of Texas Press, 1941, p. 27.

55. *Life on the Mississippi*, p. 166.

56. *Mark Twain's Letters, Volume 1: 1853–1866*, ed. Edgar Marquess Branch, Michael B. Frank, and Kenneth M. Sanderson (Berkeley: University of California Press, 1988), pp. 80–81.

57. For more on Clemens's response to Henry's death, see Edgar Marquess Branch, *Men Call Me Lucky: Mark Twain and the Pennsylvania* (Miami, Ohio: Friends of the Library Society, 1985); and Forrest G. Robinson, "Why I Killed My Brother: An Essay on Mark Twain," *Literature and Psychology* 30 (1980): 168–81.

58. *Roughing It* (New York: Oxford University Press, 1996), p. 19.

59. James M. Cox, *Mark Twain: The Fate of Humor* (Princeton: Princeton University Press, 1966), p. 17. For a detailed account of the feud with Laird, see Paul Fatout, *Mark Twain in Virginia City* (Bloomington: Indiana University Press, 1964), pp. 196–213.

60. Paine, *Mark Twain: A Biography*, 1:287.

61. Branch et al., eds., *Mark Twain's Letters, Volume 1*, p. 322.

62. For more on the lectures, see Paul Fatout, *Mark Twain on the Lecture Circuit* (Carbondale: Southern Illinois University Press, 1960), ch. 3 and passim.

63. Branch et al., eds., *Mark Twain's Letters, Volume 1*, p. 368.

64. *The Innocents Abroad* (New York: Oxford University Press, 1996), p. 645.

65. Howells, *My Mark Twain*, p. 288.

66. Kaplan, *Mr. Clemens and Mark Twain*, p. 96.

67. Hoffman, *Inventing Mark Twain*, p. 309.

68. Justin Kaplan's handling of Clemens's relationship with Grant is especially insightful. See *Mr Clemens and Mark Twain*, pp. 225–27, 274–75, and 296–97.

69. Smith and Gibson, eds., *Mark Twain-Howells Letters*, p. 212.

70. Paine, *Mark Twain: A Biography*, 2:609.

71. For more on McGuinn, who went on to a distinguished legal career, see Shelley Fisher Fishkin, *Lighting Out for the Territory: Reflections on Mark Twain and American Culture* (New York: Oxford University Press, 1997), pp. 99–107.

72. Other well-known essays on social issues—"Battle Hymn of the Republic (Brought Down to Date)," "As Regards Patriotism," "The United States of Lyncherdom," "Corn-Pone Opinions," and "The War Prayer"—were written during these years but not published in Clemens's lifetime.

73. Bernard DeVoto, *Mark Twain at Work* (Cambridge: Harvard University Press, 1942), pp. 115–16.

TWAIN IN
HIS TIME

"A Moralist in Disguise"

Mark Twain and American Religion

Harold K. Bush, Jr.

Around the summer of 1874, Mark Twain rapidly read and digested W. E. H. Lecky's *History of European Morals from Augustus to Charlemagne* (1869), writing the following in the margins: "If I have understood this book aright, it proves two things beyond shadow or question: 1: That Christianity is the very invention of Hell itself; 2 & that Christianity is the most precious and elevating and ennobling boon ever vouchsafed to the world."[1] The first half of this inscription constitutes by far the most popular critical approach to Twain's treatment of religion: he mocked and ridiculed it. However, much less has been said about Twain's affinities for and his deep attractions to the "invisible domains" of faith, as signified by the second half of the inscription.[2] This attraction can be seen throughout Twain's life, from his highly religious courting letters to Livy, to his close friendships with clergymen (especially the Rev. Joseph Twichell), his regular attendance and charitable giving to Twichell's Asylum Hill Congregational Church, and more generally to his lifelong championing of moral causes and his cagey deployment of Christian rhetoric. Despite the very abundant criticisms of religion throughout his corpus, it is vitally important to see much of Twain's greatest achievement in religious and/or moral terms—so much so, it would seem that we can summarize that achievement in much the same way that he once summarized himself—as "a moralist in disguise."[3]

Strikingly similar conflict marked much of American religion during Twain's life. In an oddly reductionist albeit somewhat convincing manner, Twain's own spiritual evolution mirrored many of the major trends and developments in American religion.[4] His movement from a rather primitivistic form of Protestant Christianity, through deism, and later into more scientific and psychological forms of belief roughly squares with the general movement of the nation as a whole. Twain, a highly curious and widely read cultural observer, dabbled at various times in scientific theories that bore on religious belief, such as those of Darwin and Spencer; religious eccentricities ranging from the Mormon movement, to spiritism and the occult, to Christian Science; and scholarly breakthroughs in areas as diverse as astronomy, biblical criticism, and anthropology that directly related to issues of faith. Moreover, when we look at what Paul Carter has called "the spiritual crisis of the Gilded Age" (fostered by such "modernist" movements as Darwinism and the German Higher Criticism of the Bible), it is hard not to notice how much it coincides with Twain's arduous struggles, as well as the emergence of his darker, more utilitarian approach to religion.[5] Thus, the major trends and developments in American religion throughout the Gilded Age, roughly 1865–1910, during which Mark Twain published his most important literary works, provide a fascinating lens through which his literary life and works can usefully be perceived.

The story begins with the frontier Protestant fundamentalism that characterized Twain's childhood in Missouri, and which marked many of his fondest memories of that childhood, even though later he would earnestly critique it. The first Sunday school which Twain attended for about three years was in a tiny brick Methodist church on the public square of Hannibal called the "Old Ship of Zion." Around 1843, his mother Jane Clemens became a member of the Presbyterian church, in whose basement young Sam attended the Sunday school whose lessons would stay with him throughout his life.[6] It was there that young Clemens was trained, as William Dean Howells once put it, "to fear God and dread the Sunday School."[7] The church Twain attended with his family (minus his freethinking father John Clemens) based its doctrine on the Bible, with emphasis on Old Testament texts about God's power, majesty, and wrath. Young Sammy was required to know the Bible: like others of his age, he had to memorize many passages, and by his own admission had "read the Bible through" before he was fifteen.[8] Despite the later, serious attacks by evolutionists, comparative religionists, infidels, and the German higher critics, as Sherwood Cummings puts it, "The Bible's imprint on his mind remained indelible under the palimpsest of later scientific knowledge."[9]

The positive imprint of the Bible and frontier religion, as rendered in sentimentalized and often humorous anecdotes about churchgoing, do appear in some of Twain's best work. The sections of *The Adventures of Tom Sawyer* covering church life, for instance, despite a clearly satirical tone, contain as well sentimental details, such as the moment when the sermon reaches its climax: "[Tom] was really interested for a little while. The minister made a grand and moving picture of the assembling together of the world's hosts at the millennium when the lion and the lamb should lie down together and a little child should lead them."[10] While it is true that Twain does immediately deflate this transcendent vision by explaining Tom's inability to grasp it, the sheer wonder represented is a telling detail. These sentimental tendencies, deeply religious in certain aspects, underscore a very positive and idealistic view of the perfectability of mankind.[11] On the other hand, many critics have emphasized the negative portrayals of his religious upbringing: noting, for instance, the oppressive tone of Twain's Sunday school or church passages in *Tom Sawyer*, *The Gilded Age*, *Adventures of Huckleberry Finn*, and elsewhere. Certainly, Twain often poked fun at the silliness of the churches of his youth. In *Tom Sawyer*, the key features of church life appear to be "showing off" and brainless conformity, such as in the story of the boy who "once recited three thousand verses [of scripture] without stopping; but the strain upon his mental faculties was too great, and he was little better than an idiot from that day forth."[12] This comic episode suggests (and criticizes) the way religious language is consumed by the general populace: memorization without meaning or reflection that precludes any in-depth examination of the religious texts themselves. In many ways, the idiot child of Twain's anecdote is representative of all the evolving (or devolving) generations, who consume the language without reflection and are won over by the art and in turn have forsaken the underlying reality (attitudes memorably captured in the posthumously published essay, "Corn-Pone Opinions"). Later, Tom is able to trade a variety of materials for the colored tokens in order to be presented with the prize Bible before the learned and honored guests by Judge Temple, who takes the opportunity to wax eloquent about this fine young Christian boy: "it's all owing to right bringing up."[13]

In *The Gilded Age*, the corrupt Senator Dilworthy addresses a Sunday school with reverence and pious charm:

> Now, my dear little friends, sit up, straight and pretty . . . let me tell you about a poor little Sunday School scholar I once knew. . . . [he] was always in his place when the bell rang, and he always knew his lesson. . . . He would not let bad boys persuade him to go to play on Sunday. . . . And by and by the people made him governor—and he said it was all owing to the Sunday School. . . . he remembered the fate of the bad little boy who used to try to get him to play on Sunday, and who grew up and became a drunkard and was hanged. He remembered that, and was glad he never yielded and played on Sunday. . . . *That man stands before you!* All that he is, he owes to Sunday School.[14]

The irony of the speech consists of the allusion to the Sunday school as a source of "all that he is"—by which is meant, hypocrisy, hidden corruption, and the ability to manipulate institutional religion to foster docility and conformity. This insight offers much to explain the morality of southern Christianity on display in *Huckleberry Finn*, where the feuding Grangerfords and Shepherdsons attend the same church, guns in tow, and attend to a sermon "about brotherly love, and such-like tiresomeness."[15] The Sunday school culture that Twain knew so well was satirized in his numerous other works. In pieces like "Disgraceful Persecution of a Boy" (where a boy is jailed for stoning a Chinese man on his way to Sunday school) and "The Story of the Good Little Boy Who Didn't Prosper" (which makes fun of the sin of literalness regarding morality and virtue), Twain undercuts the pious and uncritical acceptance of the Sunday school message.

These examples and many more underscore a religious skepticism that attacks the prevailing myth of the small town and the Sunday schools—a myth of which Twain became profoundly aware at an early age. The small town, with the church and its Sunday school squarely at its center, became reified in the minds of many Americans as an abstract symbol of all things good, pure, and right about their society. Children of the second half of the nineteenth century had been indoctrinated with such a view of midwestern civilization through texts like the McGuffey school readers. William H. McGuffey, called by one scholar an "apostle of religion, morality, and education," tried to inculcate a small town ideal in his readers that might "bolster midwestern civilization against the dangers inherent in pioneering new frontiers."[16] As a result, his readers, of which approximately 100 million copies were sold between 1850 and 1900, depicted small towns in largely mythical and didactically moralistic terms that asserted the superiority of village and country life over that of the rapidly developing cities of the late nineteenth century.

The mythic concept of the town was attacked by a number of savage critics of middle-class American civilization, who reached an apogee of influence just after World War I, but the revolt began in the antebellum period with the masters of southwestern humor and reignited just after the Civil War ended and the Gilded Age commenced. In Edward Eggleston's *The Hoosier School-Master* (1871), for example, one long and memorable chapter entitled "The Hardshell Preacher" pokes good fun at the small-town church run by the "Hardshell" type of minister: "prodigiously illiterate, and often vicious. Some of their preachers are notorious drunkards."[17] Besides the sheer delight of Eggleston's remarkable ear for dialect, this chapter is easily compared with similar sections in *Tom Sawyer* and *Huckleberry*

Finn: the long, drowsy sermon; Tom playing with a pinch-bug (in Eggleston's book, a green lizard); and the satirical references to old-time revivalism, when the King in *Huckleberry Finn* becomes a revivalist at a camp-meeting associated in antebellum times with such groups as the "New York Perfectionists," the "Millerites," and the "Campbellites." Twain often poked fun at this sort of revivalism—as in the brief autobiographical note recorded in his youth: "Campbellite revival. All converted but me. All sinners again in a week."[18] Twain's personal "revolt from the village" rises to perhaps its greatest height in his later story, "The Man That Corrupted Hadleyburg," which reveals a vision of small-town religion that is both powerless to change the hearts of the people and highly negotiable when money is on the table.

Money and greed, of course, were central themes of Twain's critique of the Gilded Age, a lifelong project that commenced in his early journalism days. In particular, Twain's skepticism toward religion often revolved around his awareness of how closely it was intertwined with issues of wealth and its corrupting influence on human morality. One might consider, for instance, the "Open Letter to Commodore Vanderbilt" that appeared in *Packard's Monthly* (March 1869). Vanderbilt, who had achieved great wealth by that time, seemed to Twain to symbolize a particularly immoral and selfish version of the American tycoon. In his scathing "Open Letter," Twain chastizes Vanderbilt for his activities: "All I wish to urge upon you now is, that you crush out your native instincts and go and do something worthy of praise—go and do something you need not blush to see in print—do something that may rouse one solitary good impulse in the breasts of your horde of worshippers . . . shine as one solitary grain of pure gold upon the heaped rubbish of your life."[19] In such pieces as "The Revised Catechism," a brief satirical essay that appeared in the *New York Tribune* of September 27, 1871, Twain excoriates the underlying lust for money at any cost as becoming essentially the reigning religious paradigm of the nation after the Civil War. This brief piece takes the form of a question-and-answer session in the field of "Moral Philosophy":

Who is God?

A. Money is God. Gold and greenbacks and stock—father, son, and the ghost of the same . . . these are the true and mighty God . . . and William Tweed is his prophet.[20]

Twain's interest in and understanding of all sorts of capitalistic claims can be contextualized by considering the massive industrial growth in general throughout many sectors of the postwar society. The invention of modern advertising, for instance, has been attributed by many to the likes of P. T. Barnum, whose *Struggles and Triumphs* (1855; 1869) was one of the biggest self-promotional bestsellers in American history. Barnum's exploits, even though admired by Twain, can nonetheless be included among those industries that greatly fostered the rise of the greedy Gilded Age economy scorned in much of Twain's best work. As might be expected, Twain's simultaneous admiration for and disillusionment with crass capitalism manifested itself as the definitive anxiety and ambivalence notable throughout his major writings.

Similar anxieties abound throughout a particularly crucial period of Twain's personal spiritual journey: the several years from roughly 1867 (when he traveled to Europe and the Holy Land, and met his future wife) through 1873 (when the move to Hartford appeared permanent with the purchase of a large lot in the Nook Farm neighborhood). According to Jeffrey Steinbrink, these years make up the period during which the former Sam Clemens worked at "getting to be Mark Twain." This process, in which the wild bohemian of the West reinvented himself as a Christian husband and parishioner (another sort of religious "claim") in one of liberal Protestantism's most prominent locations, engendered a virtual transformation in his outward behaviors and demeanor. Much has been made of Twain's embrace of Christianity during this crucial period at the outset of his eastern literary career, all set in motion when he fell in love with Olivia Langdon, daughter of the genteel, self-made businessman Jervis Langdon of Elmira, New York. Livy Langdon was a complex figure with intellectual and moral concerns that were representative of much of Victorian American culture. The sentimentalized religious piety that resonates throughout the courtship letters of 1868–1869 has led some critics to make the dubious assertion that Twain's "conversion" to Christianity was nothing much beyond a mere rhetorical move initiated to ensure that the Langdons would part with their refined daughter to such an outlandish, somewhat boorish roughneck from the Far West. Clearly, Twain was a rhetorical genius as a writer; and without a doubt, it is a difficult business discerning the real from the fake in any writer's personal letters. Nevertheless, in Twain's letters of this period, one confronts numerous bald statements of Christian faith: in February 1869, for instance, when Twain writes to Livy's mother, "But now I never swear; I never taste wine or spirits upon any occasion whatsoever; I am orderly, and my conduct is above reproach in a worldly sense; and finally, I now claim that I am a Christian."[21]

Some critics have not accepted Twain's confession, describing Twain as merely "[a]cting the part of returned prodigal, of sinner turned Christian," thus pointing out its trickery over its authenticity.[22] Moreover, whereas some have tended to belittle and/or condescend to what they consider to be Twain's vaguely spiritual turn for greater gain, the ambiguity of this topic has resulted in many ambivalent reactions from some critics. Susan Harris, for example, while at first stating that Twain's religious proclivities constituted "a series of feints designed to convince the entire Langdon family that he was a viable suitor," later admits that it is imaginable that Clemens was in fact "genuinely struggling to become a Christian."[23] More forthrightly, James D. Wilson asserts that the love letters reveal "graphically and, I think, convincingly the depth and sincerity of his quest for religious faith. . . . During the period from Christmas 1868 to the Epiphany, 6 January 1869, Clemens seems Augustinian in his concentrated and agonized examination of conscience."[24] Clearly, shortly after the marriage, much of the piety did disappear, and Twain began to slip away from whatever orthodoxy he may have attained. And yet, the passionate quest for faith revealed in these letters is symptomatic of a profoundly religious nature. Furthermore, as Wilson has noted, this religious impulse had been fully awakened in Twain well before his encounter with Livy.[25]

Simultaneously, during these crucial years when he was forging his own "Christian" identity, Twain completed and published two early masterworks that attack and disparage institutional religion and romantic idealism. His first bestseller, *The Innocents Abroad* (1869), spends much of its energy lambasting the hollow spirituality of Twain's fellow passengers on the voyage to Europe and the Holy Land. A major theme is the crass commodification of the cultural and religious sites being visited. Twain directs much of his critique toward the fictitious William Grimes, the supposed author of a highly romantic and pietistic travel book called *Nomadic Life of Palestine*. Grimes was a thinly disguised pseudonym for William Cowper Prime, whose own *Tent Life in the Holy Land* (1857) was the common guide for many of Twain's companions. Richard Lowry discusses Twain's investigation of and interest in the various kinds of "claims" made by not only touring companies, tour guides, and guidebooks, but also prospectors, famous authors, and newspaper writers themselves, who were often given shares in stocks and then asked to trump them up in their columns. In this thoroughly modern scheme of things, value is always already mere expectation, promotion, and finally recirculation—all of which is fraught with anxiety and fear.[26] In this way, *Innocents* criticizes the deceptive ways of the social negotiation of value throughout Gilded Age culture.

More important, *Innocents* reveals a strong anti-Catholic prejudice along with more generally a distaste for the excesses of institutionalized religion. His prejudice mirrored the sentiments of the Masonic Lodge of which he became a member, as well as the growing nativism in the 1880s.[27] According to this view, Twain equated Catholicism with ignorance, while the desire for knowledge and progress is frequently shown to be blasphemous in the eyes of the church. The church, in fact, is actively engaged in deception (e.g., "Jesuit humbuggery"),[28] while the churchgoers are gullible and often base. These views culminate in his visit to Italy:

We were in the heart and home of priestcraft—of a happy, cheerful, contented ignorance, superstition, degradation, poverty, indolence, and everlasting unaspiring worthlessness.

And we said fervently, It suits these people precisely; let them enjoy it, along with the other animals. . . . *We* feel no malice toward these fumigators.[29]

Twain's anti-Catholic strain would remain throughout his career: a much more vitriolic criticism of Romanism, influenced by his reading of Lecky's *History of European Morals* in 1874, is seen throughout *Connecticut Yankee*, where the church is depicted as the main reason for the stupidity and backwardness of the entire civilization; it also provides the opening context of *No. 44, The Mysterious Stranger*. These attitudes also reflect the thorough revulsion toward Rome dictated by his Protestant youth, a revulsion influenced by popular anti-Catholic diatribes like Samuel F. B. Morse's *Foreign Conspiracy* or Lyman Beecher's *Plea for the West* (both 1834). Twain undoubtedly also encountered anti-Catholicism in sermons by Horace Bushnell and other Congregational preachers that he heard during the Hartford years.

In *Roughing It* (1872), similar attacks are brought to bear on social structures of the Wild West. Forrest Robinson writes, "Nothing in [Twain's] response to [the] world is at all stable or predictable. . . . Humans are everywhere in thrall to fictions of their own devising."[30] Thus, Twain's pioneer is infected by a "vision of a whole mountain of gold and silver [which] overwhelmed the senses of thousands of investors and brought them to financial ruin."[31] At one point, describing the mounting anticipation of crossing "an absolute desert," Twain ends his commentary on the romance and drama of the situation by writing, "The poetry was all in the anticipation—there is none in the reality."[32] One religious reality considered is Mormonism, another marginalized group eschewed by nativists and Masons alike, particularly in a long section ranging through much of chapters 12–17 and then in an extended appendix at the end of *Roughing It*. When he encounters a Mormon "Destroying Angel," he responds with, "but alas for all our romances, he was nothing but a loud, profane, offensive, old blackguard!"[33] The section also contains a lengthy dismissal of the Book of Mormon: "so 'slow,' so sleepy; such an insipid mess of inspiration. It is chloroform in print."[34]

These two books epitomize irreverence, an antireligious flippancy so prevalent that Louis Budd has labeled it the "dominant quality" of Twain's achievement.[35] Despite his irreverent lampoons, however, both books also contain moments of strong sentimentality, exemplified in *Innocents*, for instance, one dark evening in Palestine, when Twain waxes eloquently about the Saviour:

> In the starlight, Galilee has no boundaries but the broad compass of the heavens, and is a theater meet for great events; meet for the birth of a religion able to save the world; and meet for the stately Figure appointed to stand upon its stage and proclaim its high decrees.[36]

The regularity of such observations has caused Leland Krauth to go so far as to assert that, "while it is seldom acknowledged, the moments of seriousness in the text far outnumber those of comedy. . . . Twain's moral outlook [in *Innocents*] is almost stodgily traditional. . . . the heart of civilization . . . is predictably religion and the morality that derives from it."[37] Krauth is surely correct in pointing out what many have obviously missed—yet the critical consensus continues to highlight the nearly complete undermining of any such traditional belief, exemplified by Forrest Robinson's emphasis on the romantic traveler's eventual "discovery of hollowness, pointlessness, collapsed illusions, willful deception, hapless self-deception, and defeat."[38]

Despite his antireligious satire, Twain desired to move into the higher realms of the staid eastern establishment, and thus we should consider how these critiques encode a conservative impulse. This impulse accounts for Twain's numerous social, moral, and ultimately religious criticisms, all worthy of inclusion in the tradition of the American jeremiad. According to Perry Miller, the historic jeremiad consisted of "lamentations over the 'declension' of New England and tirades against its lengthening list of sins." Like John the Baptist's similar wailings, these rhetorical creations were meant to be delivered publicly: "on the great occasions of communal life, when the body politic met in solemn conclave to consider the state of society, the one kind of sermon it attended . . . was a jeremiad in which the sins of

New England were tabulated over and over again."[39] Though clearly much more secular in tone, nevertheless, I would argue that a vast amount of Twain's work can be understood as an ongoing contribution to the long line of American prophets who utilized their favored mode, the jeremiad. As a raving Jeremiah speaking out against the social and ethical injustices of an age, Twain becomes much more than merely "a moralist in disguise"[40] He becomes, rather, a profoundly religious and spiritual presence.

Here, we must once again note the ambivalent regard of a man torn between the sentimental and the real. As often as he drew upon the Garden of Eden and American Adam motifs in describing an idyllic youth, Twain just as often invoked such ideologies and myths as the targets of some his most sarcastic attacks. Nevertheless, Twain remained sympathetic to and even a disciple of what has often been called America's civil religion. In an essay focused on the realm of the "religious," we must continually recall the close intertwining in American social and cultural history of religion with political and other forms of thought. Indeed, the close connection of these two realms provides the term "civil religion" itself, pointing as it does simultaneously to the kingdoms of this world and to the Kingdom of God. This civil religion, as defined by Robert Bellah,

> borrowed selectively from the religious tradition in such a way that the average American saw no conflict between the two. In this way, the civil religion was able to build up without any bitter struggle with the church powerful symbols of national solidarity and to mobilize deep levels of personal motivation for the attainment of national goals.[41]

Twain's symbolic manifestations of ideological versions of the regnant American myth are myriad in his fiction and essays. For example, the sacred act of declaring independence from corrupt authority and then incarnating a national ideal, a peculiarly American ideology that I have outlined in detail elsewhere,[42] is embodied in arguably some of the most famous acts in Twain's literary works: the "lighting out for the territory" motif, depicted in his real life at the beginning of *Roughing It* and then most famously at the end of *Huckleberry Finn*. Although we may be tempted to view these as radical acts of rebellion, they can also be understood as the most conservative and even primordial religious acts of the American civil religion: they embody, that is, what Sacvan Bercovitch has called a "consensus through dissensus" and ultimately serve to support and glorify the peculiarly American religion.

These tendencies to glorify the nation and its reigning myths (such as liberal individualism, the march of progress, American newness and regeneration, and biblical typology) are notable throughout many of Twain's writings. In 1879, when Civil War hero and former president Ulysses S. Grant returned to America from a long stay abroad, Twain participated in a reunion of the Army of the Tennessee in Chicago. Twain, who "worshipped" Grant, was "transfigured by oratory," as he listened to the patriotic rhetoric throughout the course of the evening. Here is his reaction to Colonel Robert Ingersoll's impassioned speech at the same dinner: "[Ingersoll is] the most beautiful human creature that ever lived"; as Twain wrote later to Howells, "I doubt if America has ever seen anything quite equal to it."[43] Further instances of Twain's ready embrace of standard American civil religion are myriad: his near-worship of mythic heroes of the republic, including especially General Grant but also William T. Sherman and other Civil War leaders; his ready embrace of earlier mythologized accounts of America like George Lippard's *Legends of the American Revolution*;[44] his high admiration of finely crafted political oratory and pomp, as in the numerous patriotic celebrations in which he actively participated (often with Twichell); and his regular enthusiastic response to Twichell's often patriotic speeches and sermons. Twain's own forays into similarly conservative strains of patriotic rhetoric include his letter "To Walt Whitman," included in a commemorative volume of tributes addressed to the aged poet in 1889. Twain's brief yet enlightening contribution focused on the "greatness" of the Gilded Age era and echoed the fervent patriotic optimism and quasi-religious mysticism of Whitman's most memorable verse: "Wait till you see that great figure appear, and catch the far glint of the sun upon his banner; then you may depart satisfied, as knowing you have seen him for whom the world was made."[45] Twain's paean contains no ironic detachment: instead, it rings with the authentic hope and fervent cultural optimism that was a fundament of America's civil religion.

All of this is important if we are to grasp the pervasive ideological structures, many of them religious in nature, that reigned in the eastern states where Twain resided for the most productive and important period of his career. During the post–Civil War period, and to some extent in response to the war's massive destruction, the desire to forge a cultural harmony fostered what may have been the most coherent national literary culture that America has ever had.[46] Twain's engagement with this culture runs very deep: he lived for almost two decades as a member of the genteel community of Nook Farm outside of Hartford, where his neighbors included some of the most influential thinkers and writers of the period, such as Horace Bushnell, Harriet Beecher Stowe (with numerous visits by her brother Henry Ward Beecher, perhaps the most famous preacher of the nineteenth century), Isabella Beecher Hooker, and Charles Dudley Warner. Moreover, the neighborhood also featured several other ministers, three in particular who were all disciples of Bushnell and who all became close friends of Mark Twain: Nathaniel Burton, Edwin Pond Parker, and of course Joe Twichell, who was Twain's best friend during his time in Hartford (and arguably for the remainder of his life). All three of these young Congregational ministers were dedicated to the liberalized "social gospel" instincts of their mentor, Bushnell, a stalwart who was one of the three or four most influential American theologians of the century. In short, to understand fully the religious ethos of Twain's most productive years as author requires a deep immersion in "the golden age of liberal theology."[47]

The rise of liberal theology is fundamentally a phenomenon of the nineteenth century—the century labeled by some historians as the "Great Century" in Christian history.[48] Instead of focusing on man's sinful nature due to the Fall, as traditional Calvinists might, liberal theologians described faulty child-rearing, poor ethical and moral training, or lack of social reform as the fundamental causes of human error. Thus, liberal theologians placed heavy emphasis on moral teaching and ethical preaching, the so-called social gospel, and in so doing they argued for the creative, autonomous, and nearly godlike nature of the human spirit. Among the many key figures of this movement were Henry Ward Beecher, Josiah Strong, and Phillips Brooks—all of whom, more or less, preached visions of a Christianized America of abundance, progress, civil religion, vaguely social Darwinistic theories of race, the superiority of Anglo-Saxons, and the providential history of the American nation.

Despite the great impact of numerous leaders, it is probably accurate to claim that Horace Bushnell was the leading light of this movement and, theologically speaking, its most important influence. His famous volume, *Christian Nurture* (1847), for example, can be considered the cornerstone of the shift toward undermining the dogma of original sin and initiating a new system of religious and moral education. Among other things, Bushnell also propounded a complex theory of the American civil religion, forcefully asserting that America was founded on the twin ideals of Protestantism and republicanism; "It was Protestantism in religion producing republicanism in government."[49] Moreover, his essay "City Planning" (1864), along with his active profile in the city of Hartford, showed his strong desire to develop a holistic view of an urban area and to create within that area an embodiment of ethical and moral society.

The ethos of the Bushnellian social gospel, and liberal theology in general, with its pragmatic call to active participation in life's cosmic struggle toward some vaguely utopian future, typifies the postbellum Hartford into which Twain wanted to fling himself at the outset of his most important career stage—becoming a "respectable" author of books. Twain demonstrated a very strong desire to settle his family in Hartford after visiting there several times and becoming fast friends with Joe Twichell. For Twain, Hartford was much more than just one of the strongholds of the New England aristocracy—a growing and monied metropolis benefiting from the infancy of a major American industry (insurance). It featured in Nook Farm what appeared to be one of America's newest, most pleasant, and intellectually stimulating environments for the likes of the Stowes, the Beechers, the Hookers, and the Warners. Moreover, Hartford maintained just enough distance from the stultified Brahminism that Twain associated with the "hub of the universe," Boston—an almost religious ethos that both he and Howells would satirize and sacralize, depending on their present moods.[50] In short, the milieu of Hartford should be understood as a profoundly important aspect of Twain's emerging sense of self and ideology. This aspect appears early when, for example, Twain writes Twichell in February 1869: "my future wife wants me to be surrounded by a good moral & religious atmosphere (for I shall unite with the church as soon as I am located), & so she likes the idea of living in Hartford."[51] During the Buffalo years, Twain maintained his desires for a Hartford lifestyle. Steinbrink correctly underlines the key attribute: "from the outset what had chiefly drawn him to the city was his sense of its upright and elevating character."[52]

Thus, we should consider in somewhat more depth the extent to which Twain's genuine quest for faith informed his career, especially throughout the major period that essentially ended with his departure from Hartford in 1891.[53] One might focus, for instance, on the deep friendship with the Bushnellian disciple Joe Twichell—a topic of the utmost concern (though generally neglected) in any attempt to come to terms with Twain's views of religion and the Christian life throughout the Hartford years. Strangely, numerous scholars have labored under the quite inaccurate impression that these two brilliant men carried on a friendship that was decidedly unreligious, so much so that this odd notion has risen almost to the level of a myth of Twain biographical criticism that must first be rejected as utterly false. Twain's initial biographer Albert Bigelow Paine was responsible for the beginning of an inaccurate portrait of this friendship as somehow being of a nonreligious variety. For Paine, the decisive moment was in Switzerland in 1878, at which time Twain supposedly confessed his own lack of belief to Twichell. This, claimed Paine, ended for all practical purposes any talk that these two friends would ever have on religion again: "So the personal side of religious discussion closed between them and was never afterwards reopened."[54] Indeed, not all of the blame for this myth of

Twain biography can be attributed to Paine: Howells himself appears to have believed the same thing; and many critics have either dismissed Twain's religious sentiment or have dismissed the orthodox commitments of his closest friends. One wrote, "his closest friends, after all, were hardly orthodox"; another claimed that "the religion of these preachers [including Twichell] was not evangelical."[55]

However, abundant evidence removes any doubt that Joe Twichell was both orthodox and evangelical in his faith.[56] It is clear from the surviving correspondence, as well as from the personal papers and journals of Twichell (held mainly at Yale University's Beineke Library), in tandem with scrutiny of the letters Twichell sent to Twain (mostly held at Berkeley), that these two men carried on a friendship that was powerfully shaped by the religious belief and the ethical and moral character of Twichell, a minister of unusual gifts and of wide-ranging intellectual interests. All contemporary accounts of Twichell speak only in the most glowing admiration for this funny, rigorous, and muscular preacher. If we agree with Steinbrink's claim that the major influence in the decision of the Clemens family to move to Hartford was the attraction of its "upright and elevating character," then we must surely recognize that this character was most competently incarnated in Joe Twichell. In any case, theirs was a lasting and deep relationship—probably the most important male friendship of Twain's life. Certainly, this idea is confirmed in Twain's own words: "I am resolved to store up and remember only the charming hours of the journeys and the times when I was not unworthy to be with you, and share a companionship which to me stands first after Livy's."[57] Their personal letters are so brimming with filial piety and genuine devotion that one critic has labeled them as "love letters."[58]

Twain's pious affirmation of his deep relationship with Twichell also brings to mind some advice Twain received while in Hawaii from Anson Burlingame, a highly intellectual, moral, and talented diplomat whose attention and interest Twain prized very highly at this early stage of his career: "What you need now is the refinement of association. Seek companionship among men of superior intellect and character. . . . Never affiliate with inferiors; always climb."[59] Burlingame's words seemed to be enacted in Twain's relationships with several Easterners, including Livy, her father Jervis Langdon, and his literary mentor Howells; however, the words above written to Joe Twichell indicate a similar if not deeper arrangement. Joe Twichell, a man of impeccable character combined with true intellectual powers and a keen wit, was the embodiment of the type of person Burlingame insisted that Twain should pattern himself after. Beyond the merely personal, Burlingame's focus on progress, refinement, and the goal to "always climb" resonates with the entire religious culture of the Victorian North, as seen, for example, in the teachings of Twichell's mentor Bushnell, as well as in the pious boys' books of Horatio Alger and Jacob Abbott.

The Twain-Twichell correspondence, despite the earlier misconceptions that the religious aspects of the friendship diminished or even disappeared after 1878, is filled with numerous mentions of and at time serious reflection on religious topics and concerns. Despite what many have been led to believe, Twain regularly participated in the social and religious activities of the Asylum Hill Congregational Church, pastored by Twichell, throughout his major period from 1871 to 1889. Innumerable newspaper reports attest to his and Livy's regular attendance: as late as 1887, for example, one paper reported that Twain "attends church regularly, being fond of the eloquent sermons of his friend, Dr. Twichell."[60] He often helped with collections for missionary work, despite his later chastisements of American missionary efforts. According to Leah Strong's close scrutiny of the parish records, Twain's name appears "on a great many" of the lists of contributors to foreign missions.[61] Perhaps most strikingly, Twain provided a yearly contribution to Twichell's local mission project, the American Chinese Educational Mission, which sponsored Chinese students for study in the United States, culminating at Yale University.[62] The mistaken characterizations of the Twichell-Twain friendship misconstrues the fundamental affinity that these two men shared. A good deal of that affinity tended toward the religious, but part of it had to do with Twichell's role as provocateur, creative stimulus, and old-fashioned storyteller who inspired many of Twain's works.[63]

Many other features of Twain's social life and activities attest to the strong draw that Christianity maintained for him. One of his first outings with Twichell, in fact, was a ministry visit to an alms house, where Twain "helped him preach and sing to the inmates (I helped in the singing, anyway)."[64] Edwin Pond Parker later recalled that sometimes, when Twichell was out of town, "Mr. and Mrs. Clemens would stray away from their accustomed place of worship and come to the South Church, to hear—as he was fond of telling me—the music there."[65] Parker's comment shows not only that the Clemenses were regular attenders of Twichell's church, but it also indicates Twain's genuine enjoyment of the elaborate choir music featured at Parker's South Church. He was a great admirer of the Fisk Jubilee Singers, and once (appropriately enough, in a letter to Twichell) called their music "utterly beautiful . . . and it moves me infinitely more than any other music can."[66] Frequently, Twichell records in his journal episodes of Twain having sung Negro spirituals and other religious hymns at public meetings and private parties. On October 26, 1877, Twichell wrote: "to MT's to attend a neighborhood reception given by him to Yung Wing and wife. . . . MT and Gen. Hawley sang negro religious songs."[67] Twichell's entry for March 8, 1884: "Friday, after a charming morning in Brooklyn (M.T. sang negro "spirituals" at the piano, deliciously) we went over to New York."[68] Another time, as Twain's housekeeper Katy Leary later reported, "Suddenly Mr. Clemens got right up without any warning and began singing one of them Negro spirituals. . . . When he got to the end, to the glory Hallelujah, he gave a great shout—just like the Negroes do—he shouted out the "Glory, Glory, Hallelujah."[69] While one might argue that these episodes speak more to aesthetic appreciation than spirituality, the religious content cannot be entirely ignored.

Generally, Twain surrounded himself with the liberal Christianity of his main environments. The Monday Evening Club of Hartford (founded by Horace Bushnell) regularly featured topics of religious concern. He listened attentively to the sermons of Twichell in Hartford and the Rev. Thomas K. Beecher in Elmira, at whose church the Langdons were longtime members. When Beecher was roundly criticized for offering Sunday meetings in the Elmira Opera House in 1869, Twain became one of his strongest supporters.[70] Twain was also attracted to the brand of "muscular Christianity" proffered by the likes of Beecher and fully incarnated in Twichell, a tall, strong, and handsome Civil War veteran, who was an accomplished athlete while at Yale and who frequently took lengthy hikes up and down steep grades with Twain. According to Strong, Christian manhood was a frequently recurring topic of Twichell's sermons: the call, that is, to being a "man's man" in spite of outer circumstances, and to embody the best of human dignity and ethical virtue.[71] In short, and especially as indicated by his strong friendship with Twichell, Twain remained both ethically and philosophically committed to a highly liberalized yet recognizably theistic Christian moralism throughout his major period.

By all accounts, however, this is not to discount the sustained and intense critique of religion, Christianity, and idealism, in general, that might be said to constitute a preoccupation of Twain's achievement. Even as he was spending considerable efforts to reform, win Livy, and establish himself as a good Christian husband in arguably the capitol of liberalized Protestantism in America, Twain was keeping abreast of the sweeping intellectual changes of the day. During the period of Twain's artistic maturity, Christianity and religion, in general, underwent several philosophical attacks that issued in some of the most sweeping changes in the entire history of the church. Much has been made of the spread of theories of evolutionism into mainstream American culture, and generally how the ideas of Darwin, Herbert Spencer, and Thomas Huxley affected traditional beliefs about the creation as narrated in the book of Genesis.[72] Darwin's explosive volume, *The Descent of Man* (1871), is particularly relevant, for it is there that Darwin took up the problem of human origins. Darwin's explicit claim was that humans are directly related to the animal kingdom—a far cry from traditional explanations of the special creation through Adam and Eve. A loud public outcry greeted Darwin's pronouncements. The famous Presbyterian leader Charles Hodge, for example, published his response, *What is Darwinism?*, in 1874, and answered the title's question quite clearly: "it is atheism."[73] Perhaps the most popular interpreter of Darwin for evangelicals was T. DeWitt Talmage, who opined in his diatribe of 1886, *Live Coals*: "I tell you plainly, if your father was a muskrat and your mother an opossum, and your great aunt a kangaroo, and the toads and the snapping turtle were your illustrious predecessors, my father was God."[74]

Less recognized today is the rapid popularization in America of the so-called German higher criticism of the Bible. This movement, which submitted the Bible to rigorous scientific and historical analysis, proved to be one of the most crucial challenges the American churches were to face. The upshot of much of this scholarship was to demythologize the biblical narrative— meaning, for instance, that ostensibly historical personages like Adam were merely the eponymous constructions of mythologization.[75] Again, Talmage became the most well-known conservative spokesperson for the evangelicals on a number of issues related to biblical criticism that threatened orthodox Christianity. His most famous sermon, "The Splendors of Orthodoxy," delivered hundreds of times, was essentially a lengthy jeremiad aimed primarily at the "advanced thinkers' who sought to destroy simple faith in God's word."[76] Rather than singling out the emergence of Darwinism as more important than the biblical criticism movement, it is more accurate to emphasize the uncanny emergence of these two philosophically related phenomena at almost exactly the same time (and, more to the point, during the major period of Twain's career), as a devastating double-barrelled attack on the traditional dogmas of the Christian church.

Twain well understood the implications of both Darwin and modern biblical criticism with regard to traditional Christian theology. Both were frequent topics of the Monday Evening Club and of lectures and sermons of the period, including Twichell's. Twain devoured *The Descent of Man* almost immediately after it appeared in 1871, filling it with numerous notes and underlinings. He knew, as well, the two best-selling novels of 1888 that centered on the controversy over biblical criticism: *John Ward, Preacher* by Margaret Deland and *Robert Elsmere* by the British author Mrs. Humphrey Ward. These novels both dramatize the falling away of once idealistic and zealous young evangelical preachers, mainly as a result of their encounters with attacks on the nature and fallibility of Scripture. Twain owned both volumes and on different occasions commented that he had read them (he greatly satirized Deland's book but strongly praised Ward's). In a tongue-in-cheek response to the religious dilemma being posed, in 1879 Mark Twain enlisted many of the most prominent members of Elmira society into his rather preposterous scheme to erect in their town a memorial to Adam, "the Father of the Human Race." A committee, called the "Adam Monument Association of Elmira," was appointed to select a sculptor, with the prominent local minister Thomas K. Beecher as president. In his essay entitled "A Monument to Adam" (1905), Twain recalled some of the reasons for his idea: "Darwin's *Descent of Man* had been in print five or six years, and the storm of indignation raised by it was still raging in pulpits and periodicals. In tracing the genesis of the human race back to its sources, Mr. Darwin had left Adam out altogether."[77] It is not too much to argue that the entire "Monument to Adam" episode can be read as an acutely complex (and surely ambivalent) response to these emerging religious conflicts.

Additional attacks on orthodox Christianity came from the widely publicized heresy trials of several leading clergymen, such as David Swing and Charles Briggs. Between 1878 and 1906, almost every major Protestant denomination experienced at least one heresy trial, usually of a seminary professor, and almost always highly publicized and politicized.[78] This tendency is best exemplified by the Henry Ward Beecher trial of 1874–1875—surely one of the great symbolic trials in American history—in which America's greatest preacher stood accused of adultery as well as, in effect, heresy. Beecher is even more relevant because of his status as the preeminent cultural icon of the liberal Protestantism of his day. Twain's admiring connection with Beecher reached back to pre-Hartford days: he visited Beecher's Plymouth Congregational Church as early as 1867, where he was mesmerized by Beecher's rhetorical brilliance. Twain mentioned his reading of Beecher sermons in his courting letters to Livy and was disappointed when Beecher was unable to go on the Quaker City voyage (organized by the Plymouth Church) that issued in *The Innocents Abroad*.[79] More generally, Beecher frequently visited his sister Harriet Beecher Stowe in the Nook Farm neighborhood, visits during which he often met with Twain. Throughout the Beecher trial, Twain publicly supported his friend and even attended the trial with Joe Twichell.

At virtually the same time that the culture was digesting the sustained critical deconstruction of the Bible, traditional Christianity, and romanticized cultural icons like Beecher, it appears that Twain was undergoing similar spiritual struggles. These conflicts can be seen, for instance, in Twain's famous metaphorical distinction between the Pilot and the Passenger, which is an especially lucid and elastic construction that can be related to a multitude of social and cultural conversations that marked the latter half of the nineteenth century in America and, indeed, the West.[80] Twain spelled out this distinction in one of the most charming and thoughtful works he was to create, "Old Times on the Mississippi" (a series for the *Atlantic* which later was greatly expanded into the book *Life on the Mississippi* [1883]). "Old Times" depicts the young cub pilot as looking in wonder on the work of the steamboatman as the "one permanent ambition" of his boyhood.[81] This magical vision changes very quickly once the young Clemens is employed full time under a strong and challenging tutor: the pilot Horace Bixby. "I began to fear that piloting was not quite so romantic as I had imagined it was"; for the boy, harsh reality begins to set in when Bixby calmly assures him that "there's only one way to be a pilot, and that is to get this entire river by heart. You have to know it just like A B C."[82] This monumental change, which is unfolded in one of the most beloved passages in all of Twain's corpus, laments the transition of the boy from mere passenger to savvy and mature pilot: "The face of the water, in time, became a wonderful book—a book that was a dead language to the uneducated passenger."[83] This image is a suggestive religious metaphor in which the river stands in as the Bible and/or simple Christian faith. The "face of the water" echoes the opening lines of Genesis: "the spirit of God was moving on the face of the waters" (Gen. 1:2). The river is directly called a "book"— one written, like the Bible, in a "dead language." This book "utters" its "secrets" with a "voice"; it also is one that needs to be read "every day." For "uneducated" readers, this book remains filled with "grace, beauty, and poetry"; however, once educated, it no longer is.[84] When read in the context of the sustained critical deconstruction of the Bible as text that was becoming arguably the most important challenge facing traditional faith, this passage nicely evokes the pros (and cons) of scientific progress and its implications in matters of the demystification of the sacred. As such, it represents the inherent tensions of the spiritual crisis of the culture-at-large.

In addition to the famous passages from "Old Times," Twain published many other deconstructions of religious romanticism, perhaps most memorably in his long story, "Extract from Captain Stormfield's Visit to Heaven" (which, along with other similar tales, such as those of "Rev. Sam Jones" and "Captain Simon Wheeler," "Captain Stormfield's Visit" forms a distinct set). "Captain Stormfield's Visit," written mostly around 1867–1871(?) but withheld from publication until 1907–1908 in *Harper's*, describes one person's long journey to and in the heavenly realm. [85] Specifically, "Stormfield" responded to the romanticized view of the afterlife that predominated throughout much of women's fiction of that period—much of it in reaction to the horrific deaths of loved ones in the Civil War.[86] Twain took umbrage with the glorified views of death and the afterlife offered in this and similar novels, a view reflecting the widespread acceptance of a "domestic heaven." Perhaps the best example of this was Elizabeth Stuart Phelps's bestseller of 1868, *The Gates Ajar*, which offered "homes restored, families regathered, and friends reunited."[87] According to Ann Douglas, *The Gates Ajar* constitutes the culmination of an entire genre of fiction that she labels "consolation literature": "All the logic of *The Gates Ajar* . . . suggests to the reader: you are going to end up, if you are well-behaved and lucky, in a domestic realm of children, women, and ministers (i.e., angels), so why not begin to believe in them now?"[88] Evidently, Livy Clemens shared such a romantic view of the afterlife.[89]

For Twain, such a view was much too small, greatly overexaggerating the similarities between Heaven and earth. Thus,

"Stormfield" (along with, e.g., the posthumous *Letters from the Earth*) can be read as Twain's satirical rebuke of the smallness of the American concept of God and His Heaven. In "Stormfield," much of the opening section is devoted to the lengthy adventure involved in simply approaching Heaven, part of which involves racing a comet. Upon arrival, we learn that there are billions of planets, and that the earth itself is of such small consequence that it is called the Wart. The mistaken and sentimental ideas about Heaven are condescendingly allowed to dictate the actions of the angels and the redeemed—when a believer from America arrives, expecting a huge welcome, that is exactly what they get. Heaven's substantially broader scope is marked by the surprising fact that it is populated by far more people of color than whites. New arrivals learn quickly how deceived they were on earth about the nature of the afterlife. Like much of Twain's attack on romanticism, he ascribes much of the guilt to the romantic ideas as presented in various written works on the subject. Furthermore, he names several historical figures, such as T. DeWitt Talmage and Dwight Moody, who bear responsibility for misrepresenting Heaven to their flocks. In short, "Captain Stormfield's Visit" offers a striking alternative vision of Heaven from the deistic Twain—one that transcends the sentimental version he seeks to dismiss.

The final two decades of Twain's life, featuring the deaths of many of his beloved friends and family members in concert with devastating financial ruin and a growing disillusionment with American politics both at home and abroad, resulted in a dark turn in the tone and content of Twain's moral and religious thought. Simultaneously, and perhaps not coincidentally, his literary achievement took a sad and permanent fall. As a result, the vision of the alienated, grief-ridden curmudgeon shaking his fist at God has become the standard reading of the final period of Twain's life.[90] This mood of despair is perhaps best captured in the rather startling denunciations of biblical Christianity contained in the autobiographical dictations of June 1906.[91] Obviously, one cannot deny Twain's utter rejection of institutional religions and biblical orthodoxy in general—for instance, he regularly read *The Truth Seeker*, the major journal of Free

Thought espousing the views of the movement's founder Robert Ingersoll, perhaps the most famous freethinker (and infidel) of the century. It is worth noting that Twain renewed his subscription to *The Truth Seeker* the month before he died.[92] However, these sorts of attitudes can be documented well before the final years. By 1874, for instance, he had written to his sister that he considered himself "an entire and absolute unbeliever"; and it is true that Twichell frequently destroyed letters sent to him by Twain, containing "blasphemies or other indiscretions which Twichell did not want to survive because of the possibility of later misinterpretations."[93] Apparently, Twichell, genuinely concerned about Twain's postmortem reputation, was unable to burn other untoward documents of Twain's later period, filled as many are with similar "indiscretions"—as Strong speculates, perhaps Twichell understood that much of this material served more as "equilibrium restorer" than as purely sincere statements of belief.

And yet, even while the final period of Twain's publishing career was undeniably marked by depression, cynicism, and finally a sort of deterministic nihilism, traces of religious fervor still appeared from time to time. John Tuckey, in fact, has challenged Hill's standard account by asserting that "this notion of a sustained despair is beginning to look like a disposable myth of Mark Twain's criticism."[94] Here, for instance, is a telltale statement from the Old Man's gospel in *What Is Man?*: "your ideals upward and still upward toward a summit where you will find your chiefest pleasure in conduct which, while contenting you, will be sure to confer benefits upon your neighbor and community." John Hays has read this and other sections as Twain's recognition of his own inability to live with determinism and his final embrace of a sort of social uplift.[95] Moreover, much of the unpublished late work is narrated through such religious figures as Adam and Eve, Methusaleh, and Satan.

In the context of a consideration of the religiosity of Twain's later period, one of the most interesting phenomena must surely be the extensive work and unusually focused and sustained level of attention that he put into his last published novel, *Personal Recollections of Joan of Arc* (1896). This historical novel, written in

Italy and France between 1893 and 1895, was produced at a time of extreme financial despair and personal trauma, yet it foregrounds Twain's lifelong awareness of the conflict between organized religion and genuine faith. The high regard that both Twain and Howells gave to this novel can be partially explained in view of certain cultural and religious contexts of the time. First, it is often noted that Twain's great idolization of innocent young women, and particularly of his virgin daughter Susy, reflects the culture's preoccupation with the sacralization of innocent young children.[96] In a sense, "Joan resembled the innumerable dying children of Victorian novels—descendants of Little Eva and Little Nell. All died young and undefiled, their innocence preserved forever." Tribute to the likes of Joan of Arc offered Twain, perhaps, "a vicarious escape from adult moral and sexual anxieties."[97] Also, Twain's connection of Joan with a strongly pro-American ideology that weds the Christian ethics of the Sermon on the Mount with a zealous patriotism for country constitutes a classic expression of the American jeremiad: "She was the Genius of Patriotism—she was Patriotism embodied, concreted, made flesh, palpable to the touch and visible to the eye."[98] Thus, although it is tempting to write this work off as perhaps the most trivial and uncharacteristic of Twain's longer works, as many modern and contemporary critics have done ("a good example of the failure of modern critics to fully recognize religious values," according to Frederick),[99] *Joan of Arc* should nevertheless be understood as a profound documentation of Twain's lingering religious sensibility and the very real and consistent place that religion had in his fictive world. Rather than dismiss this novel, perhaps we should regard it as a particularly clear confession of Twain's continued spiritual sensibility—a frank affirmation of the better angels of humanity's nature.

These better angels, manifested quite often in the form of Twain's moral outrage toward social injustice, became increasingly a regular feature of his late career. For a world-famous author, who supposedly abandoned religion much earlier, Twain certainly maintained and acted on profoundly moral imperatives during his final decades. His long private criticism of Czarist Russia became public in 1905, for example, with the appearance of

"The Czar's Soliloquy." His attacks on Western imperialism in such far-flung locales as South Africa, China, Cuba, the Congo, and the Philippines are illustrated in such pieces as "To the Person Sitting in Darkness" and "King Leopold's Soliloquy"; he equates imperialist motives more specifically with the work of the church in his "To My Missionary Critics." In 1901, Twain was so appalled by the injustices of the lynching of African Americans that he proposed to write a book on it. The result, "The United States of Lyncherdom," though it is one of his most powerful rhetorical tours de force, was not published until after his death. Twain addressed the deep anti-Semitism of the Gilded Age in such works as "Stirring Times in Austria" and "Concerning the Jews"; he also complained to President Cleveland in 1885–1886 to protest the abuse of Native Americans in the western lands.[100]

Finally, we should consider the seemingly unquenchable curiosity that Twain had throughout his life for all manner of spiritual phenomena, whether marginal or even outright bizarre. His knowledge of and at times even direct participation in spiritual activities beyond the pale of orthodoxy is stunning. Christian Science and Mary Baker Eddy's huge following prompted many scathing responses, but in his first reports on the movement Twain was impressed with accounts of healings by the group. Later, Twain collected his writings on this religion, added to them, and published them as *Christian Science* (1907). Among other things, that volume focused on Twain's fears that Christian Science would grow rapidly and Eddy would gain great power as a religious leader; the movement was satirized more elaborately in the unfinished fiction, "The Secret History of Eddypus, The World-Empire." Much of his interest in Eddy's success probably stemmed from Twain's long-standing interest in the occult and various sciences of the mind: mediumship, seances, mental telegraphy, amanuensises, mesmerism, poltergeists, phrenology, animal magnetism, and other raging fads of the day were endlessly fascinating to Twain.[101] Twain and his wife experimented with several spiritualists in 1900–1901, desiring to communicate with their deceased favorite daughter Susy.[102] In fact, the Nook Farm neighborhood experimented with seances so frequently (largely spurred on by Isabella Beecher Hooker, an eccentric suffragist who slipped into a delusional idea that one day she would reign over a matriarchal government) that Kenneth Andrews has claimed it "reached an excess of abnormality unduplicated in Hartford."[103] Although he attacked spiritualism in several places, notably chapter 48 of *Life on the Mississippi*, Twain clearly believed in the ability of humans to have simultaneous or duplicate thoughts, as he admitted in "Mental Telegraphy" (1891). Twain was a member of the English Society for Psychical Research for nearly twenty years: Their reports on "ghost stories, haunted houses, and apparitions of the living and the dead" greatly fascinated Twain, so that he "read their pamphlets with avidity as fast as they arrived."[104] He was deeply intrigued by reports of a Scottish spiritualist named Daniel Dunglas Home, "the most famous nineteenth-century medium in Britain and Europe," who claimed he could levitate and fly via mental power.[105] Many other instances of Twain's obvious affinities with the supernatural could be recounted; for now, we can readily agree with Randall Knoper's conclusion: "despite the abuse he unleashed in *Christian Science* . . . Eddy's ideas about the primacy of mind or spirit over matter resonated with Twain's thinking."[106]

Definitive conclusions about Twain's engagement with and understanding of American religion of the Gilded Age remain difficult. One useful approach might draw upon one of the oldest tricks in the trade—his doubleness, the classic expression of which may be the title of Justin Kaplan's biography, *Mr. Clemens and Mark Twain*. Framed in religious terms, we might draw upon Leland Krauth's distinction between what he calls the "transgressive Twain" and the "bounded Twain."[107] Krauth has correctly pointed out the critical preoccupation with the transgressive Twain—to the regrettable exclusion of a full consideration of the bounded, or "proper" Mark Twain, a hole in Twain scholarship that Krauth's volume aims at filling. Strikingly, however, these very categories obscure the fact that religious, and indeed Christian impulses (such as the act of repentance as rebellion or the rhetorical stylings of the jeremiad), played crucial roles in Twain's (and America's) transgressive mode.[108] As a result, Krauth's work underplays the role of Christianity and gives almost no attention to Twain's evangelical friends—or indeed to the ways that they, by challenging the prevailing culture, operated according to the transgressive mode. Horace Bushnell, for example, was considered in his day a radically innovative theologian and social engineer, whose theories flew in the face of more traditional thought. Thus does Krauth ironically echo the majority of recent critical commentary on Twain's iconoclastic approach to religion, with its emphasis on the transgressive Twain, by his dismissal of the evangelical piety and the prophetic awareness of social injustice inherent in the better angels of America's Christian tradition.

Examples from Twain's obituaries verify that his own contemporaries perceived and appreciated both religious impulses. *The Truth Seeker*, the major journal of Christian infidelism, described him this way: "We conclude that the religious views of Mark Twain, so far as they concerned the Christian system, were substantially those of Robert G. Ingersoll. We are told privately, by one having immediate knowledge of the fact, that Twain was less reverent than Ingersoll."[109] Conversely, his childhood girlfriend Laura Hawkins Frazier (the model for Becky Thatcher) wrote in 1923: "the last time I saw him [at Stormfield], he told me goodbye twice, came back the third time and said, 'We will meet in Heaven, Laura,' pointing upward. He was a Christian."[110] Another boyhood friend, John L. Robards, did not agree with the inscription "His Religion was Humanity" on the Missouri state commemorative statue to Twain because "Mark Twain was not an Infidel but . . . the inscription made him out one."[111] Likewise, Katy Leary, the faithful household servant, recalled Twain saying to her, "Oh, Katy! [Jean's] in heaven with her mother. . . . Oh, I think—I am sure he believed in the hereafter. But he was pretty serious in arguing about religion."[112]

Perhaps it is best to go to the person who may have known him best at his death. Joe Twichell, often called upon to offer eulogies in his large urban church setting, usually made clear assertions about the Christian faith of the deceased.[113] Thus, it is significant that he only indirectly made similar statements about Twain in any of his published remarks about him after his death. He most certainly did comment on Twain's "character"—his gentleness, humility, and care for others, including surprisingly and memorably his tenderness toward animals. However, on topics specific to Christian doctrine, Twichell maintained a public silence—probably because he knew firsthand of Twain's infidelity on key aspects of dogma; partly, perhaps, because of his desire not to add to the rather widely held opinion of Twain as a blasphemer or at least infidel. In any case, Twichell certainly never went on record defending Twain as an actual Christian believer. On the other hand, Twichell remained loyal and strongly attracted to the memory of the better angels of Mark Twain's character—framing him, like some of the others, as the "moralist in disguise" he most admired—and which Twain, apparently, most aspired to be.

NOTES

1. Quoted in Howard Baetzhold, *Mark Twain and John Bull: The British Connection* (Bloomington: Indiana University Press, 1970), 138. Regarding Lecky's volume, it is worth noting what many scholars have unfortunately overlooked in their analyses—that Lecky's work describes the teachings of Jesus as "an agency which all men must now admit to have been, for good or for evil, the most powerful moral lever that has ever been applied to the affairs of men." Clearly Lecky sought to highlight the profoundly valuable effect of Jesus' life and teachings on the history of ethical behavior in the West— and yet the opposite reading is most often emphasized.

2. The term comes from Jenny Franchot's suggestive article describing the theoretical premises that have led to the exclusion of matters of faith in much recent American literary scholarship. See Franchot, "Invisible Domain: Religion and American Literary Studies," *American Literature* 67 (Dec. 1995): 833–42.

3. Jeffrey R. Holland, "Soul Butter and Hogwash: Mark Twain and Frontier Religion," in *"Soul Butter and Hogwash" and Other Essays on the American West*, ed. Thomas Alexander (Provo, Utah: Brigham Young University Press, 1978), 14, 15. My use of the phrase "religious and/or moral terms" is meant to indicate an awareness of the ways these terms compare and contrast. While Twain vigorously denounced at times institutional religion, it must not mitigate the fact that much of his moral philosophy derives from a Christian ethical

framework—in particular, from the frontier gospel of his youth and later from a liberalized social gospel that permeated the New England Congregational culture of Hartford—points which will be developed later in this essay.

4. Sherwood Cummings, *Mark Twain and Science: Adventures of a Mind* (Baton Rouge: Louisiana State University Press, 1988) and John Q. Hays, *Mark Twain and Religion* (New York: Peter Lang, 1989) are both convincing on this point.

5. See Paul Carter, *The Spiritual Crisis of the Gilded Age* (DeKalb: Northern Illinois University Press, 1971), passim.

6. Dixon Wecter, *Sam Clemens of Hannibal* (Boston: Houghton Mifflin, 1952), 86.

7. William Dean Howells, *My Mark Twain: Reminiscences and Criticisms* (New York: Harper, 1901), 125.

8. Cummings, *Mark Twain and Science,* 18; for excellent coverage of Twain's use of biblical metaphor and allusion, see especially Allison Ensor, *Mark Twain and the Bible* (Lexington: University of Kentucky Press, 1969); Susan K. Harris, *Mark Twain's Escape from Time: A Study of Patterns and Images* (Columbia: University of Missouri Press, 1982); and Stanley Brodwin, "Mark Twain's Theology: The Gods of a Brevet Presbyterian," in *The Cambridge Companion to Mark Twain,* ed. Forrest G. Robinson (New York: Cambridge University Press, 1995), 220-48.

9. Cummings, *Mark Twain and Science,* 18.

10. *The Adventures of Tom Sawyer,* 57. All quotes from Twain, unless otherwise noted, are from *The Oxford Mark Twain,* ed. Shelley Fisher Fishkin, 29 vols. (New York: Oxford University Press, 1996).

11. Gregg Camfield, *Sentimental Twain: Samuel Clemens in the Maze of Moral Philosophy* (Philadelphia: University of Pennsylvania Press, 1994), is particularly strong on this point.

12. *Adventures of Tom Sawyer,* 46.

13. *Adventures of Tom Sawyer,* 51.

14. *The Gilded Age,* in *The Oxford Mark Twain,* 481-2.

15. *Adventures of Huckleberry Finn,* in *The Oxford Mark Twain,* 148.

16. See Lewis Atherton, *Main Street on the Middle Border* (Chicago: Quadrangle, 1966), 65 ff., for an abundance of evidence from the McGuffey readers. The quote above is from 65.

17. Edward Eggleston, *The Hoosier School-Master* (1871; Bloomington: Indiana University Press, 1984), 102. This chapter, and the entire

novel, are also remarkable for their specific awareness of, and attack against, the charges of Charles Darwin's *The Descent of Man*—specifically, the charge that humans are mere animals. Here, Eggleston sketches the small town as being populated mainly by near-animals until the advent of the heroic title character Ralph Hartsook.

18. Quoted in Wecter, *Sam Clemens of Hannibal*, 88.

19. Reprinted in Louis Budd, ed., *Mark Twain: Collected Tales, Sketches, Speeches, and Essays, 1852–1890* (New York: Library of America, 1992), 287.

20. Budd, ed., *Collected Tales*, 539.

21. Quoted in James D. Wilson, "Religious and Esthetic Vision in Mark Twain's Early Career," *Canadian Review of American Studies* 17 (Summer 1986): 166.

22. Ensor, *Mark Twain and the Bible*, 39.

23. Susan K. Harris, *The Courtship of Olivia Langdon and Mark Twain* (New York: Cambridge University Press, 1996), 70, 78. Harris further admits candidly and somewhat autobiographically that "retrospection facilitates our skepticism. . . . [It is] difficult not to be struck by [the love letters'] apparent sincerity. . . . Clemens's struggles to achieve faith were perfectly sincere", 79. Penetrating analysis of Twain's relationship with Livy is found throughout Harris's volume, as well as in Laura E. Skandera-Trombley, *Mark Twain in the Company of Women* (Philadelphia: University of Pennsylvania Press, 1994), esp. 1–64, and Resa Willis, *Mark and Livy: The Love Story of Mark Twain and the Woman Who Almost Tamed Him* (New York: Atheneum, 1992), passim.

24. Wilson, "Religious and Esthetic Vision in Mark Twain's Early Career," 167, 168.

25. See especially Wilson, "Religious and Esthetic Vision in Mark Twain's Early Career," 155–57. Cummings, *Mark Twain and Science*, 23–28, is also enlightening on this.

26. See Richard S. Lowry, *"Littery Man": Mark Twain and Modern Authorship* (New York: Oxford University Press, 1996), esp. 16–65. See also Hilton Obenzinger, *American Palestine: Melville, Twain, and the Holy Land Mania* (Princeton: Princeton University Press, 1999).

27. On anti-Catholicism in *Innocents*, see Hays, *Mark Twain and Religion*, 44–7; in *Connecticut Yankee*, see Leo F. O'Connor, *Religion in the American Novel: The Search for Belief, 1860–1920* (Lanham, Md.: University Press of America, 1984), 225–30; on the connection of nativism with anti-Catholicism, see Sydney Ahlstrom, *A Religious History of*

the American People (New Haven: Yale University Press, 1972), 852–56; on Bushnell's views see Jenny Franchot, *Roads to Rome: The Antebellum Protestant Encounter with Catholicism* (Berkeley: University of California Press, 1994), xviii and 229–33; on antebellum attitudes toward Catholicism, see Franchot, *Road to Rome*, passim; Twain's important encounter with Lecky is covered in Baetzhold, *Mark Twain and John Bull*, 134–43, 155–56, and 218–28, as well as Cummings, *Mark Twain and Science*, esp. 59–60, Camfield, *Sentimental Twain*, 113–4 and 160–1, and Alan Gribben, *Mark Twain's Library*, 2 vols. (Boston: G. K. Hall, 1980), 400–02.

28. *The Innocents Abroad*, in the *Oxford Mark Twain*, 57.

29. *The Innocents Abroad*, in the *Oxford Mark Twain*, 209.

30. Forrest G. Robinson, "The Innocent at Large: Mark Twain's Travel Writing," in *The Cambridge Companion to Mark Twain*, 30.

31. Robinson, "The Innocent at Large," 33.

32. *Roughing It*, in *The Oxford Mark Twain*, 143.

33. *Roughing It*, in *The Oxford Mark Twain*, 106.

34. *Roughing It*, in *The Oxford Mark Twain*, 127.

35. Louis Budd, *Our Mark Twain: The Making of His Public Personality* (Philadelphia: University of Pennsylvania Press, 1983), 25.

36. Hays, *Mark Twain and Religion*, 53.

37. Leland Krauth, *Proper Mark Twain* (Athens: University of Georgia Press, 1999), 54, 61.

38. Robinson, "The Innocent at Large," 34.

39. Perry Miller, *Nature's Nation* (Cambridge: Harvard University Press, 1957), 23. In particular, see Miller's chapter "Declension in a Bible Commonwealth," 14–49. Further discussion of the jeremiad tradition in American culture can be found in Sacvan Bercovitch, *The American Jeremiad* (Madison: University of Wisconsin Press, 1979), passim; and Harold K. Bush, Jr., *American Declarations: Rebellion and Repentance in American Cultural History* (Urbana: University of Illinois Press, 1999), 1–11 and passim.

40. Holland, "Soul Butter and Hogwash," 14, 15.

41. Robert Bellah, "Civil Religion in America," *Daedalus* 96 (1967): 13. More consideration of this topic, which is surely one of the major thematics of Americanist scholarship over many decades, can be found in already cited works by Bercovitch, Bush, and Miller; see also Ernest Lee Tuveson, *Redeemer Nation: The Idea of America's Millennial Role* (Chicago: University of Chicago Press, 1968), and

Garry Wills, *Inventing America: Jefferson's Declaration of Independence* (Garden City, N.Y.: Doubleday, 1978).

42. Bush, *American Declarations*, passim.

43. Justin Kaplan, *Mr. Clemens and Mark Twain: A Biography* (New York: Touchstone, 1966), 225–6.

44. Gribben, *Mark Twain's Library*, vol. 1, 412.

45. Reprinted in Budd, ed., *Collected Tales*, 940. The letter appeared originally in *Camden's Compliment to Walt Whitman*, ed. Horace Traubel (Philadelphia: David McKay, 1889), 64–5.

46. Richard Brodhead makes this claim in "Literature and Culture," in *The Columbia Literary History of the United States*, ed. Emory Elliott et al. (New York: Columbia University Press, 1988), 472–3.

47. See Ahlstrom, *Religious History*, 765–804.

48. Martin Marty, for instance, has commented on "the extent of the evangelical triumph" during the Gilded Age—a victory consistently noted by foreigners who visited the United States: "Wherever one turned, signs of progress, growth, and success could be documented. . . . All these signs were impressive to partisans of Christianity and seemed oppressive and overpowering to its antagonists." See Martin Marty, *The Infidel: Freethought and American Religion* (Cleveland: World, 1961), 139.

49. Howard A. Barnes, *Horace Bushnell and the Virtuous Republic* (Metuchen, N.J.: American Theological Library Assoc., 1991), 17; more information about Bushnell's vision of what Barnes calls the "virtuous republic" is in 3–62. The tone of this period's millennialism is nicely evoked in Timothy Smith, "Righteousness and Hope: Christian Holiness and the Millennial Vision of America, 1800–1900," *American Quarterly* 31 (Spring 1979): 180–98.

50. For a consideration of Twain's and Howells's mixed feelings about Boston and the prestige it had accumulated by this period, see Bush, *American Declarations*, 124–46; and Lowry, *"Littery Man,"* 16–44.

51. Jeffrey Steinbrink, *Getting to Be Mark Twain* (Berkeley: University of California Press, 1991), 31–32.

52. Steinbrink, *Getting to Be Mark Twain*, 189.

53. Not incidentally, 1891 is also identified by Sherwood Cummings as a crucial moment of religious and philosophical change in Twain's view of religion; see Cummings, *Mark Twain and Science*, 29 ff.

54. Albert Bigelow Paine, *Mark Twain: A Biography,* 4 vols. (New York: Harper, 1912), 2: 632.

55. Thomas D. Schwartz, "Mark Twain and Robert Ingersoll: The Freethought Connection," *American Literature* 48 (1976): 183–93 191; Kenneth Andrews, *Nook Farm: Mark Twain's Hartford Circle* (Cambridge: Harvard University Press, 1950), 51.

56. Admittedly, part of the problem may have to do with the historically vexed definition of the term "evangelical." A succinct definition is in Mark Noll, *The Scandal of the Evangelical Mind* (Grand Rapids, Mich.: Eerdmans, 1994), 7–10; see also Noll's notes to this discussion. Noll emphasizes four major aspects of evangelical theology (conversionism, biblicism, activism, crucicentrism), all of which, I would argue, Twichell embraced throughout his ministry years. A similar definition is found in James Davison Hunter, *American Evangelicalism: Conservative Religion and the Quandary of Modernity* (New Brunswick, N.J.: Rutgers University Press, 1983), 7–9.

57. Quoted in Leah Strong, *Joseph Hopkins Twichell: Mark Twain's Friend and Pastor* (Athens: University of Georgia Press, 1966), 82.

58. Andrews, *Nook Farm,* 71.

59. Quoted in Andrew Hoffman, *Inventing Mark Twain: The Lives of Samuel Langhorne Clemens* (New York: Morrow, 1997), 108. On Burlingame's influence, see Krauth, *Proper Mark Twain,* 37–41.

60. Quoted in Jim McWilliams, *Mark Twain in the St. Louis Post-Dispatch, 1874–1891* (Troy, N.Y.: Whitson, 1997), 212.

61. Strong, *Joseph Hopkins Twichell,* 120.

62. Yung Wing, the first Chinese student at Yale who went on to lead the Mission and become a key spokeman for Chinese-American activists, was an acquaintance of Twain and a very close friend of Twichell. Twain apparently embraced Wing's work, hosting, for instance, a reception for him in his Nook Farm home in 1877. More important, Twain personally arranged at least two meetings between Twichell, Yung Wing, and General Grant in New York in 1880, with the goal of helping them arrange letters of support from Grant in an attempt to avert the closing of the Mission (Grant voluntarily offered his services). On one of these occasions, Twain himself personally escorted Wing to New York and participated in the meetings with Grant. In connection with his interest in and sympathy for the Chinese students, we should nonetheless recall the range of Twain's response over the years to this ethnic group: from the eight scathingly critical articles on Chinese persecution he published

in the *Galaxy* in the early 1870s to the embarrassingly stereotyped burlesque/drama (suggestive of Twain's halting response at times to issues of race) he authored with Bret Harte in 1877 called *Ah Sin*. On Twain's involvement with Wing and Grant, see Strong, *Joseph Hopkins Twichell*, 85–87 and Hoffman, *Inventing Mark Twain*, 283 and 310. On Twain's articles on the Chinese in the *Galaxy* see Hays, *Mark Twain and Religion*, 74–5. For an interesting reading of *Ah Sin* with regard to Twain's thinking at this time on issues of race, see Randall Knoper, *Acting Naturally: Mark Twain and the Culture of Performance* (Berkeley: University of California Press, 1995), 46–8.

63. Leah Strong has gone so far as to argue that some of Twain's greatest work may be attributable to what she calls a "Twichell effect"—and evidence from letters indicates that Twain was himself aware of the very positive air of creativity that he sensed when he spent time with Twichell as opposed to the long periods of time that they spent apart. Perhaps that is why he asked Twichell if he could set up an office in an empty room in Twichell's house when he was struggling to write *Connecticut Yankee;* or why Twain asked Twichell to accompany him on several writerly occasions, such as the "Tramp Abroad" excursion. See Strong, *Joseph Hopkins Twichell*, esp. 109–50.

64. Quoted in Cummings, *Mark Twain and Science*, 24.

65. Quoted in Strong, *Joseph Hopkins Twichell*, 96.

66. Quoted in Milton Meltzer, *Mark Twain Himself: A Pictorial Biography* (New York: Crowell, 1960), 219. For information on the Fisk Jubilee Singers and Twain's connection with them, see Andrew Ward, *Dark Midnight When I Rise: The Story of The Jubilee Singers Who Introduced the World to the Music of Black America* (New York: Farrar, Straus and Giroux, 2000), esp. 164–5, 224–5, 282–4.

67. In Joseph Twichell Journal, #3, page 16. Used with permission of the Beineke Library, Yale University.

68. In Joseph Twichell Journal, #5, page 34. Used with permission of the Beineke Library, Yale University.

69. Katy Leary, *A Lifetime with Mark Twain* (New York: Harcourt, Brace, 1925), 213.

70. For information on the incident, see Myra C. Glenn, *Thomas K. Beecher: Minister to a Changing America, 1824–1900* (Westport, Conn.: Greenwood, 1996), 127–9; for Twain's published response to the criticism, see "Mr. Beecher and the Clergy," *Elmira Daily Advertiser,* 10 April 1869; reprinted in Budd, *Collected Tales*, 291–5.

71. See Strong, *Joseph Hopkins Twichell*, 120, 124. On "muscular

Christianity," see Donald Hall, ed., *Muscular Christianity: Embodying the Victorian Age* (New York: Cambridge University Press, 1994).

72. For an excellent analysis of Darwin's reception in America, see Cynthia Eagle Russett, *Darwin in America: The Intellectual Response, 1865–1912* (San Francisco: W. H. Freeman, 1976). See also, for instance, Ahlstrom, *Religious History*, 767–72; William Hutchinson, *The Modernist Impulse in American Protestantism* (Cambridge: Harvard University Press, 1976), 88–90; and Carter, *The Spiritual Crisis of the Gilded Age*, 21–62. For Twain's encounter with Darwin, see Cummings, *Mark Twain and Science*, 54–67 and 180–83.

73. Ferenc Morton Szasz, *The Divided Mind of Protestant America, 1880–1930* (University, Ala.: University of Alabama Press, 1982), 5.

74. T. DeWitt Talmage, *Live Coals* (Chicago: Fairbanks, 1886), 271.

75. For background on this critical movement, see Szasz, *The Divided Mind*, esp. 15–41, as well as Jerry Wayne Brown, *The Rise of Biblical Criticism in America, 1800–1870: The New England Scholars* (Middletown, Conn.: Wesleyan University Press, 1969).

76. Quoted in Szasz, *The Divided Mind*, 38.

77. Quoted in Robert D. Jerome and Herbert A. Wisbey, Jr., eds., *Mark Twain in Elmira* (Elmira, N.Y.: Mark Twain Society, 1977), 85–85.

78. See Ahlstrom, *Religious History*, 805–15.

79. See Holland, "Soul Butter and Hogwash," 18–19.

80. Many excellent readings of this passage are available. Leo Marx's *The Pilot and the Passenger* (New York: Oxford University Press, 1988) is a good place to start. See also Cummings, *Mark Twain and Science*, chap. 4, "The Science of Piloting" (especially 61–64) for a reading of the passage with emphasis on Darwinism.

81. *Life on the Mississippi*, in the *Oxford Mark Twain*, 62.

82. *Life on the Mississippi*, in the *Oxford Mark Twain*, 84, 87–8.

83. *Life on the Mississippi*, in the *Oxford Mark Twain*, 118.

84. *Life on the Mississippi*, in the *Oxford Mark Twain*, 118–9.

85. For the lengthy, troubled, and in large part still mysterious reconstruction of the composition of this tale, see Howard Baetzhold and James McCullough, eds., *The Bible According to Mark Twain* (New York: Touchstone, 1997), 129–38.

86. On romantic views of the afterlife throughout this period in America, see Ann Douglas, *The Feminization of American Culture* (New York: Knopf, 1977), 220–226.

87. Douglas, *Feminization*, 223.

88. Douglas, *Feminization*, 224.

89. See Alan Gribben, "'When Other Amusements Fail': Mark Twain and the Occult," in *The Haunted Dusk: American Supernatural Fiction, 1820–1920*, ed. Howard Kerr et al. (Athens: University of Georgia Press, 1983), 177.

90. As Hamlin Hill once memorably put it, "Until 1900 Mark Twain managed to retain control over his universe, over his despair, pessimism, frustration, and insensitivity, by his artistic capacity. . . . [but after 1900] the bitterness which permeated *What Is Man?*, "Letters from the Earth," the "Mysterious Stranger" fragments, much of the autobiography, and most of the shorter political writings was a rage at the obscenity of life." See Hamlin Hill, *Mark Twain: God's Fool* (New York: Harper and Row, 1973), 272, 274.

91. See, in particular, the autobiographical dictations of 6/19, 6/20, 6/22, 6/23, and 6/25, all 1906—all in the Mark Twain Papers, University of California, Berkeley, Calif. Together these dictations were edited and published by Charles Neider, as "Mark Twain: Reflections on Religion," *Hudson Review* 16 (1963): 329–52.

92. Schwartz, "Mark Twain and Robert Ingersoll," 191; according to Schwartz, the journal was founded by D. M. Bennett, "an outspoken atheist whose hatred of Christianity made the *Truth Seeker* the most vehemently anti-Christian of the free-thought periodicals": 191n23.

93. Cummings, *Mark Twain and Science*, 26; Strong, *Joseph Hopkins Twichell*, 111.

94. John S. Tuckey, "Mark Twain's Later Dialogue: The 'Me' and the Machine," *American Literature* 41 (Jan. 1970): 532.

95. Quoted in Hays, *Mark Twain and Religion*, 185; for Hays's unusually uplifting reading of *What Is Man?*, see 179–211.

96. See, for instance, John Cooley, ed., *Mark Twain's Aquarium: The Samuel Clemens Angelfish Correspondence, 1905–1910* (Athens: University of Georgia Press, 1991), xxiii, 282.

97. T. Jackson Lears, *No Place of Grace: Antimodernism and the Transformation of American Culture, 1880–1920* (Chicago: University of Chicago Press, 1981), 151.

98. *Joan of Arc*, in *The Oxford Mark Twain*, 461.

99. John T. Frederick, *The Darkened Sky: Nineteenth-Century American Novelists and Religion* (Notre Dame: University of Notre Dame Press, 1969), 165.

100. On these matters, see Louis Budd, *Mark Twain: Social Philosopher* (Bloomington: Indiana University Press, 1962); and Philip S. Foner, *Mark Twain: Social Critic* (New York: International, 1958). On Twain and anti-Semiticism, see Carl Dolmetsch, *"Our Famous Guest": Mark Twain in Austria* (Athens: University of Georgia Press, 1992), especially 160–80. Regarding the protest to President Cleveland, see Budd, 107 and Foner, 236–7.

101. Twain's interest in and knowledge of mental sciences is thoroughly covered in Knoper, *Acting Naturally*, especially 119–40 and 170–92.

102. Hill, *Mark Twain*, 33–4.

103. Andrews, *Nook Farm*, 62; on the spiritualism of the Nook Farm community, see Andrews 53–66; on Twain's familiarity with various forms of spiritism, see Howard Kerr, *Mediums, Spirit-Rappers, and Roaring Radicals: Spiritualism in American Literature, 1850–1900* (Urbana: University of Illinois Press, 1972), 155–89; on spiritualism in general, see Carter, *The Spiritual Crisis of the Gilded Age*, 99–106 and Ahlstrom, *Religious History*, 488–90.

104. Other instances of Twain's use of mediumship in his fiction are noted in Gribben, "'When Other Amusements Fail,'" 178; see also Kerr, *Mediums*, 188.

105. Quoted in Gribben, "'When Other Amusements Fail,'" 179.

106. Knoper, *Acting Naturally*, 185.

107. See Krauth, *Proper Mark Twain*, passim, but especially 1–6, for this distinction.

108. See Bush, *American Declarations*, passim, on how Christian thought has contributed significantly to the transgressive and rebellious aspects of American cultural ideology.

109. Quoted in Schwartz, "Mark Twain and Robert Ingersoll," 192–3.

110. Letter written by Laura Hawkins Frazier 23 Jan. 1923, in Twichell papers, Beinecke Library, Yale University.

111. Letter, B. Q. Stevens to Willard Morse, 12 Dec. 1922, in Twichell papers, Beinecke Library, Yale University.

112. Quoted in Jerome and Wisbey, *Mark Twain in Elmira*, 93.

113. This is clear from the many published obituaries (most from the *Hartford Courant*) that Twichell kept and pasted into his journals, now housed at the Beinecke Library at Yale University.

A Republican Artisan in the Court of King Capital

Mark Twain and Commerce

Gregg Camfield

> Honest poverty is a gem that even a King might feel proud to call his own, but I wish to sell out. I have sported that kind of jewelry long enough. I want some variety. I wish to become rich, so that I can instruct the people and glorify honest poverty a little, like those good, kind-hearted, fat, benevolent people do.
>
> —Mark Twain to the *Alta California*, May 26, 1867

The term "venture capitalist" had not yet been coined, but Mark Twain played the role for James W. Paige, a mechanic and inventor who held patents for a typesetting machine. Twain was spellbound by the machine's potential. Having worked as a compositor, writer, and publisher, he knew the high cost of the compositor's bottleneck in the printing industry, and while he knew the Paige machine had competitors, he was confident that Paige's machine would carry the day.[1] It did not, and when the machine's proclivity to break down under hard use proved insurmountable, the losses Twain experienced helped bankrupt both his publishing firm and himself.

Then again, if the financial panic of 1893 and ensuing major economic depression hadn't cramped credit, Twain probably could have withstood the loss. But during the panic, not only could he not secure funding through commercial banks, but also his wife's wealthy family was too pinched to help.[2] If supercapitalist H. H. Rogers, one of the principals of the Standard Oil Company, hadn't come to Twain's rescue, telling him where and how to cut his losses, helping him decide how to use his literary fame to create income, negotiating with creditors for him, and investing the proceeds of his literary ventures, Twain probably would not have recovered.

This well-known story is part of a large-scale pattern of commerce in the nineteenth century. Old ideas of commerce as familial and cautious gave way to increasingly impersonal entrepreneurship; advances in machine technology cut labor costs; expansion of the national market created economies of scale; consolidation of businesses into ever larger enterprises demanded greater capitalization; and the pressure resulted in frequent, massive dislocations in the money supply. Consequently, failure was more common than the colossal successes for which America became known.

It was a time of high expectations and great fear. On the one hand, statistics prove that America's new economy created unparalleled wealth over the course of Mark Twain's life. The general condition of even the working classes improved—real wages rose about 50 percent in manufacturing between 1870 and 1890. On the other hand, the share of the nation's total wealth became concentrated into fewer hands. Moreover, half of the wage increase took place in the 1880s, and because these were the result of deflation of costs, most workers didn't really feel happy about their statistical improvement. What they saw was falling wages, not rising ones. That combined with massive unemployment in the frequent depressions—most notably the depressions of 1873–1879 and 1893–1897—created real anxieties about the economic order that was developing.[3]

Such anxieties find their way into Mark Twain's works, most obviously in those works that decry greed, such as "The Man That Corrupted Hadleyburg" (1899) or "The $30,000 Bequest" (1904)[4] or the posthumously published "3,000 Years among the Microbes." All of these were written after Twain's bankruptcy and stand in stark contrast to the happy-ending "Million Pound Banknote" of 1893, written before Twain's hopes of speculative wealth were shattered, but when he had enough stress on his finances to make his vision of wealth seem more dream than plausibility. The contradiction here between the earlier praise of wealth made through speculation and an attack on greed per se is easily explicable as a reaction to simple personal experience.

This easy answer, though, does not explain the same pattern of denunciation and appreciation of wealth that pervades Twain's work from the earliest. *Roughing It* is virtually a hymn in praise of the enterprising spirit of the West, made all the richer against the dissonant countermelody of potential failure. In another vein, such pieces as "Open Letter to Com. Vanderbilt" (1869), *The Gilded Age* (1873), and the posthumously published "Letter from the Recording Angel" (written about 1887) all attack America's love affair with money. Something larger than mere personal experience drove these attacks as well as drove Twain's own hunger for wealth. At first blush, this appears to be a typically Twainian contradiction.

When addressing money and commerce, Twain's expressed attitudes toward money don't provide readers with their only puzzle. As much as the business of America finds its way into Twain's books, when one looks at all the pieces Twain wrote that in one way or another address the major changes the American economy experienced over his lifetime, they seem odd by comparison with his contemporaries's writing on similar subjects. Twain's good friend William Dean Howells, for example, worked steadily to develop social realism. In the correspondence between Howells and Twain, the two seemed to agree that realism was a moral imperative in art. Yet Twain's typical mode when writing about the economy was to use some combination of burlesque, allegory, and melodrama. The allegorical *Connecticut Yankee* (1889) is the most obvious example, but in the burlesque *The*

Gilded Age from the 1870s, the allegorical "Blue-Jay Yarn" and the allegorical representation of the range wars personified in "*Sheperd*sons" and "*Grangerfords*" in *Huckleberry Finn* from the 1880s, the melodramatic *American Claimant* from the 1890s, and the allegorical "3,000 Years among the Microbes" from the 1900s, we see this antirealistic tendency spanning his career.

As odd as his attitudes toward money and realism may be, in no case is the puzzle of Twain's reaction to the changing economy more perplexing than in his attitudes toward what was commonly referred to as the labor problem, which lay at the center of industrialization. In his 1875 series of *Atlantic Monthly* essay, "Old Times on the Mississippi," Twain describes the riverboat pilots' union in remarkably supportive terms, precisely when the kinds of people who read the *Atlantic* were being whipped into a frenzy over unions as a threat to the American way of life. A rash of railway strikes in 1873–1874 and prolonged labor disputes in the coal industry had northeastern elites worried. Some went so far as to hire Pinkerton detectives to break the "Molly Maguires," the supposed secret society that was organized in the coal fields. So while the educated readers of the *Atlantic* and similar journals were worked up over "foreigners" corrupting America's labor force, Twain's depiction of the pilot's union instead praises workers for their steadfastness, manliness, and ultimately for improving safety on the river. The union men won, Twain tells us, when the insurance companies, those most conservative of capitalistic forces, backed them.

A decade later, after the labor violence of the 1877 railroad strikes but just before the Haymarket riot in May of 1886, Twain drafted a rousing essay supporting the Knights of Labor. In this essay, "The New Dynasty," which he read to the Hartford Monday Evening Club on March 22, 1886, Twain personified the labor union as the world's king, the real nation that kings are supposed to embody. Robert Weir discusses Twain's ideas about the Knights in greater depth in an essay later in this volume. For my purposes, it is worth noting that, although Twain never published this essay, he did, ironically, have it set on the Paige typesetter, which, had it been successful, would have thrown thousands of compositors out of work, supplanting their skill with the dumb labor of a machine.

Twain was not unaware of the irony, but the contradiction between his support of labor and his investment in a labor-supplanting machine seems more poignant in the context of his *January* 18, 1886 talk to the "Typothetae," a nationwide printers association that annually celebrated Benjamin Franklin's birthday. In 1886, Twain was invited to speak at the New York celebration, held in Delmonico's. In comparing a rejected draft speech to the one he finally gave, we can discern Twain's anxiety about his relationship to labor. The rejected draft praises the invention of movable type as the founder of all material and intellectual progress, an event akin to the creation of the earth itself. But it laments that while presswork has changed to match the progress of the nineteenth century, composition remains the same as it was in the beginning. He challenges compositors to accept inevitable advances when he announces that he is among many who are investing in composition machines.[5] The speech he actually gave, on the other hand, is nothing but reminiscences about his apprenticeship in Hannibal, Missouri. His depiction is deliberately nostalgic, discussing a period that he himself had seen pass in his brief stint as a printer. It seems that he was feeling guilty enough to avoid the challenge in favor of a eulogy, a eulogy that would say, in effect, "I am one of you," when his actions were those of an adversary.

The contradiction here is emblematic of Twain's reaction to the economic conditions and practices of his day. Of course, to say that Mark Twain contradicts himself is hardly revolutionary, and critics have for generations tried to explain the causes—psychological, ideological, sociological. When it comes to business, Twain apparently outdoes himself in contradictions. Or so it seems in hindsight, when we have developed intellectual models that explain the political economy of the late nineteenth century in terms that justify, or at least explain, our own economic conditions. Most Americans now regularly accept capitalism and democracy as synonymous. As such, they tend to determine value as a function of capital, even to the point of describing labor itself as "human capital" and therefore supporting education not to mold citizens but to make the United States economically competitive. Even those who do not accept that democracy and capitalism are coterminous tend to view the world through macroeconomic lenses, accepting that society is a complex affair best explained through economics. We have grown accustomed to the political and economic relations that were new and perplexing in Twain's day, and two world wars and a cold war—fought substantially, though not exclusively, over economic ideology—have hardened us to see the world (how accurately only time will tell) in such terms.

From such standpoints, Twain's attitudes toward the world of commerce seem confused and contradictory. How can he be prolabor while working to undermine labor? How can he rail against massive accumulations of wealth while pursuing it? Why does he turn to allegory, melodrama, and burlesque, in other words, why does he turn backward, when addressing economic issues? Simply because he was of his time and addressed political economy in the terms shared by most of his contemporaries. Twain used the intellectual coin of his nation, the ideology of democratic republicanism, that saw the entire nation, including merchants, artisans, and laborers, as part of the same antiaristocratic class, and that saw the virtue of labor as the fundamental underpinning of a republican gentility. For once, Twain is remarkably consistent. The apparent inconsistencies arise in the gap between Twain's worldview and the economic realities that changed as he aged. The wide variation in his reactions depends on his very personal approach to economic issues, an approach often challenged but never superseded by new and competing ideologies of commerce being offered to justify or attack the modern industrial economy even as they explained it. One can see this by tracing Mark Twain's involvement in commerce, showing that his point of view was forged in an antebellum context, one predicated on individual character rather than on macroeconomic trends or cost-benefit analyses, on the labor theory of value rather than on investment.

He began his work life in 1848, about a year after his father died in March of 1847.[6] The family's circumstances were already straitened before his father's death. In his autobiography, Twain blamed his father's ill fortune on his aristocratic notion of being above labor and having foolishly speculated in land on the assumption that land itself would provide his family with ultimate wealth. But John Marshall Clemens had moved his family repeatedly during the depression of 1837–1844, each time trying to establish himself as either merchant or lawyer or both, and one cannot help but speculate that a man trying to deal in dry goods or work as an attorney out on the nation's fringe would have a hard time establishing business during an economic downturn. The facts are less revealing than is Twain's explanation; by arguing that land is an aristocratic basis for wealth, Twain reveals his essential democratic-republicanism, holding labor as the source of value.[7]

Be that as it may, eleven-year-old Samuel was, like his brother Orion before him and brother Henry after him, apprenticed to the printing trade. He learned his trade first with Joseph Ament, publisher of Hannibal's *Missouri Courier*. In Hannibal, industrial practices had not come to the trade, so Twain learned everything, from composition to presswork, much as it had been practiced since the fifteenth century. As he put it in his "Compositor" speech at the Typothetae dinner:

All things change in the procession of the years, and it may be that I am among strangers. It may be that the printer of today is not the printer of thirty-five years ago. I was not stranger to him. I knew him well. I built his fire for him in the cold winter mornings; I brought his water from the village pump; I swept out his office; I picked up his type from under his stand; and, if he was there to see, I put the good type in his case and the broken ones among the "hell matter"; and if he wasn't there to see, I dumped it all with the "pi" on the imposing stone— for that was the furtive fashion of the cub, and I was a cub. I wetted down the paper Saturdays, I turned it Sundays—for this was a country weekly; I rolled, I washed the rollers, I washed the forms, I folded the papers, I carried them around at dawn Thursday mornings. The carrier was then an object of interest to all the dogs in town. If I had saved up all the bites I ever received, I could keep M. Pasteur busy for a year. I enveloped the papers that were for the mail—we had a hundred town subscribers and three hundred and fifty country ones. (Fatout, 200–201)

In such a shop, the master owned the plant and personally handled or supervised every aspect of the entire business, from reporting, to printing, to distribution, and trained his apprentices in all aspects of the trade.

Young Twain became a good compositor, by country standards, good enough for his brother Orion to want to take over training him in 1851, and good enough, when Sam grew tired of what he perceived as his brother's abuses of a master's authority, to find work in St. Louis in 1853. He then briefly lived the life of an itinerant journeyman compositor in New York and Philadelphia, where he made a pilgrimage to the grave of Benjamin Franklin.

Granted that it is one of the first mass-production industries, as Twain came to know it, printing was still organized around the principles of craft guilds, principles that, though adapted to meet American ideas of republican virtue, were essentially hierarchical, with masters owning plant and goodwill and hiring the work of journeymen for wages and the labor of apprentices in exchange for education in the craft. But the social organization mitigated the hierarchy. The typical craftsman's house included a shop on the ground floor with living quarters upstairs (though print shops often were separated from living quarters). Apprentices often roomed and boarded in the master's house, as, for that matter, did journeymen. The pace of labor fluctuated with business but always included a social element, with shared meals and entertainments part of the daily routine. The workplace was at once hierarchical and egalitarian, paternalistic and social, with the experience of different workers depending very much on the personality and economic conditions of individual masters (Laurie, 35–46, Licht, 31–32).

Apprentices, at the bottom of the hierarchy, handled the meanest of the work, learning the skills of a journeyman between the dirtier chores. Hazing was an acceptable part of the initiation into the "mysteries" of a guild, as Mark Twain depicts in "Old Times on the Mississippi" and in his late unfinished work, *No. 44, The Mysterious Stranger*. While on the one hand, hazing was intended to enforce the hierarchy, on the other hand, it served to establish one of the essential principles of American craft labor, the idea of "manliness."[8] We can see this at the end of the fifth installment of "Old Times," when Twain describes a trick his master played on him to teach him to have confidence in his knowledge and to teach him "when you get into a dangerous place, don't turn coward."

In the republican terms of the late eighteenth century, terms that governed labor's self-definition through the nineteenth century, manliness was a key principle. It may explain Twain's obsession with it in his works of the mid- to late 1880s, precisely when the labor question was so much on his—and everyone else's—mind. What it means to be a "man" as Twain describes it in *Connecticut Yankee* is best understood as the worker's creed, that a worker, to prevent his enslavement at the hands of management and owners, must insist on a manly bearing toward authority.

This attitude prompted most of the workers' strikes prior to 1890 in the United States, with work stoppages not planned by unions and agreed to by most members, but rather arising from the spontaneous response of one or more key workers to a perceived "outrage." The frame for *Connecticut Yankee* depends on this, with Hank Morgan as a foreman in a physical altercation with one of the men he supervises. In this case, labor gets the better of management. In *No. 44*, too, the workers strike to protest violations of their privileges, and in "The Compositor" speech, Twain recalls the free exercise of derision as a prerogative of labor:

> [The editor] was full of blessed egotism and placid self-importance, but he didn't know as much as a 3 em quad. He never set any type except in the rush of the last day, and then he would smouch all the poetry. . . . He wrote with impressive flatulence . . . and whenever his intellect suppurated, and he read the result to the printers and asked for their opinion, they were very frank and straightforward about it. They gen-

erally scraped their rules on the boxes all the time he was reading, and called it "hogwash" when he got through. (Fatout, 202)

This idea of free and independent manliness that Twain praises persisted well into the factory system of the late century. The operative manifestation of early nineteenth-century labor radicalism, then, was essentially political, not economic, predicated on the idea of political equality that outweighed economic hierarchy, and that insisted on the free contract of a man's labor. At any moment he might refuse work—regardless of economic consequence either to himself or his master.

Thus, the American guild system, unlike its European predecessor, was built on a deep egalitarianism, based on the idea that labor, not land, is the source of wealth. The artisan saw his life's task as accumulating a competency, not as amassing power through wealth. As cooper turned lawyer Tristram Burgess put it in 1800, the craftsman strove for a financial "condition below the dissipation of wealth and above the solicitude of necessity" (Laurie, 47, 57). The master as well as the apprentice was therefore on the same path of what Twain called "plodding prosperity." In this sense, artisans often opposed capitalism as a system of gambling money to make unearned money, but they rarely opposed property rights or wealth (Laurie, 63–71). In this context, Twain's February 23, 1867, letter to the *Alta* from New York makes sense as a deep conservatism, an anticapitalistic conservatism in favor of a republican idea of industry as a personal virtue. Attacking New York's "Shoddy" millionaires in a bubble economy, Twain anticipated the comeuppance of these speculators, writing, "a part of the crash is already here; and the sooner it comes in its might and restores the old, sure, plodding prosperity, the better."[9] While hoping for a crash could be construed as Marxist, Twain's hopes to *restore* the antebellum elites do not accord with modern ideas of labor radicalism, but they are very much in keeping with American antebellum labor radicalism, one that took a far different path than that of labor in Europe.

In short, American artisans considered themselves the urban equivalent of the yeoman farmer ideal on which republican principles, like those articulated by Jeffersonian democratic-republicans, depended.

> Simply put, [republicanism] posed an enduring tension between virtue and commerce, the self and the market. Eighteenth-century Americans attached different meanings to virtue but agreed that it signified the subordination of self-interest to the good of the whole. To them, the market stimulated the cupidity that lurked in all men and compromised the self-reliance and moral probity essential for republican rule. They understood the idle rich and dependent poor to be "parasites" living off the state or the labor of others, and revered the sturdy yeoman and independent artisan of middling ranks who kept the market at arm's length. (Laurie, 49)[10]

This rhetoric of fundamental equality governing social relations gave Americans a sense of political stability in the midst of economic fluidity until economic conditions changed radically. Then the language of parasitism failed, but without a language to replace it, people groped in a moral vacuum.

Twain's "The Facts Concerning the Recent Carnival of Crime in Connecticut" (1876) manifests this difficulty. Twain may have intended the piece, as I have argued elsewhere,[11] to challenge the moral terminology used by his Hartford peers, but the action turns substantially over how to treat the army of unemployed, what the narrator calls "tramps." His republican terminology makes no room for unemployed though physically fit young men, but when Twain wrote this piece in January of 1876, the United States was in the middle of a six-year depression that saw up to two million industrial workers unemployed. In this context, he could challenge the process by which we discern morality by addressing these conditions. He has his narrator tell "a tramp the square truth, to wit, that, it being regarded as bad citizenship to encourage vagrancy, I would give him nothing," but such a response strikes him with remorse. Yet he is also stricken with remorse for any other possible response. The language of his day and class is inadequate to new conditions.

Still, when Twain served as an apprentice tradesman, the language still seemed to work. Such a vision of economic fluidity within political equality allowed for tremendous economic inequality but militated against radical exploitation, though this often did take place when market lures encouraged masters to take on too many apprentices without fully planning to educate them. Local economies discouraged such exploitation while not preventing it. Traditions of socializing with hands, of keeping work paces slow enough to allow the frequent shared pint of ale, and of retiring from labor after securing a competency rather than a fortune also militated against exploitation (Laurie, 35–37, 43–44).

The essence of status within such conditions was a combination of trade skill and "industry"—the very shift of the meaning of this term over the nineteenth century compresses the history of economic consolidation in a single word. While "industry" was a character virtue, skill was a question of talent. Artisanal jobs were manual labor jobs, but they were also brain jobs, and the industry and talent of individual workers made for a meritocracy, whereas the point of industrialization in the late nineteenth century was to eliminate the need for skilled labor, replacing it instead with machines.

Ironically, it was the tradition of skill that created and sanctioned the machine revolution. In the mechanic trades, masters and journeymen were often inventors, improving their means of production at the same time they demonstrated their mechanical skills. The functions of labor and professional engineer were combined in the artisanal organization of work (Bruchey, 325; Licht, 31–32). Again, Franklin serves as a prime example. As a craftsman, he was raised in an empirical methodology that led more to practical tinkering than to systematic thinking. That Franklin took the next step toward philosophical speculation speaks to his own genius, but that in America a mechanic could also be a philosopher speaks to the high esteem in which artisans were held in America and to the republican bias against idle gentility.

As befits an avid youthful admirer of Benjamin Franklin—his sketch "The Late Benjamin Franklin" notwithstanding—Twain admired inventors as the ultimate artists. As he put it in a June 12, 1870, letter to his sister: "An inventor is a poet—a true poet—and nothing in any degree less than a high order of poet" (*Letters* 4:151).[12] His own poetic output included three inventions for which he secured patents: a self-pasting scrapbook that actually made him some money, and a self-adjusting garter and a history game that did not. His other inventions, including a notebook with tear-away tabs to allow him easily to find his place, an improved bed clamp, and a perpetual calendar, never made it to the patent stage, although he had some of the notebooks made up for his own use. He endorsed the ideal of technological progress embodied in the founders' ideal of the republic so much that he had Hank Morgan parrot the idea in *Connecticut Yankee*: "The very first official thing I did, in my administration—and it was on the very first day of it, too—was to start a patent office; for I knew that a country without a patent office and good patent laws was just a crab, and couldn't travel any way but sideways or backwards."[13]

Such was the commercial context in which Twain was raised, and all the changes in the economy notwithstanding, the image of commerce he developed as an artisan worker stuck with him through his career. But though this image governed his thinking, his behavior was shaped by the forces that transformed the nation's economy over his lifetime. No doubt if he had remained a country printer, young Twain would have tried to do as his brother did, that is, to move from apprentice, to journeyman, to master and would have failed equally badly as market conditions drove such small artisans out of business. In running East, however, he instead participated in a new phase of American commerce, industrialization, a phase coming into its own in the 1850s and rapidly accelerating after the Civil War.

Actually, the major industrialization that we think of as typifying the late nineteenth century was one of four revolutions of the nineteenth century: revolutions in transport, in the market, in industrial production, and in finance. All are inextricably bound, and moved in fits and starts according to their interdependent development, but the concentration of industry into large factories was a late development. Of these four revolutions,

transport, market, and industrialization may have had some resistance among yeoman farmers, but were all seen primarily as
agents of progress.[14] The concomitant development of financial
instruments to capitalize these changes, however, created substantial unease among Americans, whose widely held labor
theory of value could not accept the role that commercial banks,
insurance companies, mortgage companies, and investment
banks held in shaping the conditions of commerce, and thus of
industry and employment (Laurie, 68–69).

Twain was essentially connected to the market from the beginning, partly because he grew up more in town than on a farm,
partly because newly opened western lands were, unlike earlier
yeoman subsistence farms in the East and North, market-driven
from the beginning. But being born in a slave state complicated
his connection to republican values. Southern agriculture from
the beginning had been connected to world markets under a
mercantile system, and while its change in emphasis from to-
bacco to cotton tied it into the postmercantile markets of the
nineteenth century, its attitudes toward commerce remained patrician. In coming into his identity as an artisan rather than as a
landowner, Twain came to see southern attitudes toward land
and labor as essentially feudal and backward. His attacks on the
South in *Life on the Mississippi* all depend on this antiaristocratic,
republican ideal.

For that matter, his sense of the backwardness of his begin-
nings manifests itself in his mockery of how far even the West
had to go to reach market standards. Much of Ament's business
was paid for in kind rather than in cash. "The town subscribers
paid in groceries and the country ones in cabbages and cord-
wood. . . . We had one subscriber who paid cash, and he was
more trouble to us than all the rest. He bought us, once a year,
body and soul, for two dollars. . . . If we ever tried to reason
with him, he would threaten to stop his paper, and, of course,
that meant bankruptcy and destruction" (Fatout, 201). In these
comments, he expresses his sense of the value of the symbolic
market, the full exchangability of money as opposed to barter,
though at the same time, he expresses a sense of the loss, rather
than the gain, of freedom when participating in a cash economy.

Though fairly comfortable with the idea of a market rather than a subsistence economy, Twain discovered the impact of industrialization when he left home to work, not as a printer per se but as a compositor. Benjamin Franklin in his Autobiography notes that as early as his first trip to Britain, he discovered that specialization had already begun in Britain while it had not in America. He notes that he was more physically fit for having mixed press work with composition, and thus argued that the yeoman artisan of America had a distinct advantage over the industrial worker of Britain. Of course, America followed, at an accelerating pace, with each economic dislocation leading to a further erosion of the value of skill through the division of labor. A widely cited anecdote describes a Marblehead, Massachusetts, shoemaker who grew prosperous enough in the 1860s to study and then practice law. The panic of 1873 destroyed his law practice, so he returned to the shoe business, only to find the work he used to do alone was now divided among 64 workers performing different tasks in the production of a single shoe. He came to describe himself as "one 64th of a shoemaker" (Bruchey, 330).

Printing was among the first American industries to magnify its scale sufficiently to justify division of labor (Laurie, 38–39), and when Twain hit the road in 1853, it was as a compositor, not as a printer. By 1850, eastern shops had been transformed by the development of new presses. In a letter for his brother's Muscatine Iowa, *Journal*, Twain wrote with happy awe of the contrast between Franklin's London press he saw in a museum and Richard Hoe's rotary press, first used in 1846 but quickly adopted by most eastern newspapers shortly thereafter, "What vast progress has been made in the art of printing! This press is capable of printing about 125 sheets per hour; and after seeing it, I have watched Hoe's great machine throwing off its 20,000 sheets in the same space of time, with an interest I never before felt" (*Letters* 1:42, 44). The flip side of that interest was the consequence in the work place for labor itself. In separating the skilled tasks from unskilled, proprietors moved away from shop floors into editorial offices, and typographers, the only skilled labor left and managed by foremen rather than owner-artisans, were paid by piece-work scales that encouraged work speed-ups. The collegiality of the workplace, too, was destroyed, with editorial and production staffs separated, damaging the old sense of labor and management jointly, if not equally, engaged in productive labor.

Twain's letters home reflect his astonishment, "The office I work in is John A. Gray's, 97 Cliff street, and, next to Harpers, is the most extensive in the city. In the room in which I work I have forty compositors for company. Taking compositors, pressmen, stereotypers, and all, there are about two hundred persons employed in the concern" (*Letters* 1:9). He learned in the process that with specialization came high standards, standards to which he had been introduced in St. Louis, but that at the time he felt were excessive:

> They are very particular about spacing, justification, proofs, etc. and even if I do not make much money, I will learn a great deal. I thought Ustick [in St. Louis] was particular enough, but acknowledge now that he was not old maidish. Why, you must put exactly the same space between every two words, and *every line must be spaced alike*. They think it dreadful to space one line with three em spaces, and the next one with five ems. (*Letters* 1:9)

He was learning the discipline to be a machine employee, to specialize and systematize. He took the challenge as if he were in control, but found, to his dissatisfaction, that he could not match his fellows. When he moved to Philadelphia in October, presumably for better wages working as a sub on the Philadelphia *Inquirer*, he found himself unable to keep up the pace. Writing his brother and fellow printer, Orion, he said:

> I will try to write for the paper occasionally, but I fear my letters will be very uninteresting, for this incessant night work dull one['s] ideas amazingly.
>
> From some cause, I cannot set type near so fast as when I was at home. Sunday is a long day, and while others set 12 and 15,000, yesterday, I only set 10,000. However, I will shake this laziness off, soon, I reckon. (*Letters* 1:29)

In good republican fashion, he takes the blame, naively unaware of the connection between the two adjacent paragraphs. As a compositor, working long hours in the nights, he could not function, too, as a writer for his brother's paper, but his artisanal ideals of labor made him unable to accept cause and effect.

Working as a compositor, Twain was working in one of the guilds that was among the aristocracy of American labor, though his time in New York and Philadelphia did not bring this reality home. New York's compositors were split into two competing guilds, so they could not set wages as well as they did in St. Louis or in Philadelphia. Moreover, larger conditions than skill alone changed employment. Yellow fever in the South in the summer of 1853 sent compositors north. Twain notes that he "did very well to get a place at all, for there are thirty or forty—yes, fifty good printers in the city with no work at all" (*Letters* 1:9). Worse, in December of 1853, fire destroyed the publishing houses of both Harper & Brothers and George F. Cooledge and Brothers, throwing many New York printers out of work (*Letters* 1:45). Twain could not thrive in the increasingly competitive climate of those years.

Still, compositors, like other highly skilled workers, transformed their guild system into labor unions, which gave skilled workers definite advantages in the increasingly competitive labor markets of the last half of the nineteenth century. Craft guilds not only set working conditions and negotiated wages, but they also created benevolent societies to provide for the personal development of their members. Predicated on their republican beliefs in the need for an educated citizenry, craft organizations sponsored debates and lectures and built libraries. Mark Twain stages the activities of such a "Mechanics Club" in chapter 10 of *The American Claimant*, in which an editor praises the value of a free press and democratic values, and in which a mechanic affirms the value of an educated working class that has advanced the material well-being of America not only through its labor but also through its labor-saving inventions. Here he is continuing his internal debate about the worthiness of his own efforts to develop labor-saving machinery, and, again, the language is not that of late nineteenth-century industrial capitalism but of early nineteenth-century artisanal labor. If he didn't first learn this language as a printer, he certainly had opportunity then to take it to heart. In his first letter home from New York, Twain boasted, "The printers have two libraries in town, entirely free to the craft; and in these I can spend my evenings most pleasantly. If books are not good company, where will I find it?" (*Letters* 1:10).

In assuring his mother that books are good company, Twain is assuaging his mother's concern that he would fall into evil company and begin drinking, a reasonable concern given that a newly mobile, young, and unskilled labor force in the large eastern cities was increasingly notorious for gang rowdyism under the influence of alcohol. Twain's letters from Philadelphia suggest his disgust at such behavior, especially insofar as many of the young laborers were recent immigrants. Indeed, the labor movement in its early years, with its emphasis on worker improvement coming out of the republican tradition of craft guilds, included much temperance activity. This in many ways struck at the heart of the old guild mentality, in which shared ale was one of the social glues between master, journeyman, and apprentice. But in the increasingly mechanized industries of the urban Northeast, temperance was a basic matter of safety. More important, it was a way for the skilled guilds to maintain their status. Indeed, temperance became one of the causes associated with respectability and drinking became associated with foreignness.

One of Twain's letters from Philadelphia suggests as much:

The printers, as well as other people are endeavoring to raise money to erect a monument to Franklin, but there are so many abominable foreigners here (and among printers, too,) who hate everything American, that I am very certain as much money for such a purpose could be raised in St Louis, as in Philadelphia[.] I was in Franklin's old office this morning— the "North American" (formerly "Philadelphia Gazette"), and there were at least one foreigner [*sic.*] [to suggest an Irish brogue] for every American at work there. . . . I always thought the eastern people were patterns of uprightness; but I never before saw so many whisky-swilling, god-despising heathens as I find in this part of the country. (*Letters* 1:28–29)

Such comments were not unusual for skilled labor in the middle of the nineteenth century. Craft unions tended to discriminate against immigrants, actively participated in nativist politics, and, in their first postbellum consortium, the Knights of Labor, promoted the Chinese exclusion act as one of the cornerstones of their *industrial* policy.[15] Again, the sense of republicanism as the fundamental orientation should be clear: these were workers who saw their work not as oppressed or oppressive, but as the source of their dignity. Regardless of the changing conditions of work as shops industrialized into large-scale, impersonal enterprises, the skilled workers strove to maintain their respectability, as readily working to distinguish themselves from the mob as from the capitalist and quickly identifying foreign labor as the cause of their decreasing status.

Furthermore, these guilds shared the capitalist's distrust of government, with good cause as the course of labor history in the last half of the century would suggest. Unions were rarely victorious in courts and often had strikes broken by state and federal troops. Not surprisingly, craft guilds took it upon themselves not only to educate and entertain their members, but also their benevolent societies bought accident and life insurance for members. Ironically, insofar as they purchased insurance, they helped fund the capitalization of machine-based manufacturing that would undercut their positions.[16] Still, such craft-based unions were very much in keeping with American traditions of self-help through common action, even as big business and big government were viewed with equal suspicion.

Even so, as Twain's own experience as a compositor showed, self-help and skill were not enough to sustain the power of craft unions. The transportation revolution that made a market for industrial production also made labor mobile, and as much as steamboats and railroads made it possible for Twain to go East to find work, he was one of a crowd of skilled migrant laborers from the United States and Europe, who depressed wages in the Atlantic coast industrial centers. Twain left publishing temporarily for another craft guild, that of steamboat pilot, so that his second career put him closer to the way technology and industry changed commercial conditions. Pilots, he discovered, were a labor elite, who had, by law, tremendous autonomy in practicing their trade, and who had, by the rarity of their skills and the importance of those skills to a major industry, economic clout that put them in a different league than the other laborers in the industry. As he puts it in the sixth installment of "Old Times,"

> [A] pilot, in those days, was the only unfettered and entirely independent human being that lived in the earth. . . . In truth, every man and woman and child has a master, and worries and frets in servitude; but in the day I write of the Mississippi pilot had none. The captain could stand upon the hurricane deck, in the pomp of a very brief authority, and give him five or six orders, while the vessel backed into the stream, and then that skipper's reign was over. The moment that the boat was under way in the river, she was under the sole and unquestioned control of the pilot. . . . He was treated with marked courtesy by the captain and with marked deference by all the officers and servants.[17]

Here Twain lauds the pilot's independence, exactly the kind of independence on which the republic depends, according to Jeffersonian ideals, but Twain quickly slips from independence to superiority. A pilot, he tells us, becomes the "novelty of a king without a keeper, an absolute monarch who was absolute in sober truth and not by a fiction of words" (721), even though it is the law—that is, a fiction of words, that grants the pilot his independence.

Be that as it may, the pilot rises from mere laborer to being able to *play* gentleman because the importance of his services renders him too valuable to exploit:

> In those old days, to load a steamboat at St. Louis, take her to New Orleans and back, and discharge cargo, consumed about twenty-five days, on average. Seven or eight of these days the boat spent at the wharves of St. Louis and New Orleans, and every soul on board was hard at work, except the two pilots; *they* did nothing but play gentleman, up town, and receive the same wages for it as if they had been on duty. (721–22)

The $300–$400 a month Twain describes as the antebellum wages on the upper Mississippi amounts to about twelve times the income of the typical worker of the day, all the more remarkable considering that the average gap between skilled and unskilled workers in 1850 was only 50 percent, rising to a high of 300 percent by the 1880s (Laurie, 128).

It is no surprise that Twain wanted to join such a club, and he was able to do it because he could borrow money from his brother-in-law to pay Horace Bixby to train him. As a fully autonomous member of a craft, Bixby could train whom he would, but so many pilots were hiring apprentices that they began to undercut their own craft. They had power only if their skill was a bottleneck, and they could maintain that bottleneck only if they surrendered the autonomy that they saw as the center of their republican virtue. The chapter in which Twain describes the pilot as completely independent is the same chapter in which he describes the pilots forming a union, one resisted by boat owners and many older pilots alike, but without which the craft would not have been able to maintain its status:

> A by-law was added forbidding the reception of any more cubs or apprentices for five years; after which time a limited number would be taken, not by individuals, but by the association, upon these terms: the applicant must not be less than eighteen years old, of respectable family and good character; he must pass an examination as to education, pay a thousand dollars in advance for the privilege of becoming an apprentice, and must remain under the commands of the association until a great part of the membership . . . should be willing to sign his application for a pilot's license. All previously-articled apprentices were now taken away from their masters and adopted by the association. (728)

Clearly, the pilots who joined paid with their independence for their continued status.

But that, too, escaped them quickly. The Civil War itself ended commercial travel for years, merely confirming the end already in the works, as railroads began to take the lucrative and prestigious passenger trade and the use of barges cut the costs and skills required for freight hauling. "[I]n the twinkling of an eye, as it were, the association and the noble science of piloting were things of the dead and pathetic past!" (730).

One of the things Twain discovered as a pilot was that he had spare income, and as such, he had a choice to become either profligate in spending it or could invest it to make more. He became something of a petty capitalist, buying various commodities at one end of his river runs and trying to sell them at the other for a profit (*Letters* 1:103–104). His letters show that he was usually quite bad at it; while he recognized the price differentials from place to place were a source of potential profit, he never seemed to recognize that the transportation revolution that gave him his job leveled local markets into larger regional and national markets. His buying and selling was rarely timely enough to beat the leveling that such large markets created. Nor, as a small-scale capitalist, did he shift from the commodities themselves to buying and selling futures. The futures market, though decried by producers and consumers alike as it came to determine prices, was where money was to be made as an investor (Bruchey, 299). Given Twain's own republican outlook, one locked in the tangible products and in the idea of local markets, he naturally lost money in a transforming economy.

Similarly, his efforts in the West merely brought him up against the new realities of capital intensive industries without forcing him to surrender his antebellum orientation. He acted as a prospector, hoping to use pick and shovel to find silver and gold. But most of the real money could only be made when extracted through capital intensive industrial processes. In chapter 58 of *Roughing It*, Twain says the boom times in Virginia City were over when the territory of Nevada voted to become a state; yet the real money came long after Twain left. Even as he was writing and publishing *Roughing It*, large capital moved into Virginia City, as Twain does mention in a footnote at the end of chapter 52, in an effort that dwarfed any Twain had seen in his time there in the 1860s. The new efforts began to pay off in 1873 and didn't play out until 1882 (Bruchey, 284).

Twain did have some inkling of how the game was really played; in *Roughing It*, he describes how stock selling was where the real money was, though he saw stocks as a bubble economy, not one predicated on real wealth. Similarly, in *The Gilded Age*, he and Warner described stocks as a way to bilk investors, not as a way to give them dividends. Certainly that was his own experience, since repeatedly in his life he invested in stocks. Often he invested reasonably, diversely, with an eye both to dividends and to appreciation. His 1882 notebook lists about $100,000 of such investments in 23 different stocks and bonds.[18] But much of his investment was speculative, often in transportation stocks. One of these, his investment in the Oregon & Transcontinental Company, was a complete bust. He purchased $15,000 worth of stock (200 shares) on a margin in January of 1883, then threw good money after bad when he bought another 100 shares in September (*N&J* 3:29). By the following May, he unloaded the lot for $12 a share. He had a good enough sense of humor about his bath to plan to "Write [a] Wall st play of 'O.T.'" (*N&J* 3:44).

More characteristically, he invested in inventions, either his own, as in the case of his self-pasting scrapbook, or those of others, such as in Dan Slote's "Kaolatype" lithography, or in Paige's typesetting machine, or even after Paige's machine helped bankrupt him, in a process for making powdered skim milk. Usually he lost money, as befits a person who invests in what he called "true poetry." But that didn't stop him from trying. When Howells's father invented a kind of grape shears in 1883, Howells asked Twain if he was willing to back the new invention. Twain's reply, half apologetic as if he were revealing a character flaw, half proud to be involved in progress, was that if he didn't sink his money in manufacturing and marketing his own invention of a history game, "I shall wish to be counted in on the grape-scissors, for I must speculate in something, such being my nature."[19]

Of course, Twain hoped to make mountains of money out of his investments, but he saw them in very narrow terms, having to do with a personal connection to the promoter of an investment or to the kind of product itself. In this way he is nothing like professional venture capitalists today. He was, rather, participating in a then new trend that helped transform the national economy. Long a debtor nation, deriving its capital from European investors, postbellum America saw a great rise in internal investment, with many moderately well-off or quite well-to-do but not independently wealthy people investing money regularly. This flow of capital taxed extant monetary systems, and with a widespread antigovernment attitude prevailing as part of the nation's dominant republicanism, no real national government control of the money supply existed beyond the chartering of banks into the correspondent banking system.

The so-called state-chartered wildcat banks, that is, banks operating where wildcats still roamed, had long fueled western expansion but had also created local currency panics. Hence, their notes were usually heavily discounted. From such banks, Twain derived his commonly used term "wildcat" to describe dime novels and other cheap, less than respectable products. After the Civil War, as it retired the greenbacks it had issued to fund the war, the government changed the banking rules to centralize the monetary system without nationalizing it. It set up the correspondent banking system, requiring heavy capitalization of banks that would in turn correspond with regional banks to meet their cash needs. The system was biased in favor of New York banks, and consequently, currency moved away from the capital needs of the emerging West. Furthermore, commercial banks were not allowed to lend for long-term capitalization and theoretically operated under the "real bills" banking doctrine. Their charters forbade mortgage lending in favor of commercial lending for seasonal cash-flow needs (Bruchey, 313). The model of agriculture created the system, but it was too rigid for an industrializing economy. Bankers often made loans with short-terms, as required, and then rolled these over as a matter of course to provide capital for industries (Bruchey, 311–20). Webster & Co., Mark Twain's publishing firm, had many such loans; the failure of banks to roll these loans over after the panic of 1894 contributed to Webster's failure.

The correspondent banking system allowed any cash crunch to ramify through the system, and by requiring private banks to be lenders of last resort, a role now exercised by Federal Reserve

Banks, this system in fact magnified local panics into national ones. Certainly, the Clemens family letters reveal how important the world of finance was to Twain. In 1873, for instance, the revelation of stock watering in Union Pacific stock in the Credit Mobilier scandal created one such panic, which sparked a six-year depression. The panic caught Twain low on cash when he was on a European trip. He jokingly wrote of the impact in an 1873 bread-and-butter letter to his new English friend, Dr. John Brown: "The financial panic in America has absorbed about all my attention & anxiety since Monday evening when I laid down this pen. However, I feel relieved, now—of L600 sterling, & so am able to take up my letter again & go on & finish it" (*Letters* 5:439). In today's terms, that's about $60,000, hardly matter for jest. His real feelings are revealed more accurately in his wife's September 25, 1873, letter home when their New York bank, Henry Clews and Company, suspended payments between September 23, 1873, and January 1874:

> Last night when we returned from the theater we had a notification that our bankers had suspended payment—After we went to bed Mr Clemens could not sleep, he had to return to the parlor and smoke and try to get sleepy—He said the reason that he could not sleep was that he kept thinking how stupid he had been not to draw out our money after he heard that J. Cook & co. had failed, said he kept thinking what the "boys" (meaning Mr Slee, Theodore, & Charlie [the partners in J. Langdon & Co]) were saying at home—"Well, it is 24 hours since J. Cook suspended and Clemens will have drawn his money out of the bank—now it is 48 hours since J. Cook failed and of course Clemens is all safe, he will have his money drawn out &c &c" . . . We fortunately have by us the L200 that Charlie sent for you and L43 that Pamela sent—but we owe several quite heavy bills and shall have to have more money from home unless Clews & co resume payment in a few days. Mr Clemens is inclined to think they will—If they do not you will probably get a dispatch from us before this reaches you— . . . We do wish that we knew how you are all feeling at home financially, it seems as if this *terrible* panic must effect [sic] all business men. (*Letters* 5:443–44)

Olivia Clemens's large perspective is correct; what is peculiar is
how narrow a perspective Twain himself took, berating himself
for being stupid in the face of international financial calamity,
which isn't to say he wasn't wise to protect himself in a financial
system that had no protections for individual investors. Later in
life, he was less trusting of banks, deciding, for instance, that "a
bank might break" so that Webster & Co. would put a large
amount of money "into government bonds or a safety deposit
vault; . . . this in order that none of us may get crippled. . . .
[A] wise nervousness, I think."[20] He persistently saw finances in
personal terms, befitting his republican ideal of an economy
composed of independent self-interested agents, who succeeded
or failed according to their own merits.

That small-scale sense of the economy, the idea that it really
was a simple question of being shrewd or being taken, governed
his economic thinking in almost every case. Emblematic of this
thinking is his September 1870 *Galaxy Magazine* sketch, "Political
Economy," in which he parodies this earliest social science as out
of touch with business realities. The abstracted narrator can
gush that "Political economy is the basis of all good government" and that "The wisest men of all ages have brought to bear
upon this subject the . . . richest treasures of their genius"
(*Tales*, 434–35), but in not watching his own interests, he discovers
that the economy is about confidence men selling too much, too
often, to the ignorant.[21] In *The Gilded Age, A Connecticut Yankee*,
and *The American Claimant*, Twain makes much the same point,
with the difference between modern business and antebellum
cons merely a matter of scale. As much as he wanted to see himself as a successful *man*, he wanted to make money on the new
scale precisely because at some level he felt business success to be
a measure of his personal worth and acumen.

Such a small-scale approach to business made him uneasy
with the tools of finance. The stock market, not industry, after all
is what brings down Camelot in *Connecticut Yankee*. And in his
speech "Accident Insurance," etc., he could make fun of the large
social forces of industrialization that turned making a living into
gambling with one's life, but there's a grimness underlying his
humor that makes one wonder how comfortable he was with the

new financial institutions he regularly invested in without fully understanding what they did. In a different mood, he blamed the panic of 1907 on the behavior of one man: "A blight has fallen everywhere and Mr. Roosevelt is the author of it."[22] Without even bothering to explain the president's power to create a panic, he foists it off on the head of state partly out of a sense of personal animosity at what he felt was an impending American monarchy with Roosevelt on the throne, and partly out of his tendency to collapse the distinction between individual action and social forces.

In this sense Twain's republicanism is of a piece with America's deepest—and still living—traditions of political satire, in which allegorical attacks encapsulate large-scale movements in personified form. Twain, in an autobiographical dictation of February 16, 1906, could apparently seriously say, "Jay Gould taught the entire nation to make a god of the money and the man, no matter how the money might have been acquired. In my youth there was nothing resembling a worship of money or of its possessor" (*MTE*, 77), a comment patently absurd if taken literally. Dan Beard, Twain's illustrator for *Connecticut Yankee*, could make virtually the same point visually in drawing Jay Gould as slave driver.

Twain and Beard attacked monopoly capital in the person of Gould because Gould, as an investment banker, helped consolidate industries into monstrous businesses. He and his kind were taking advantage of the Supreme Court's crippling of common law restrictions of monopolies. The big-business magnates were expressly against competition, having learned in the free-competition of the 1880s that free-competition in heavily capitalized industries often forced them to operate at a loss. Overproduction in part caused the deflation of the postwar period, and anticompetitive pools, combinations, and interlocking directorates were the response that large capital took to competition. As George W. Perkins, one of the partners in J. P. Morgan & Company, put it in 1905, "The old idea that we were raised under, that competition is the life of trade, is exploded. Competition is no longer the life of trade, it is cooperation" (Bruchey, 343).

In this context, Twain and Beard promoted not an idea of proletarian rebellion, but a return to the idea of free labor and full competition. They saw changes to the republican ideals they held as damaging to the body politic. In the political rhetoric of republicanism, they personified these novelties in order to make sense out of them. They thus attacked individuals as representing untoward changes in the political-economic order as they understood it, as is clear in Twain's chapter 33, "Sixth-Century Political Economy," in *Connecticut Yankee*. Much of this chapter's discussion of labor and wages lectures labor about the advantages of real buying power versus the emotionally seductive symbolism of high wages. It's an antilabor touch in a book that as often attacks the plutocracy. But this passage concludes with a paean to labor unions as part of free labor! Beard's cartoons emphasize the allegorical nature of the chapter and suggest more explicitly the republicanism of Twain's ideas, that is, that Twain is advocating individual rights and individual access to the means of labor, and even as he sees capital pools as anticompetitive, he sees labor unions as guilds that regulated real value without stifling competition.

Considering all financial dealings as the operation of cold calculation of individual operators rather than as the large-scale workings of a complex economy, Twain could alternately burn with indignation over such behavior as politically and morally corrupt or mock it with humorous good will, but never did he understand it in any but personal terms. In this way, his writings about the economy participate in an older, but still vital form of discussion, one that is allegorical, bringing complex political ideas down to the personal level.

Howells, of course, had tried to convince Twain that socialism was the appropriate response to industrialization, and Twain politely acceded, at times. But his remark to Edward Bellamy fan Sylvester Baxter on Bellamy's *Looking Backward*, a book that helped popularize socialism among larger groups of Americans than had hitherto been the case, as "the last and best of all the bibles," suggests as much skepticism as enthusiasm, considering that the Bible was not, for Twain, a source of absolute truth. On the contrary, his ideals were founded less on the Bible than on Thomas Paine's *Rights of Man*, and as such, he was interested in an older form of radicalism, a republican individualism. His attacks on big business, big party, big anything are very much in keeping with this older ethos. Even as he often rejected intellectually such individualism in his sense of human beings as machines out of control of their own destinies, his heart was essentially republican, and he promoted the autonomy of the individual to act out of virtue and industry above all, especially when dealing with matters of money.

As such, he came finally to see himself as a hypocrite, seeing that he much preferred to make his money in speculation than in labor. But even in discovering his hypocrisy, he registers surprise that he and the America he has come to live in have one set of values they believe in and another they live by. In "3,000 Years among the Microbes" he writes:

> "I know of a country . . . where the dignity of labor is a phrase which is in everybody's mouth; where the *reality* of that dignity is never questioned; where everybody says it is an honor to a person that he works for the bread he eats; that earned bread is noble bread, and lifts the earner to the level of the highest in the land; that unearned bread, the bread of idleness, is tainted with discredit; a land where the sayers of these things say them with strong emotion, and think they believe what they say, and are proud of their land because it is the sole land where the bread-earners are the only acknowledged aristocracy. And yet I do see, that when you come to examine into it—"
>
> "I know the land you mean! It's G[et]R[ich]Q[uick]! Honest, isn't it GRQ?"[23]

Perhaps, however, he is registering not so much hypocrisy as the gap between the political ideals of his youth and the economy of his age.

NOTES

1. Perhaps the machine appealed to him because it operated on the same principle as hand composition, sorting and setting movable type. His error in believing that such a machine would supplant

human workers is all the more surprising, given that he saw in New York in early 1867 a crude version of a typesetter that worked on different principles, much like those of the ultimately successful linotype.

2. Justin Kaplan, *Mr. Clemens and Mark Twain* (New York: Simon & Schuster, 1966), 320.

3. Given that studies of nineteenth-century economic conditions usually begin from a political position either praising capitalism or attacking it, the degree of consensus about what the economy was actually doing is startling. I derived this specific information and indeed most of the general information in this essay from Stuart Bruchey, *Enterprise: The Dynamic Economy of a Free People* (Cambridge: Harvard UP, 1990), p. 361, Bruce Laurie, *Artisans into Workers: Labor in Nineteenth-Century America* (Urbana: University of Illinois Press, 1989), pp. 14, 127–28, and Walter Licht, *Industrializing America* (Baltimore, Md.: Johns Hopkins University Press, 1995), pp. 41–45, 181–85. Subsequent references to all three will be cited parenthetically in text.

4. It seems hard to imagine people losing their heads over $30,000, but if one uses the crude multiple of 20 to 25 to calculate what 30,000 1904 dollars would be in current dollars, one begins to understand. Even so, the fantasy wealth Saladin and Electra Foster build on substantial though still modest *promised* capital is the tale's point.

5. Paul Fatout, ed., *Mark Twain Speaking* (Iowa City: University of Iowa Press, 1976), pp. 204–5. Subsequent references will be cited parenthetically in text.

6. Michael J. Kiskis, ed., *Mark Twain's Own Autobiography* (Madison: University of Wisconsin Press, 1990), p. 273, n.6.

7. Such an idea persisted even late in the nineteenth century when the Homestead Act was passed and amended. The key to securing land was to improve it through active labor on the assumption that real wealth, and thus legitimate title to property, depended not on investment of capital but on labor.

8. David Montgomery, "Workers' Control of Machine Production in the Nineteenth Century" (1976), rpt. in *The Labor History Reader*, ed. Daniel J. Leab (Urbana: University of Illinois Press, 1985), p. 113.

9. Franklin Walker and Ezra Dane, eds., *Mark Twin's Travels with Mr. Brown* (New York: Alfred A. Knopf, 1940), p. 107.

10. See also Licht, pp. 90–96, for a more carefully nuanced reading of republican ideology in the antebellum period, showing that within ideas of a commonweal, different attitudes toward the market and toward government regulation run along two axes—an economic one, running from self-sufficiency to accumulation, and a political one, running from a weak state to a strong state. While Licht's analysis explains, in part, how the political and economic system carried the seeds of change within itself, my point is that it did not carry the ideas that would explain the change.

11. See my *Sentimental Twain* (Philadelphia: University of Pennsylvania Press, 1994), p. 112–21.

12. Victor Fisher and Michal B. Frank, eds., *Mark Twain's Letters*, vol. 4 (Berkeley: University of California Press, 1995), p. 151. Subsequent references to this and to the other volumes in the series will be cited parenthetically in text as *Letters*.

13. Mark Twain, *A Connecticut Yankee in King Arthur's Court* (1889; rpt. Berkeley: University of California Press, 1979), p. 118.

14. Leo Marx, *The Machine in the Garden* (New York: Oxford University Press, 1964), chap. 4, "The Machine," pp. 145–226.

15. See chap. 16, "The Chinese and the Labor Question, " and chap. 19, "Declaration of Principles of the Knights of Labor," in *The Labor Movement: The Problem of To-Day*, ed. George E. McNeill (1887; rpt. New York: Augustus M. Kelley, 1971). McNeill describes himself on the title page as "First Deputy of Mass. Bureau of Statistics of Labor; Sec-Treas. of D. A. 30, Knights of Labor."

16. "In the period after the Civil War life insurance companies emerged as the most important nonbank intermediary for the mobilization and interregional transfer of capital . . . [with] assets increas[ing] more than twenty-fold between 1869 and 1914" (Bruchey, 318).

17. Mark Twain, "Old Times on the Mississippi," *Atlantic Monthly* 35 (June 1875), p. 721. Subsequent references will be cited in text by page number.

18. Frederick Anderson, Lin Salamo, and Bernard L. Stein, eds., *Mark Twain's Notebooks and Journals*, vol. 2 (Berkeley: University of California Press, 1975), p. 491. Subsequent references to this and to the other volumes in the series will be cited parenthetically in text as *N.&J*.

19. Henry Nash Smith and William M. Gibson, eds., *Mark*

Twain-Howells Letters (Cambridge: Harvard University Press, 1960), p. 439.

20. Hamlin Hill, ed., *Mark Twain's Letters to His Publishers* (Berkeley: University of California Press, 1967), pp. 200–201.

21. Louis J Budd, ed., *Mark Twain: Collected Tales, Sketches, Speeches, & Essays, 1852–1890* (New York: Library of America, 1992), pp. 434–35.

22. Bernard DeVoto, ed., *Mark Twain in Eruption* (New York: Harper & Brothers, 1940), p. 5. Subsequent references to this edition will be cited in text as *MTE*.

23. "3,000 Years Among the Microbes," in *The Devil's Race-Track* ed., John S. Tuckey (Berkeley: University of California Press, 1980), p. 234.

Mark Twain and Race

Shelley Fisher Fishkin

In the earliest of his letters that survives to this day, seventeen-year-old Sam Clemens wrote his mother from New York in 1853, "I reckon I had better black my face, for in these Eastern States niggers are [thought to be] considerably better than white people."[1] Sam's sarcastic quip was clearly an exaggeration: for although free African Americans in the North may have been spared the lash that terrorized their enslaved brothers and sisters in the South, they were nonetheless subjected to countless indignities and humiliations solely for having black skin. It is not surprising that this teenager away from home for the first time spouted the racist views to which he had been exposed since his birth into a slaveholding family in the slave state of Missouri. What *is* surprising, however, is that this garden-variety knee-jerk racist would eventually go on to upend hierarchies of racial superiority with a daring that could shock even some of his most progressive peers and with a subtlety that would continue to derail his critics nearly a century after his death.

The America into which Sam Clemens was born in 1835 was marked by an ideology of racial hierarchy so pervasive and so firmly entrenched that it is sometimes difficult to recall that this ideology, like America itself, was less than a century old at the time. Although racial prejudice, as Stephen Jay Gould suggests, "may be as old as recorded human history,"[2] the colonists of the seventeenth century and early eighteenth century rationalized their enslavement of Africans on grounds other than race. They justified their actions on the basis of Africans' heathenism or their status as captives or prisoners of war in their own societies, as Thomas Gossett, George Fredrickson, Winthrop Jordan, and others remind us.[3] From the late seventeenth century on, Southerners had a major social and economic stake in creating a class of hereditary bondsmen. But it was not until the eighteenth century that arguments for the allegedly "natural superiority" of the white race were widely advanced.

Some of the earliest arguments were largely aesthetic. In 1751, for example, Benjamin Franklin asked, "why increase the Sons of Africa, by Planting them in America, where we have so fair an Opportunity, by excluding all Blacks and Tawneys, of increasing the lovely White and Red?"[4] The first ideological justifications for white supremacy in the New World surfaced around the same time that the first rumblings of independence among the American colonists did. Jamaican physician Edward Long made the case in 1774 that blacks were a lower order of humanity than whites—a different species—suggesting that this hypothesis itself might provide a sufficient justification for slavery.[5]

For Thomas Jefferson, the slaveholding author of the Declaration of Independence, this line of argument had a special appeal. The hypocrisy of slaveholders clamoring loudly for their own freedom had not eluded British observers. The charge of hypocrisy could be mitigated somewhat, however, if blacks were recognized as an inferior branch of humanity. This insight may have helped prompt Jefferson to write in *Notes on Virginia* that he suspected blacks to be "inferior to the whites in the endowment both of body and of mind."[6] (Later, much later, Mark Twain would sardonically revise Jefferson's more famous sentence from the Declaration of Independence by inserting the assumed-but-unspecified qualification: "'ALL WHITE MEN ARE BORN FREE AND EQUAL.' Declaration of Independence."[7]) Jefferson considered blacks well suited to physical labor, requiring less sleep than whites and being "more tolerant of heat, and less so of cold." Jefferson found blacks emotional, impulsive, and lacking in "forethought"; he found them dull and unimaginative, and incapable of uttering "a thought above the level of plain narration."[8] And if their reason was "much inferior" to that of whites, their ability to withstand pain was greater since, in Jefferson's view, their "griefs are transient."[9]

Jefferson suspected strongly that black "inferiority," rather than being "the effect merely of their condition of life," was natural—inborn, rather than a function of environment.[10] As abolitionist pressure mounted, Jefferson's line of argument appealed more and more to slavery's apologists. In 1851, for example, the prominent southern physician S. A. Cartwright, echoing Jefferson, argued that blacks were insensitive to physical pain: "When the unfortunate individual is subjected to punishment, he neither feels pain of any consequences . . . [nor] any unusual resentment, more than stupid sulkiness. In some cases . . . there appears to be an almost total loss of feeling."[11] Cartwright opined that the adult negro had the capacities for learning of a white infant; because he stood in such dire need of white control, "republican institutions were not only unsuited to his temperament but actually inimical to his well-being and happiness."[12]

Those who argued that the races had separate origins and separate abilities (such as Dr. Samuel George Morton and Louis Agassiz) thought that they could be ranked on a scale, with whites on top. Those who believed that we were all one race (such as the Reverend John Bachman of South Carolina) found the justification for white supremacy in religion, arguing that the Bible established that blacks are the descendents of Noah's third son Ham—everywhere the "'servants of servants'"—supporting the contention "that in intellectual power the African is an inferior variety of our species."[13] While the debate between the polygenists and the monogenists continued throughout the mid-nineteenth century, all sides tended to agree from the 1830s on that members of nonwhite races showed no evidence of high intelligence or capacity for civilization, unless they had at least one white ancestor. When Darwin's theory of evolution at mid-century challenged the basis of much of contemporary race theory, it did not challenge the idea that some races are superior to others, and his work sparked yet other chapters of pseudo-

science (measuring crania, jaws, etc.) that bolstered white supremacy.[14] Indeed, Abraham Lincoln gave voice to what he assumed to be the conventional wisdom on the topic in 1858: "there
must be the position of superior and inferior," he assumed, "and
I as much as any other man am in favor of having the superior
position assigned to the white race."[15]

Sam Clemens came into the world at a time when the "black
inferiority" argument—bolstered by both religion and pseudoscience—reigned as the preeminent justification for slavery. In his
"schoolboy days," Twain recalled in his autobiography, he "had
no aversion to slavery." He was "not aware that there was anything wrong about it." No one around him challenged the institution; local churches taught that "God approved it, that it was a
holy thing." "In those old slave-holding days," he recalled, "the
whole community was agreed as to one thing—the awful sacredness of slave property. . . . To help steal a horse or a cow was
a low crime, but to help a hunted slave . . . or hesitate to
promptly betray him to a slave-catcher when opportunity offered
was a much baser crime, and carried with it a stain, a moral
smirch which nothing could wipe away. . . . It seemed natural
enough to me then."[16] Settled mainly by slaveholders from Kentucky and Virginia, Marion County had a history of violently
running out of town anyone with abolitionist sympathies.[17] (Indeed, sympathy for the colonization movement elicited just as intensely vicious antipathy.)[18] Clemens's father, John Marshall
Clemens, served on a jury that sent three abolitionists (or "slave-
stealers") to the state penitentiary. For the most part, Clemens's
family and other residents of the town accepted without question the legitimacy of slavery and the alleged natural inferiority
of blacks that justified it. The church and the law were unanimous on the inherent justice of the status quo. Although slaves
were not taught to read and write, their religious education was
not neglected. As the first historian of the county recalls, "the
Pauline precept, 'Servants obey your masters,' was constantly
cited to them as one of the teachings and commands of the
Bible."[19]

Slavery in Missouri—based, as it was, in small farms—may
not have been "the brutal plantation article,"[20] but it was slavery

nonetheless, with the all too familiar mix of pain and powerlessness. Emma Knight of Hannibal was born a slave near Florida, Missouri, Mark Twain's birthplace. When she and her sisters outgrew the shoes their master gave them only once a year, they had to go barefoot. "Our feet would crack open from de cold and bleed. We would sit down and bawl and cry because it hurt so," she told an interviewer years after freedom had come.[21] Her family had been separated, her father sold at auction—and not simply to settle an estate (a Missouri law passed the year of Sam Clemens's birth provided that slaves be sold to pay off debtors of the deceased):[22] "My father was took away. My mother said he was put upon a block and sold 'cause de master wanted money to buy something for de house.'"[23] Clay Smith, another slave from Hannibal, recalled that her aunt Harriet "was sold on de block down on Fourth Street right here in Hannibal."[24] A businessman named John Armstrong traded hay, grain, and slaves four blocks from Sam Clemens's home.[25]

All slaves were vulnerable to being sold away from friends and family; indeed, as Twain tells us, his own father was responsible for one such sale, having exiled a slave named Charley "from his home, his mother, and his friends, and all things and creatures that make life dear." In 1842, John Marshall Clemens, who had received the slave in settlement of a long-standing debt, took Charley with him on a trip to collect $470 he was owed by a man in Mississippi. John Clemens found the financial trials of the Mississippi man so moving that he "could not have the conscience" to collect the debt (as he wrote home). But he had no qualms about selling Charley down the river for about $40 worth of tar (the price that the King and the Duke got for Jim when they sold him in the novel Twain would write some forty years later).[26]

That the Deep South held no monopoly on cruelty as far as slaves were concerned is clear not only from accounts by ex-slaves and by antislavery clergymen,[27] but also from Twain's own recollections and by recent forays into Hannibal history. At age ten, in 1845, on one of Hannibal's main streets, he had watched a white master strike and kill a slave with a piece of iron, a memory that came back to him in Bombay. "I knew the man had a right to kill his slave if he wanted to, & yet it seemed a pitiful thing & somehow wrong, though why wrong I was not deep enough to explain. . . . Nobody in the village approved of that murder, but of course no one said much about it."[28]

On another occasion he recalled the community's response to the death of a slave at the hands of a white overseer. "Everybody seemed indifferent about it as regarded the slave—though considerable sympathy was felt for the slave's owner, who had been bereft of valuable property by a worthless person who was not able to pay for it."[29] (The jarring intrusion of the fact that the murder of the slave left the owner "bereft of valuable property" resonates with the dry denouement of *Pudd'nhead Wilson*: "Everybody granted that if 'Tom' were white and free it would be unquestionably right to punish him—it would be no loss to anybody; but to shut up a valuable slave for life—that was quite another matter. As soon as the Governor understood the case, he pardoned Tom at once, and the creditors sold him down the river.")[30] Terrell Dempsey's recent research on slavery in Hannibal paints a picture of an institution as harsh and brutal in its own way as its plantation counterpart.[31] One of the first things Hannibal did after it got its city charter in 1839, the year the Clemens family moved there, was to enact a slave code to regulate the conduct of slaves. Dempsey found that the law forbade slaves to congregate in groups of more than five, or to have church services without an approved minister. He notes that the law "set out a number of penalties, up to 39 lashes, and it was enforced by John Marshall Clemens when he was justice of the peace." On one occasion, Dempsey notes, Clemens "[tried] a slave and [sentenced] him to 20 lashes with a bull whip."[32]

During Twain's childhood, it was against Missouri law to read even the Declaration of Independence or the Bible to a slave.[33] But state-enforced illiteracy failed to extinguish a rich and creative oral tradition that Twain would later come to call consummate "literary" art[34] A young Sam Clemens who as yet knew nothing of his future calling listened to it every chance he got. The slaves didn't tell this attentive little white boy how much they suffered: stories like those Emma Knight and Clay Smith shared with interviewers years after slavery were not for his ears. What they did let him hear were ghost stories and satirical orations so masterfully constructed and delivered that he would remember them all his life. He was tremendously struck by the storytelling talents of Uncle Dan'l, a slave at his uncle's farm in Florida, Missouri, whose tales he was privileged to listen to every night in the summer; in a letter Twain wrote about him in 1881, he recalled the "impressive pauses and eloquent silences" of Uncle Dan'l's "impressive delivery."[35] Twain would also recall the rhetorical performances of Jerry, "a gay and impudent and satirical and delightful young black man—a slave, who daily preached sermons from the top of his master's woodpile, with me for sole audience. . . . To me he was a wonder. I believed he was the greatest man in the United States."[36] All his life Twain would emulate the lessons in storytelling and satire he learned from Uncle Dan'l and Jerry during his Hannibal childhood, striving to reach an audience as effectively as these master-talents managed to reach him. Uncle Dan'l may have been the most accomplished storyteller Sam Clemens had ever encountered, and Jerry the most effective satirist; but the society in which they lived defined them as "inferior" because of the color of their skin. Twain would eventually understand and explode the irony and arrogance of that label.

One could see signs of things to come in his first book, *The Innocents Abroad* (1869), in which he had nasty things to say about every guide he met on the trip, save one: the child of South Carolina slaves, a black man in Venice who spoke several languages, knew his art history cold, and made more sense than any other guide the group had encountered.[37] One would be hard-pressed to find a more candidly admiring profile of an educated black man among Twain's peers in the 1860s. (Twain recorded an analogous response to a black man's intellectual gifts in the journal of his trip to Bermuda in 1875, in which "an intelligent young colored man" captured his attention.)[38]

Contact with former abolitionists in the East after the Civil War and his marriage into Olivia Langdon's abolitionist family helped prompt Twain to continue to reexamine his views in the

late 1860s. An editorial Twain wrote for the Buffalo *Express* condemning a lynching, "Only a Nigger" (1869), marked some of the
changes in his sensitivity on this subject. In this piece Twain delivered a scathing, unsubtle attack on the worldview embodied in
that offensive racial epithet, lacerating the southern "gentlemen"
who were unconcerned about a miscarriage of justice so long as
"only a nigger" lost his life in the process. Elmira, Olivia Langdon's hometown, was proud of its abolitionist heritage. It had
been a key stop on the Underground Railroad, and Twain was
fascinated by the stories of escape he heard from ex-slaves who
had made it north. While his father had been sending abolitionists to the state penitentiary, his father-in-law, Jervis Langdon, had
been funding their activities. After the war, while residents
of Hannibal were resolving "that they would not rent a negro
a foot of land, or render him any sort of aid in his efforts to
make a living,"[39] Jervis Langdon and other residents of Elmira
were bankrolling former slaves' education. In this environment,
Twain continued to probe the "naturalness" of the racist views
drummed into him during his youth and found them wanting.
He became aware of the fact that the South had no monopoly on
racism and published (in the Buffalo *Express*) the occasional dig
at racism in the North.[40]

It is interesting that it was two black speakers in the North—
Mary Ann Cord in Elmira and a young black servant in Paris,
Illinois—who stimulated Twain to understand in fresh ways a
fact that he later claimed to have understood during his childhood: the people who were most talented at the art that Twain
himself was now elevating into a calling had often, throughout
his life, been black. In "A True Story" (1874), published in the *Atlantic Monthly*, an ex-slave, in her own powerful and eloquent language, told of being separated from her child on the auction
block and of being reunited years later; the sketch won Twain
critical acclaim for his dramatic evocation of "Aunt Rachel's" pain
and joy.[41] A talkative and engaging black child he met in Illinois
in 1871, whom he profiled three years later in a New York *Times*
piece entitled "Sociable Jimmy," helped spark his awareness of
the potential of a child-narrator and contributed significantly
to the voice with which Twain would endow Huck Finn.[42]

At a time when African-American vernacular speech was widely ridiculed in the nation at large, Mark Twain recognized that African-American vernacular speech and storytelling manifested a vitality and literary potential that was rich, powerful, and largely untapped in print. He wrote no manifestoes on this topic however. What he did do was change the course of American literature by infusing it with lessons he had learned from African-American speakers. And at a time when African Americans themselves were characterized as inferior specimens of humanity by pseudoscientists, statesmen, and educators, Mark Twain recognized that such pronouncements were absurd. He wrote no manifestoes on this topic, either. But his awareness of black individuals of extraordinary courage and talent impelled him to challenge this characterization in fiction, nonfiction, quips, quotes, and unpublished meditations that he wrote from the 1870s until his death.

Twain's major imaginative works focusing on the issue of race—*Adventures of Huckleberry Finn* (1885) and *The Tragedy of Pudd'nhead Wilson* (1894)—explored the subject of racism through satire and irony, a strategy that has often led readers to miss the point entirely or to take as Twain's message the opposite of what he intended to convey. Although readers' misreading of his irony has helped prompt recent moves to ban his work as "racist," it is ironic that Twain originally developed this strategy when a direct exposé of racism that he wrote was censored.

As a young reporter in San Francisco in the mid-1860s, Twain witnessed an incident he considered outrageous: several policemen stood idly by, apparently amused, as young white hooligans attacked a Chinese man who was going about his business. Twain's publishers refused to run the account he wrote of the incident, caring more about not offending the paper's subscribers (who shared the police's prejudices) than about the truth. Twain quickly learned that exposés of racism in San Francisco would not be printed in newspapers there. So he started writing a different kind of story, one with the same subject but an alternate strategy, and published it in a paper in the next state and in a national magazine. He had already published satires on travel letters, society balls, and corporate stock prospectuses. Now he turned his skill as an ironist on its thorniest target yet—racism.

These satires were told from the perspective of an invented character too innocent or bigoted to see anything wrong with the injustices he related. In "What Have the Police Been Doing?" (1866), for example, the narrator, posing as the policemen's most loyal friend and defender, paints a devastating portrait of corrupt and brutal police officers, who constantly victimize the local Chinese population. In "Disgraceful Persecution of a Boy" (1870), Twain focuses on a community that collects unlawful mining taxes from the Chinese not once but twice, whose courts convict the Chinese not just when guilty but always, whose police stand idly by when the Chinese are mugged by gangs—all occurrences he had witnessed in San Francisco. A young boy who has been taught by his elders that it was "a high and holy thing" to abuse the Chinese answers the call by stoning "a Chinaman" on his way to Sunday school. When the boy is arrested, the narrator decries the injustice of the fact that the boy "no sooner attempts to do his duty than he is punished for it."[43]

When Twain took up the subject of racism in *Adventures of Huckleberry Finn*, the time, the place, and the race would be different. But the central question would be the same: How can a society that debases human lives on a mass scale consider itself civilized? In *Huckleberry Finn*, as in earlier works, Twain used irony to shame his countrymen into recognizing the gap between their images of themselves and reality, as he portrays a racist society through the eyes of a boy too innocent to challenge that society's norms.

Readers who are not misled by Twain's irony find his attack on racism in *Huckleberry Finn* to be effective and memorable. Consider the exchange between Huck and Aunt Sally regarding a steamboat accident Huck has invented to make conversation. "Good gracious! anybody hurt?" Aunt Sally asks. Huck answers, "No'm. Killed a nigger." Aunt Sally responds, "Well, it's lucky, because sometimes people do get hurt" (chapter 32). Huck does not correct her, despite the fact that on the basis of personal experience he rejects Aunt Sally's assumption that the two words ("nigger" and "person") refer to two different orders of being.[44] Huck knows that if he is to play his role convincingly (he has undertaken it in order to rescue Jim), he had best remain silent. A further irony stems from the fact that despite his love for Jim and his commitment to "stealing him" into freedom, Huck never achieves a larger awareness that the laws that define black people as less-than-human property are wrong. If Huck never reaches this awareness, the attentive reader, however, does. Twain himself had certainly reached this awareness by the time he wrote the novel. In 1885, for example, the year he published the book in this country, Twain provided a succinct comment on racism's shameful legacies when he wrote the dean of the Yale Law School about why he wanted to pay for one of the first black students at Yale: "We have ground the manhood out of them," he wrote, referring to black people, "& the shame is ours, not theirs, & we should pay for it."[45]

Efforts to ban *Huckleberry Finn* as racist have surfaced periodically since 1957, when the New York City Board of Education, citing some passages derogatory to African Americans, removed the book from approved textbook lists. Challenges to this novel have been mounted in Pennsylvania, Washington, Florida, Texas, Virginia, Illinois, Canada, and elsewhere. Those who charge the book with being racist say that the term "nigger," used close to two hundred times in the book, retains the power to hurt more strongly than ever and argue that the presence of demeaning minstrel stereotypes in Twain's characterization of Jim is painful in a society in which negative stereotypes of black people have not disappeared.

Twain's defenders argue that Twain used the term "nigger" because it was integral to the project of presenting and indicting a racist society, whose illegitimate racial hierarchy was embodied in the use of that word, because it was central to dramatizing the failure of everyone in that society (black *and* white) to challenge the legitimacy of the status quo and of the word that cemented and reinforced it, and because the diction was realistic to the time and characters. (This fact does not mitigate the challenge of addressing in the classroom the pain still associated with this term— a challenge that requires that the literature classroom open itself to the history of American race relations.)[46] And critics in the

1990s challenged earlier critics' willingness to link Jim to minstrel stereotypes in simple, uncomplicated ways. Building on groundbreaking essays from the 1980s by David Lionel Smith and Forrest Robinson, a growing chorus of critics in the 1990s—including myself, Jocelyn Chadwick, Emory Eliott, Ralph Wiley, David Bradley, and Jim Miller—suggested that (1) Jim—not Huck—may well be the "hero" of the book; (2) Jim may don a minstrel mask strategically, when it seems to be in his self-interest to do so, and (3) critics' failure to recognize Jim's intelligence may reveal their own limitations rather than Twain's.[47] These assumptions suggest that Twain was doing more than challenging the ideology of black inferiority that dominated his world: he was consciously inverting it, crafting a book in which the most admirable and, perhaps, the most intelligent character, was black.

Ralph Ellison wrote in 1958 in "Change the Joke and Slip the Yoke":

> Writing at a time when the blackfaced minstrel was still popular, and shortly after a war which left even the abolitionists weary of those problems associated with the Negro, Twain fitted Jim into the outlines of the minstrel tradition, and it is from behind this stereotype mask that we see Jim's dignity and human capacity—and Twain's complexity— emerge.[48]

Critics in the 1980s—with the notable exceptions of David Lionel Smith and Forrest Robinson—tended to focus on the first half of Ellison's statement (the links between Jim and minstrelsy) while ignoring the second, forgetting that Ellison refers to minstrelsy as a "mask" and ignoring his comment that Jim's dignity and human capacity emerge "from behind" this mask. In a 1984 article originally published in the *Mark Twain Journal* entitled "Minstrel Shackles and Nineteenth-Century 'Liberality' in *Huckleberry Finn*," for example, Fredrick Woodard and Donnarae MacCann assert that "Twain's use of the minstrel tradition undercuts serious consideration of Jim's humanity beyond those qualities stereotypically attributed to the noble savage; and Jim is forever frozen within the convention of the minstrel darky."[49] This view is echoed in a number of articles published in that issue of the *Mark Twain Journal* (and reprinted in *Satire or Evasion?*) and also in Anthony J. Berret's 1986 article, "*Huckleberry Finn* and the Minstrel Show."[50]

David Lionel Smith's pioneering 1984 essay, "Huck, Jim and American Racial Discourse," however, took a different tack. In the hitherto most sophisticated and complex discussion of the topic to be published, Smith argued that "Twain adopts a strategy of subversion in his attack on race. That is, he focuses on a number of commonplaces associated with 'the Negro' and then systematically dramatizes their inadequacy."[51] The issue, Smith writes, is: "does Twain merely reiterate cliches, or does he use these conventional patterns to make an unconventional point? A close examination will show that, in virtually every instance, Twain uses Jim's superstition to make points that undermine rather than revalidate the dominant racial discourse."[52] Smith and others (including Ralph Wiley and myself) read scenes that some critics have taken as examples of "superstitious behavior" redolent of minstrelsy—such as the incident in chapter 2, where Tom hangs Jim's hat on a branch and Jim devises an elaborate story about being ridden by witches—as scenes that also may be understood as demonstrating Jim's creativity and resilience. In this particular scene, for example, Smith notes that

> Jim becomes, through his own story telling, unsuited for life as a slave introduces unexpected complications. Is it likely that Jim has been deceived by his own creative prevarications—especially given what we learn about his character subsequently? Or has he cleverly exploited the conventions of "Negro superstition" in order to turn a silly boy's prank to his own advantage. . . . [Jim] turns Tom's attempt to humiliate him into a major personal triumph. . . . by exercising remarkable skills as a rhetorician. By constructing a fictitious narrative of his own experience, Jim elevates himself above his prescribed station in life. By becoming, in effect, an author, Jim writes himself a new destiny. . . . [I]t is intelligence, not stupidity, that facilitates Jim's triumph. Tom may have had his chuckle, but the last laugh clearly belongs to Jim. (109)

On this occasion, Smith maintains, "Jim's darky performance here subverts the fundamental definition of 'darky'" (110).

Smith's iconoclastic approach was echoed four years later by Forrest Robinson in his intriguing essay, "The Characterization of Jim in *Huckleberry Finn*." Robinson argued that

> Jim does what he must do to survive: he resorts to all varieties of deception. His mastery in this line is first and most vitally manifest in his seeming incapacity to deceive. Without that simulated two-dimensional face, that happy, carefree, gullible fraud that he retreats to more and more as the hostile world closes in, Jim would be helpless to defend himself. Naturally enough, in entering this perilous but obligatory game of cat and mouse, he exploits all the resources available to him. Not least among these is the deep cultural investment among white people in the conception of slaves as happy children— gullible, harmless, essentially good.[53]

Jim uses this "preposterous stereotype"—one deeply embedded in minstrelsy—to work to his own advantage. Behind "the face of the gullible 'darky' that Jim presents to the world," Robinson finds "hints and glancing suggestions that there may be an artful and self-interested deceiver at work," who knows that "this simulated identity" may be "his best defense against white cruelty and infidelity."[54]

In 1993 in chapters 5 and 6 of *Was Huck Black? Mark Twain and African-American Voices*, I pursued a related line of argument, suggesting that African-American folk traditions with which Twain was familiar, rather than minstrelsy, may have been a key source for many episodes involving Jim.[55] Jocelyn Chadwick has similarly maintained that agency and intelligence rather than minstrel-stereotypes underlie Jim's verbal performances and suggests that the complexity of Twain's satire combined with readers' prejudices—not Mark Twain's—prevent readers from recognizing this dynamic.[56]

A 1999 essay by Emory Elliott added to the growing body of criticism that credits Jim with intelligence and self-awareness. "The way in which Twain establishes Jim's intelligence and hu-

manity and his subtle paternal authority over Huck is under-
stated and easily overlooked by readers who resist the notion that
beneath Jim's foolish superstitions and seeming ignorance are
deeper forms of knowledge and perception that guide him but
which he must carefully conceal," Elliott writes.[57] Discussing the
dialogue between Huck and Jim on economics and financial
speculation in chapter 8, for example, Elliott notes

> while this humorous dialogue is entertaining and on one level
> plays upon the naivete of both characters, it also has a serious
> side at the end when Jim says that he knows he is worth $800
> on the slave market and that if he owned himself and thus had
> that money he would be a rich man. This observation on the
> moral problems of commodification involves an astute under-
> standing of the value of slave labour to the national economy
> of antebellum America and the debt that society owed to
> Africans were they to be fairly compensated for their work.[58]

Elliott traces the ways in which Twain establishes "Jim as a man
of more intelligence and perception than would be immediately
obvious to most of Twain's readers" by methodically working
through a series of key scenes in the book, affirming that Jim is
portrayed "as an intelligent man who happens to be a slave"
rather than as a laughable minstrel stereotype.[59] In a similar vein,
Ralph Wiley suggests that Jim shrewdly and consciously dons the
minstrel mask as a strategic performance, playing a minstrel role
when that is what a white person expects him to do. But it is a
role, and that is key: he plays it out of self-interest. He is smart,
sensitive, savvy, self-aware, politically astute, generous, and stun-
ningly altruistic, a compelling and intelligent father, and a slave
seeking his freedom in a racist world determined to keep him
enslaved.[60]

In the same vein, writer David Bradley argues that "to me Jim
has always been the hero of *Huckleberry Finn*."[61] He goes on to
say that while

> a lot of people—white critics, black critics, have looked at
> Jim's behavior in the novel and said that Jim is portrayed as a

buffoon, as superficial, as all those things—as a stereotypical "nigger," this is the point where Twain's use of point of view gets him into trouble because you're seeing Jim as Huck sees him. In the course of the novel Huck learns to see Jim in a different way. And so what he tells you about Jim, what he observes about Jim, how he characterizes Jim at the beginning changes as he becomes more and more aware of what Jim is doing with him and for him.

And critic Jim Miller comments,

> as the novel develops we see that what Twain is doing is peeling away the minstrel mask and showing us the complex humanity behind the posture that Jim has adopted. We learn that [Jim's] a family man, we learn something about his relationship with his wife and his children, we learn something of the way that he sees himself and the world he lives in, we see a great deal about his hopes for his family, his future, his desire for freedom. So that we move towards a very very complex portrayal of Jim as character from a historical point of view.[62]

During the 80s and the early 90s, many critics (including most of those represented in the volume *Satire or Evasion?*, as well as Eric Lott and others)[63] became convinced of the value of identifying and condemning the residues of minstrelsy in Jim as part of the admirable project of dismantling naturalized racist caricatures wherever one found them. But what had initially seemed like the progressive, politically correct move turns out to be just the opposite: a part of the process of (yet again) denying a black man his full humanity. It is one thing to credit Jim with intelligence, some might say—but do we have to give Twain credit for being that smart? A number of critics (myself included) would respond, "yes": Twain was wise enough to recognize intelligence and strength of character when he saw it, wise enough to understand the masks blacks had to wear to manipulate white people, and cagey enough to write a book that would take us over a hundred years to learn to read.

Sometimes a work of art can be a lens through which a historical moment can be seen in stunning clarity and brilliant color. *Huckleberry Finn* may well perform that function for American race relations in the period from 1876 through the early 1880s, just as *Pudd'nhead Wilson* may be thought to play that role for American race relations in the 1890s.

Twain began and abandoned *Huckleberry Finn* in the summer of 1876, during the greatest formal celebration of freedom the country had ever mounted, the centennial of the Declaration of Independence. But, like the charade of chivalry that prevented the Grangerford family from seeing the barbarity of their way of life, the rhetoric of freedom that dominated the national discourse that summer tended to blind people to the fact that the fate of freedom for black Americans was about to be dealt a near fatal blow. The summer of 1876 brought not only the centennial celebrations but also the death throes of Reconstruction. With the Hayes-Tilden Compromise and the withdrawal of federal troops from the South, America was about to enter the period historians refer to as the "nadir," the all-time low point in American race relations.

Our contemporary sense of how far off freedom was that summer of 1876 may help explain why Twain decided to smash the raft and shelve the manuscript; and the confirmation of these fears during the next seven years may well have induced him to use the unsatisfying, burlesque, artificial ending that he eventually chose for his book. Twain's failure to resolve the moral conflicts set in motion in the first part of the book underlines the troublesome complexity of those issues and the difficulty of settling them even now, more than a hundred years later, which may be one reason why the ending continues to perplex us. Like America itself, *Huckleberry Finn* is castigated for its shortcomings precisely because of the boldness and daring of the challenge it took on from its start. Is what America did to the ex-slaves any less insane than what Tom Sawyer put Jim through in the novel? The ending of *Huckleberry Finn*, does more than encode and reflect the historical moment in which it was written: with an uncanniness that is as startling as it is sad, it illuminates so much of the history that followed it, both in Twain's lifetime and beyond.

What is the history of post-emancipation race relations in the United States if not a series of maneuvers as cruelly gratuitous as the indignities inflicted on Jim in the final section of *Huckleberry Finn*? Why was the civil rights movement necessary? Why were black Americans forced to go through so much pain and trouble just to secure rights that were supposedly theirs already? *Huckleberry Finn* occupies the unique niche we have reserved for it, in part, because it dramatizes, as only a work of art can, both the dream and the denial of the dream, both the spectacular boldness of a national experiment premised on the idea that "all men are created equal" and our spectacular failure to fulfill our promise.

The year Twain published *Huckleberry Finn* in the United States also saw the publication of Congregational minister Josiah Strong's blatantly racist bestseller, *Our Country*, which sold over 175,000 copies, was translated into a number of languages, and made Strong a leading figure on the lecture circuit in the United States and England.[64] Strong's assertions about the inevitability of the "superior" Anglo-Saxon race ruling the world were echoed by "scientists" of various persuasions who supported this perspective with "data." In the early 1890s, Dr. Eugene Rollin Corson, an erudite Savannah physician, claimed to have "proven," with the help of elaborate statistics, his assertion that African Americans "lacked the intelligence to care for themselves properly." Denied the benevolent control of slaveholders, they "quickly reverted to savagery" and were "destined to disappear, a victim of 'the struggle for existence against a superior race.'"[65] *Atlanta Constitution* editor Henry W. Grady, a popular national orator in the late 1880s, asserted in a speech in 1887 that "the supremacy of the white race of the South must be maintained forever, and the domination of the negro race resisted at all points and at all hazards—because the white race is the superior race."[66]

A compendium of popular knowledge published in 1887 featured a page of drawings entitled "The Levels of Intelligence," with a black man drawn to look like an ape representing the lowest level. During the next decade pseudoscientific disquisitions on black inferiority proliferated. These included Charles Carroll's *"The Negro a Beast"; or "In the Image of God";* (1900), William P.

Calhoun's *The Caucasian and the Negro in the United States* (1902), William B. Smith's *The Color Line: A Brief in Behalf of the Unborn* (1905), and Robert W. Shufeldt's *The Negro: A Menace to American Civilization* (1907).[67]

In an enormously influential book, entitled *Race Traits and Tendencies of the American Negro* (1896), German-born insurance statistician Frederick L. Hoffman amassed copious footnotes and statistical tables to charge "the American negro" with a range of innate "race traits" including "an immense amount of immorality."[68] (Hoffman's assertions of the doomed nature of the black race made it harder for African Americans to obtain life insurance from mainstream insurance companies and contributed to the rise of black insurance companies.) In 1900, Walter F. Willcox, the chief statistician of the United States Census Bureau, pronounced that blacks would eventually "succumb to the effects of the 'disease, vice, and profound discouragement' that generally accompanied the feeble efforts of a 'lower people' to compete with their racial superiors."[69]

Critics ready to claim that Twain generally affirmed this deafening din of racial determinism often base their judgment on *Pudd'nhead Wilson* (1894), Twain's most important work of fiction of this later period, complaining that Twain echoed his racist peers when he made his thoroughly despicable villain, Tom Driscoll, part black. Tom is weak-willed, cowardly, brutally cruel, and dishonest. Michael Rogin, for example, argues that Twain makes Tom's "'one drop of Negro blood' (the Swedish title of the novel) into the sign of an explanation for his guilt. This is not just what Roxana, Tom's mother, says; it is what the novel says."[70] Carmen Subryan reaches the same conclusion: "Twain seemed to be stressing that the one drop of Black blood in [Tom's] veins" was responsible for his failure as a human being.[71]

But a passage Twain cut from the novel before he published the final version suggests a different, more complex line of reasoning. As Tom ponders his fate, he tells muses that it was the white blood that made him base, not the black blood:

> Whence came that in him which was high, & whence that which was Base? That which was high came from either

blood, & was the monopoly of neither color; but that which
was base was the white blood in him debased by the brutaliz-
ing effects of a . . . long-drawn heredity of slave-owning,
with the habit of abuse which the possession of irresponsible
power always create & perpetuates, by a law of human
nature.[72]

In this passage, Twain actually went further than any of his
white peers did in their fiction—including George Washington
Cable—in his rejection of a hierarchy of color.

Twain would upend this hierarchy on other occasions as well.
His book about his round-the-world lecture tour of the late
1890s, *Following the Equator* (1897), for example, blasts through
conventional stereotypes of "savage" and "civilized" by (1) paying
special attention to instances of intelligence, skill, courage, and
creativity on the part of the so-called savages—qualities custom-
arily associated with "civilized" human beings, and (2) calling attention to instances of so-called civilized people acting in shock-
ingly depraved—or "savage"—ways. Twain quotes comments of
whites who bear witness to the intelligence of blacks and gives
his own examples of blacks' inventiveness, noting that even the
smartest whites could not fathom how the blacks invented certain superior technologies and methods of tracking. In addition
to admiring their intelligence, Twain praises blacks' aesthetic talents and their bravery. "These were indeed wonderful people,
the natives," Twain writes. "They ought not to have been wasted.
They should have been crossed with the Whites. It would have
improved the Whites and done the natives no harm."[73] Here, as
in that cut passage from *Pudd'nhead Wilson*, Twain articulates a
notion of black superiority that went well beyond positions articulated even by his most progressive white contemporaries.[74]

If the first part of Twain's strategy for challenging the savage-
civilized binary involved championing the highly civilized qualities of blacks, as he called them, the second part involved shining
an unsparing spotlight on instances of barbarous behavior on the
part of whites. "There are many humorous things in the world,"
Twain writes, "among them the white man's notion that he is
less savage than the other savages."[75]

Twain's willingness to challenge the savage-civilized/black-white binary emerges in his unpublished private papers as well as his published work. A "Family Sketch" (1906) is a case in point. Here Twain expresses his honest admiration of a black man whom he recognizes as, in some respect, "his superior." The occasion is Twain's reminiscences about George Griffin, his former butler. Twain, whose financial acumen was notoriously shaky, had had to abandon his Hartford home for Europe in 1891, after bad investments left him seriously in debt. Back in the states during the financial panic of 1893, Twain visited Griffin in New York. Griffin, Twain recalls,

> called at the hotel, faultlessly dressed, as was his wont, & we walked up town together. . . . He had been . . . serving as a waiter a couple of years, at the Union League Club & acting as banker for the other waiters, forty in number, of his own race. . . . Also, he was lending to white men outside. . . . The times were desperate, failure & ruin were everywhere, woe sat upon every countenance. I had seen nothing like it before, I have seen nothing like it since. But George's ark floated serene upon the troubled waters. . . . he was a prosperous & happy person & about the only one thus conditioned I met in New York.

Griffin had managed to lend money to the gentlemen who frequented the club and who were bankrupted by the financial panic; he took only watches and diamonds as collateral. Of Griffin, Twain writes, "in some ways he was my equal, in some others my superior."[76] Twain suspected, correctly, that George Griffin's talent for making and holding onto money was better than his own. This was one of many instances of "black superiority" Twain had encountered—others being the superhuman strength and extraordinary altruism demonstrated by John Lewis when he stopped a runaway horse to save the lives of Twain's sister-in-law, her child, and the child's nurse in Elmira, New York, or the startling talents of the satirical slave named Jerry, whom Twain had recalled fifty years later as the greatest man in the country. Some of the most powerful, eloquent, and moving speakers Twain had ever met—such as Mary Ann Cord, Frederick Douglass, and "Uncle Dan'l"—were black; Twain appreciated their superior gifts from the vantage point of a writer who struggled all his life to have an effect on his audience equal to the effect these speakers had on him.

The meaninglessness of racial hierarchies is a theme Twain also explores in an unpublished sketch, probably dating from the 1890s, "The Quarrel in the Strong-Box," which parodies the racial discourse of his day in a fantasy, in which different denominations of money represent the culture's hierarchy of color.

> Upon a certain occasion a quarrel arose among the money in the banker's strong-box, upon matters of right & privilege. It began between a Nickel & a Copper. In conversation the Nickel chanced to make a disparaging remark about the Copper, whereupon the latter spoke up with heat & said—
> "I will have you to know that I am as good as you are."
> "Since when?" retorted the Nickel, with scorn.
> "Since the Declaration of Independence said 'all money is created free & equal.' What do you say to that?"
> "I say it is nothing but a form of speech & isn't true. You know quite well that in society I am more welcome than you are; that more deference is paid to me than to you, & that no one would grant you are equal in rank to me."[77]

The nickel is put in his place by "an emaciated half dollar," who is put in *his* place by "a Ten-Dollar Gold-Piece, who is dismissed "with asperity" by "a Hundred Dollar Bill," who is pushed to the side by "a Thousand Dollar Bond," whereupon a general free-for-all ensues, frightens away a burglar, and brings the police. The judge resolves the dispute with a disquisition on the nature of equality that makes clear the idea that while there may be differences that create inequality—differences of "strength, health, stature, weight, comeliness, complexion, intellect, & so on"— denomination (read "race") is completely irrelevant. The "Copper" and the "Thousand Dollar Bond" [in the 1890s at least] all earn "five percent."

"Deep down in my interior," Twain had written in a "Family

Sketch," "I knew that the difference between any two of those poor transient things called human beings that have ever crawled about this world & then hid their little vanities in the compassionate shelter of the grave was but microscopic, trivial, a mere difference between worms."[78] But although, as these passages suggest, race may have struck Twain as, at bottom, a meaningless category, it did not follow that the degradations of racism were without meaning. For Twain well understood that as long as people behaved "as if" race mattered, it did. The deprivations and hurts associated with racism took on a reality of their own, however much "socially constructed" race itself may have been.

A novel Twain worked on between 1899 and 1903—"Which Was It?"—explored this issue. In "Which Was It?", a slave named Jasper buys his freedom by dint of enormous energy and hard work; but the bill of sale is destroyed in a fire and his deceitful ex-master reenslaves him. As Jasper endeavors to work and save to buy his freedom a second time, his savings are stolen from him by a duplicitous poor white woman whom he has befriended. "Which Was It?", even more than the last third of *Huckleberry Finn*, lends itself to being read as commentary on the post-Reconstruction reenslavement of black Americans. Betrayed and reenslaved by whites whom he had trusted, Jasper's troubles, Twain writes, "embitter him against the whole white race. That hate has grown in vindictiveness since, year by year."[79] Free at last, Jasper is captured yet again—this time by a local constable who jails and whips him for no reason. Jasper staggers home from jail in the morning "brooding vengeance and cursing all the white race without reserve, out of the deepest deeps of his heart, and rejoicing that in fifteen years he had spared no member of it a pain or a shame when he could safely inflict it." Emboldened by the depth of his rage, Jasper takes revenge on the white race by turning the tables on the heir of his former master. Jasper blackmails the white man into enacting a charade: in public, Jasper plays the part of loyal servant; in private, however, and in reality, Jasper is the master and the white man is his slave. Jasper exercises total, absolute, brutal power over him—power not unlike that which whites have used to enslave, betray, and contain him all his life. In the process, Jasper's bearing is transformed. "The meek slouch of the slave was gone from him," Twain writes, "and he stood straight, the exultation of victory burning in his eyes."[80]

Twain also explores the toll racism takes in the unnamed fragment referred to as "The Man with Negro Blood," a plot summary for a novel about "passing" set in the post-Reconstruction North that Twain outlined sometime between 1883 and 1889, but never wrote.[81] Twain's protagonist in the novel was born before the war, in *1850*, the light-skinned child of his master and a slave. Separated from his mother and sister by some accident or sale when he is ten years old, the young man wanders in search of them after the war. While struggling to find work and gain an education, the young man tirelessly advertises and hunts for his mother and sister and finally gives them up for lost. He does not deny his black blood: in fact, he speaks of it. Seeing, however, that "even the best educated negro is at a disadvantage, besides being always insulted," the young man "clips his wiry hair close, wears gloves always," "& passes for a white man, in a Northern city." Here he achieves great success, becomes wealthy, and becomes engaged to a white woman. At a dinner in a restaurant attended by the young man, his fiancée, and other members of her family, the black waitress waiting on their table stuns the group by exposing the young man's masquerade of "passing." The waitress turns out to be the sister the young man had given up searching for years before. And, in an emotionally charged recognition scene, we learn that his mother is working at that restaurant as well. They reveal not only that the young man is 1/16 black, but also that his fiancée is really his white cousin from the plantation. The fiancée, who has been described as "noble & lovely" up to this point, immediately abhors the man who moments before she had planned to marry. The girl's cousin, who has joined them for dinner, expresses her horror as well. It is at this cousin that the young man directs *his* final revelation. While the precise nature of the blood bond that connects him to her is left a bit ambiguous, there is nothing ambiguous about the anger and defiance with which he shouts his final shot, fully aware of the impact his words will have. He tells her, 'This loathesome negro is your brother."

We have no proof, of course, that Twain planned to leave the fragments "Which Was It?" and "The Man with Negro Blood" incomplete forever. As inspiration failed him on one project, Twain would jump to another. Inventions, games, and business schemes competed with writing for his imaginative attention. But the fact remains that these particular stories did stay untold, and it's intriguing to pose some conjectures as to why.

It was important to Twain to be able to "go home again." Quite likely his sense of his place in the culture, of the role into which he had been cast and the one he embraced with such gusto, shaped his view of which stories might best be left untold. As Justin Kaplan reminds us, the "affection and admiration" he craved from his audiences "came to be the basic conditions he needed in order to be creative and happy."[82] He was, Kaplan writes, "outrageous enough to hoax, surprise, and disorient, but careful not to offend."[83] The slogan on the Mark Twain Cigar, as Louis Budd notes, was "Known to Everyone and Liked by All, "[84] qualities Twain himself painstakingly endeavored to preserve. Twain had planned to write a book on lynchings, but then thought better of the project. "I shouldn't have even half a dozen friends left after it issued from the press," he wrote his publisher."[85] He abandoned the project.

Interestingly, Twain was willing to risk his popularity during his later years by blasting racist imperialism abroad in scathing attacks on what he called the "Blessings of Civilization Trust." His friend Joe Twichell warned him against speaking out on these issues. But Twain defied him, in full knowledge of the impact these attacks might have on his public image. Still, the fact that Twain was willing to speak out publicly on racism abroad does not change the fact that he left unfinished and unpublished these fragments dealing with various aspects of racism at home.

The risks for the white writer who *did* dare to address these issues were, indeed, severe, as the experience of his friend George Washington Cable must have taught Twain. Cable's outspoken pleas for civil rights and racial justice as a journalist, and his candid treatment of the thorny issue of miscegenation in his fiction, led the South to violently reject him. Ostracized, vilified, and warned not to set foot again in certain towns if he valued his health, Cable was forced to endure a fate that Twain himself had every desire to avoid. A story of racial injustice and "passing," like the one Twain outlined in the 1880s, might well have struck him, on second thought, as too risky to pursue.

The last thirty-five years of Twain's life coincided with the period that has come to be known as the "nadir" in American race relations. On some intuitive level, Twain may have suspected that it was not the time to tell these stories—or at least, not the time for him to tell them. Some of them *were* being told, however—by black writers—who seem to have been as oblivious to Twain's interest in these themes as he was to theirs. Several years before Twain conceived of writing a book about the history and progress of lynching, Ida B. Wells had published just such a book—two of them, in fact: *Southern Horrors: Lynch Law in All Its Phases* and *A Red Record.* Twain seems to have been unaware of them. (Indeed, of the many books that have been identified as having belonged to Twain's library, less than a handful are by black writers, and only one or two are by black contemporaries.) And while Twain couldn't tell the story of "passing" he outlined in the 1880s, for black writers the theme of "passing" and the dramatic dilemmas the subject embodies would become one of the most heavily freighted crucibles of race relations in African-American fiction. Frances E. W. Harper would explore this theme in 1892 in *Iola Leroy,* and Pauline Hopkins would explore it in 1902 in "A Test of Manhood." It would form the core of such distinguished novels as James Weldon Johnson's *Autobiography of an Ex-Colored Man* in 1912, and Nella Larsen's *Passing* in 1929. And Twain's insight—in the deleted *Pudd'nhead Wilson* fragment—into the social roots of problems in African-American life prefigures the sociological analyses W.E.B. Du Bois would begin to publish seven years later in his Atlanta University studies. And if Twain forced himself to excise the direct reference to positive qualities of blacks from *Pudd'nhead Wilson* before he published the book, these ideas would resurface in the 1920s, when pride in the creative dimensions of African-American culture would be celebrated by Zora Neale Hurston and Langston Hughes, and in the 1960s, when a long roll call of poets, novelists, and dramatists proudly asserted that "black is beautiful." That stark tale of psychological violence, unleashed anger, and revenge for centuries of racial injustice that Twain began and abandoned between 1899 and 1903 ("Which Was It?") would also be told in the 1960s, in the protest literature that channeled raw pent-up rage into searing poetry and prose.

If it was impossible for Twain to tell these stories, it was by no means easy for his black contemporaries at the turn of the century to tell them either. Charles W. Chesnutt's "frank discussion of race-mixing" drew one reviewer's ire in 1900, and in 1901 Howells criticized one of Chesnutt's most controversial novels as "too bitter."[86] The country had little interest in "race problem books," Chesnutt wrote to a friend in 1902. "Books in sympathy with the higher aspirations of the Negro do not sell" Chesnutt wrote, "and mine have cost me more to write, in time spent, than I have got out of them."[87] With no market for his work and no recognition for his talents, Chesnutt turned his pen to legal stenography. Paul Laurence Dunbar similarly found that "race problem" poetry had little audience. Much as the public expected humor from Twain, it expected dialect verse from Dunbar and paid attention to little else.[88] When Chesnutt and Dunbar tried to probe some of the thornier dimensions of race and identity in America, the critics, as a rule, grew impatient. On some intuitive level, Twain may have sensed that the country wasn't ready for some of those stories he tried to tell but couldn't. A number of the issues Twain tried—and failed—to address would become some of the central themes animating African-American writing in the twentieth century. The fecundity of these subjects and themes for African-American writers confirms one's sense that Twain was on the right track, even if he was destined to be derailed. The stories on race that Twain did manage to tell have played a key role in sparking African-American literary achievements n the twentieth century: Langston Hughes, Ralph Ellison, Toni Morrison, and David Bradley have all paid eloquent homage to Twain.[89] Twain's influence—both direct and indirect—on African-American writers was profound.

Although most of the nation's attention during Mark Twain's lifetime was focused on race in black-and-white terms, Twain also wrote about racism directed against the Chinese, Jews, and aborigines. For the most part, however, Twain remained rabidly hostile to Native Americans throughout his life and is responsible for reinforcing a number of negative stereotypes. Even on this front, however, Twain demonstrated the capacity to learn and change. A late posthumously published fragment, "The Dervish and the Offensive Stranger," suggests that near the end of his life Twain may have been approaching a fuller understanding of the pain that Native Americans had endured at the hands of whites— but this understanding did not begin to approach his insight into white racism toward blacks. On this latter subject, Twain subverted and challenged his culture's ingrained pieties with a boldness and subtlety that readers are still struggling to appreciate fully.

How do we explain Mark Twain's journey from knee-jerk racist to a writer so profoundly engaged by the conundrum of racism? Twain himself gives us the answer in a paper he gave in 1884: "What is the most rigorous law of our being? Growth. No smallest atom of our moral, mental or physical structure can stand still a *year.* . . . In other words, we change—and *must* change, constantly, and keep on changing as long as we live."[90]

NOTES

For an extended discussion of the issues raised in this chapter, see the following books and articles by the author from which some of the material in this chapter is drawn: *Lighting Out for the Territory: Reflections on Mark Twain and American Culture* (New York: Oxford University Press, 1997); *Was Huck Black? Mark Twain and African-American Voices* (New York: Oxford University Press, 1993); "In Praise of 'Spike Lee's Huckleberry Finn' by Ralph Wiley," *Mark Twain Circular* (Oct.–Dec. 1999); "Mark Twain's Historical View at the Turn of the Twentieth Century," *Proceedings of the 1999 Kyoto American Studies Summer Seminar* (Kyoto, Japan: Ritsumeikan University, 2000); "New Perspectives on 'Jim' in the 1990s," *Mark Twain Review* (Korea) (Winter 1999); "The Challenge of Teaching *Huckleberry Finn*," in *Making Mark Twain Work in the Classroom*, ed. James Leonard (Durham: Duke University Press, 1999); "Racial Attitudes," in *The Mark*

Twain Encyclopedia, ed. J. R. LeMaster and James D. Wilson (New York: Garland, 1993); "False Starts, Fragments and Fumbles: Mark Twain's Unpublished Writing on Race," *Essays in Arts and Sciences* 20 (October 1991); "Race and Culture at the Century's End: A Social Context for *Pudd'nhead Wilson*," in *Essays in Arts and Sciences* 19 (May 1990).

   1. Samuel L. Clemens to Jane Lampton Clemens, 31 August 1853, in *Mark Twain's Letters, vol. 1, 1853–1866*, ed. Edgar Marquess Branch, Michael B. Frank, and Kenneth M. Sanderson (Berkeley: University of California Press, 1988), 9. The context was Clemens's visit to the Court House in Syracuse, New York, which had been the center of a widely publicized incident involving a fugitive slave originally from the Hannibal area.

   2. Stephen Jay Gould, *The Mismeasure of Man* (New York: W.W. Norton, 1996), 633.

   3. Thomas Gossett reminds us, "among the colonists of the seventeenth and early eighteenth centuries it is the heathenism of the Negroes and Indians, rather than their race, which is emphasized as a basis for their enslavement (*Race: The History of an Idea in America* [New York: Oxford University Press, 1997], 3). And, as George Fredrickson notes, "The evidence strongly suggests that Africans and other non-Europeans were initially enslaved not so much because of their color and physical type as because of their legal and cultural vulnerability" (*White Supremacy: A Comparative Study in American and South African History* [New York: Oxford University Press, 1981], 70). Fredrickson comments that "what made the slave trade seem a legitimate enterprise to Europeans was, first of all, the belief that slaves were in fact prisoners of war or criminals whose enslavement was an alternative to execution; or, to put the issue on a practical plane, that they were already properly condemned to slavery by the laws or customs of the African or Asian societies in which they originated, meaning that their purchase by European traders did not alter their condition. This was not, of course, an accurate picture of what occurred in places like the Guinea coast of West Africa. . . . But the fact that most slaves were acquired by purchase from native traders or rulers gave enough plausibility to the prevailing rationalization to put European consciences at ease" (71). He adds that "the combination of heathenness and *de facto* captivity was what made

people enslavable, not their pigmentation or other physical characteristics"(73).

4. Benjamin Franklin, "Observations Concerning the Increase of Mankind" (1751), in *Benjamin Franklin: Writings* (New York: Library of America, 1987), 374.

5. For more on Long and other figures in the early debates about the nature of race, see Maghan Keita, *Race and the Writing of History: Riddling the Sphinx* (New York: Oxford University Press, 2000), 18–26.

6. Quoted in Gossett, *Race*, 44.

7. "The Stupendous Procession" (1901), in Jim Zwick, ed., *Mark Twain's Weapons of Satire: Anti-Imperialist Writings on the Philippine-American War* (Syracuse, N.Y.: Syracuse University Press, 1992).

8. Thomas Jefferson, *Notes on Virginia, The Writings of Thomas Jefferson*, vol. 1, ed. Albert Ellery Bergh (Washington, D.C.: Thomas Jefferson Memorial Association, 1907), 195.

9. Jefferson, *Notes on Virginia*, 194.

10. Fredrickson, *White Supremacy*, 142. See also Philip A. Klinkner and Rogers Smith, *The Unsteady March: The Rise and Decline of Racial Equality in America* (Chicago: University of Chicago Press, 1999), 14.

11. Qtd. in Gould, *Mismeasure of Man*, 103.

12. John Hope Franklin, "Two Worlds of Race," in Franklin, *Race and History: Selected Essays, 1938–1988* (Baton Rouge: Louisiana State University Press, 1989), 137.

13. Quoted in Gossett, *Race*, 63.

14. See Gossett, *Race*, 67.

15. Abraham Lincoln in Douglas debates, qtd. in Gould, *Mismeasure of Man*, 66

16. Mark Twain, *Mark Twain's Autobiography*, ed. Albert Bigelow Paine, 2 vols. (New York: Harper & Brothers, 1924), 1:101.

17. See, for example, the account in Harrison Anthony Trexler, *Slavery in Missouri 1804–1865* (Baltimore: Johns Hopkins University Press, 1914), 120–2.

18. Three years before the Clemens family moved to Marion County, William Muldrow, who believed it a "Christian duty" for members of his church "to contribute their funds to purchase the freedom of slaves and send them to the colony of Liberia," was almost lynched. See R. I. Holcombe, *History of Marion County Missouri*

1884 (rpt. Hannibal, Mo.: Marion County Historical Society, 1979), 205–6.

19. Holcombe, *History of Marion County*, 809.

20. Mark Twain, "Jane Lampton Clemens," in *Mark Twain's Hannibal, Huck, & Tom*, ed. Walter Blair, The Mark Twain Papers (Berkeley: University of California Press, 1969), 49.

21. Former slave Emma Knight, 924 North Street, Hannibal, Missouri; Western Historical Manuscripts Collection, University of Missouri, Columbia; rpt. in *The American Slave: A Composite Autobiography*, 1st ser., vol. 2: *Arkansas, Colorado, Minnesota, Missouri, and Oregon and Washington Narratives*, ed. George P. Rawick (Westport: Greenwood Press, 1977), 202.

22. Revised Laws 1835, P. 40, Art.VI, ch.2, sec.32, cited in Trexler, *Slavery in Missouri*, 61.

23. Knight, *American Slave*, 202.

24. Former slave Clay Smith, 612 Butler Street, Hannibal, Missouri; Western Historical Manuscripts Collection, University of Missouri, rpt. in *The American Slave*, 263.

25. Advertisement, *Hannibal Journal*, Sept. 21, 1848, cited in J. Hurley and Roberta Hagood, *Hannibal, Too: Historical Sketches of Hannibal and Its Neighbor* (Marceline, Mo.: Walworth, 1986), 103.

26. Twain, "Jane Lampton Clemens," 51. See also Dixon Wecter, *Sam Clemens of Hannibal* (Boston: Houghton Mifflin, 1952), 74–75; Albert Bigelow Paine, *Mark Twain: A Biography*, 3 vols. (NewYork: Harper & Brothers, 1912), 1:43; and Arthur G. Pettit, *Mark Twain and the South* (Lexington: University Press of Kentucky, 1974), 17–18.

27. For references to accounts of physical cruelty toward Missouri slaves, see Trexler, "The Social Status of the Slave," in *Slavery in Missouri*, 95–6. For more on the treatment of Missouri slaves in general, see Lorenzo J. Greene, Gary R. Kremer, and Antonio F. Holland, *Missouri's Black Heritage*, rev. ed. (Columbia, Mo.: University of Missouri Press, 1980), 8–62.

28. Mark Twain, *Following the Equator* [1897], *Oxford Mark Twain* [OMT hereafter] (New York: Oxford University Press, 1996), 352.

29. Twain, typescript of notebook 28b, pp. 22–23, Mark Twain Papers; qtd. in Pettit, *Mark Twain and the South*, 15.

30. Mark Twain, *The Tragedy of Pudd'nhead Wilson*, OMT, 303.

31. Dempsey's research is described in Bev Darr, "Hannibal's

Slave History." *Hannibal Courier-Post* (online edition), January 15, 2001, Features section. See also Terrell Dempsey's four-part series on the history of slavery in Hannibal: "The Whitewashed History of Slavery in Hannibal: 'Suffer Not the Children,'" *Hannibal Courier-Post* (online edition), February 3, 2001, Features section; "Slave-owning Culture Vastly Different Than That Which Exists Today," *Hannibal Courier-Post* (online edition), Februrary 10, 2001, Features section; "History Recounts the Whitewashing of Slavery's Cruel Ways," *Hannibal Courier-Post* (online edition), February 17, 2001, Features section; and "Heroes, Previously Unnamed, Played an Important Role in Our History," *Hannibal Courier-Post* (online edition), February 24, 2001, Features section. Also informative is Terrell Dempsey, "Why Sam Clemens Was Never a Confederate . . . and a Few Other Things You Should Know about Hannibal in 1860 and 1861," Oct. 13, 2001. Electronically published on the Mark Twain Forum http://www.yorku.ca/twainweb/filelist/1861.html.

32. Terrell Dempsey, qtd. in Darr, "Hannibal's Slave History."

33. House Journal, 9th Ass., 1st sess., p. 60. Law passed House on Jan 28, 1837, and Senate on Dec. 23, 1836 (Senate Journal, 9th Ass., 1st sess.). Cited in Trexler, *Slavery in Missouri*, 134–35.

34. See Fishkin, *Was Huck Black?*, 8–9.

35. Samuel Clemens to Joel Chandler Harris, Aug. 10, 1881; in *Mark Twain Letters*, 1:402–3.

36. Twain, "Corn-Pone Opinions"[1901], *Europe and Elsewhere*, ed. Albert Bigelow Paine (New York: Harper, 1923), 399.

37. Mark Twain, *Innocents Abroad*, OMT, 240–42.

38. Clemens, May-June 1877, Notebook 13. *Mark Twain's Notebooks and Journals*, vol. 2, 22.

39. Holcombe, *History of Marion County*, 811.

40. Twain, "Life on the Isthmus," *Buffalo Express*, Oct. 4, 1870; rpt. in Henry Duskis, ed., *The Forgotten Writings of Mark Twain* (New York: Philosophical Library, 1963), 310.

41. See Fishkin, *Lighting Out*, 85–88.

42. See Fishkin, *Was Huck Black?*, 11–40.

43. Twain, "Disgraceful Persecution of a Boy," *Sketches, New and Old*, OMT, 119.

44. David Bradley has raised the interesting possibility that Huck may also be responding literally to the question, drawing a distinction between "hurt" and "killed"(personal communication).

45. See Fishkin, *Lighting Out*, 101–6.

46. For more on this topic see Fishkin, "The Challenge of Teaching *Huckleberry Finn*."

47. I would like to take this occasion to reject an earlier comment I made in *Was Huck Black?* that "Jim's voice is, ultimately, a diminished voice" (107). Over the course of the nine years since I wrote that, I have changed my mind on the subject, as I have indicated in a number of public lectures.

48. Ralph Ellison, "Change the Joke and Slip the Yoke," *Partisan Review* 25 (Spring 1958): 212–22. Rpt. in Ellison, *Shadow and Act*, 45–59 (New York: Random House, 1953), 50.

49. Fredrick Woodard and Donnarae MacCann, "Minstrel Shackles and Nineteenth-Century 'Liberality' in *Huckleberry Finn*," rpt. in *Satire or Evasion? Black Perspectives on "Huckleberry Finn"*, ed. James S. Leonard, Thomas A. Tenney, and Thadious M. Davis (Durham, N.C.: Duke University Press, 1991), 142.

50. Anthony J. Berret, "*Huckleberry Finn* and the Minstrel Show," *American Studies* 27, no. 2 (1986): 37–48.

51. David Smith, "Huck, Jim and American Racial Discourse," in *Satire or Evasion?*, 105.

52. Smith, "Huck, Jim and American Racial Discourse," in *Satire or Evasion?*, 108.

53. Forrest Robinson, "The Characterization of Jim in *Huckleberry Finn*," *Nineteenth-Century Literature* 43, no. 3 (Dec. 1988): 361–91, rpt. in Laurie Champion, ed., *The Critical Response to Mark Twain's "Huckleberry Finn*," 207–25 (Westport, Conn.: Greenwood Press, 1991), 211–12.

54. Robinson, "The Characterization of Jim," 220.

55. I expanded on these arguments in 1997 in *Lighting Out for the Territory: Reflections on Mark Twain and American Culture*. (My primary focus there, however, was on the last third of the book—the "evasion"—rather than the early portion. I offered a reading of the latter part of the book as signifying on the breakdown of Reconstruction, viewing Jim's imprisonment on the Phelps Farm as an imaginative rendering of the nation's "re-enslavement" of free blacks through a range of economic, political, and social means in the post-Reconstruction South).

56. In *The Jim Dilemma: Reading Race in Huckleberry Finn* (Jackson, Miss.: University Press of Mississippi, 1998), Jocelyn Chadwick-

Joshua expanded on this theme, asserting that to the careful reader, "Jim is a man, a father, a husband, a slave who decides to run toward an ideal—freedom—in a country where his mask and double voice are his survival tools" (xxii). Chadwick-Joshua argues that the book "compels us to confront what I call 'the Jim dilemma': the need to distinguish a richly positive and generous humanity from the confusing crosscurrents of prejudice that obscure it" (xiv).

57. Emory Elliott "Introduction," Mark Twain's *Adventures of Huckleberry Finn*, Oxford World Classics edition (New York and Oxford: Oxford University Press, 1999), xxv.

58. Emory Elliott, "Introduction," xxvi.

59. "The serious point of these humorous exchanges," Elliott observes, is that the condition of being a slave and an outcast from society enables Jim to perceive the flaws in those very arguments that are used by his enemies to justify actions that he recognizes as inhuman and unjust." Emory Elliott, "Introduction," xxvii.

60. See Fishkin, "In Praise of 'Spike Lee's Huckleberry Finn' by Ralph Wiley."

61. David Bradley in the film, *Born to Trouble: Adventures of Huckleberry Finn*, produced by the television station WGBH in Boston for PBS (Public Broadcasting System), broadcast nationally on January 26, 2000.

62. James Miller in the film, *Born to Trouble*.

63. Eric Lott, "Mr. Clemens and Jim Crow: Twain, Race and Blackface," in *The Cambridge Companion to Mark Twain*, ed. Forrest G. Robinson (Cambridge: Cambridge University Press, 1995).

64. Gossett, *Race*, 189–90.

65. George M. Fredrickson, *The Black Image in the White Mind: The Debate on Afro-American Character and Destiny, 1817–1914* (Middletown, Conn.: Wesleyan University Press, 1981), 248.

66. Qtd. in Gossett, *Race*, 264.

67. Gossett, *Race*, 280.

68. Frederick L. Hoffman, *Race Traits and Tendencies of the American Negro*, 95, cited in Fredrickson, *The Black Image in the White Mind*, 249–51.

69. Fredrickson, *The Black Image in the White Mind*, 257.

70. Michael Rogin, "Francis Galton and Mark Twain: The Natal Autograph in *Pudd'nhead Wilson*," in *Mark Twain's Pudd'nhead*

Wilson, ed. Forrest G. Robinson (Durham: Duke University Press, 1990), 74.

71. Carmen Subryan, quoted in Anon., "Experts Split on Whether Twain, His Work Is Racist," *Jet*, April 15, 1985, 39.

72. Twain [Samuel Clemens] Autograph Manuscript of *Pudd'nhead Wilson*, Pierpont Morgan Library, New York, MA 241–42, qtd. in *Was Huck Black?*, 122–23.

73. Twain, *Following the Equator*, OMT, 265.

74. For an expanded version of this argument, see Fishkin, "Mark Twain's Historical View at the Turn of the Twentieth Century."

75. Twain, *Following the Equator*, OMT, 214.

76. Twain, "A Family Sketch," qtd. in *Was Huck Black?*, 124.

77. Twain [Samuel Clemens] manuscript of "The Quarrel in the Strong-Box," Mark Twain Papers, box 7, qtd. in *Was Huck Black?*, 123.

78. Twain, "A Family Sketch," qtd. in *Was Huck Black?*, 124.

79. Twain [Samuel Clemens], "Which Was It?", in Twain, *Which Was the Dream? And Other Symbolic Writings of the Later Years*, ed. John S. Tuckey (Berkeley: University of California Presss, 1968), 315–16.

80. Twain, "Which Was It?", 415.

81. In Mark Twain Papers, Bancroft Library, University of California, Berkely, box 37, DV 128 no. 4 ("The man with negro blood"). MS notes, 4 pp. See Fishkin, "False Starts, Fragments and Fumbles," for full text of fragment and also for description of the textual and physical evidence supporting the idea that it was written between 1883–1889, rather than later, as scholars previously thought.

82. Kaplan, *Mr. Clemens and Mark Twain*, 15.

83. Kaplan, *Mr. Clemens and Mark Twain*, 30.

84. Louis J. Budd, *Our Mark Twain: The Making of His Public Personality* (Philadelphia: University of Pennsylvania Press, 1983), 216.

85. SLC to Frank Bliss, 29 August 1901, Humanities Research Center, University of Texas, Austin.

86. Sylvia Lyons Render, ed., "Introduction," *The Short Fiction of Charles W. Chesnutt* (Washington, D.C.: Howard University Press, 1981), 50–51.

87. Chesnutt to Monroe Trotter, 17 December 1902, qtd. in Render, "Introduction," 51.

88. See Charles T. Davis, "Paul Laurence Dunbar," in *Black Is the Color of the Cosmos: Essays on Afro-American Literature and Culture, 1942–1981*, ed. Henry Louis Gates, Jr. (New York: Garland, 1982), 121–66.

89. See *Was Huck Black?*, 134–41 and *Lighting Out*, 191–94.

90. Twain, paper delivered in Hartford, late 1884, qtd. in *Mark Twain's Speeches*, ed. Albert Bigelow Paine (New York: Harper & Brothers, 1923), 121.

Mark Twain and Gender

Susan K. Harris

Readers have rarely felt as strongly about the issue of gender in Mark Twain's works as they have about, say, issues of gender in Hemingway or D. H. Lawrence's writings. As Shelley Fisher Fishkin notes, most disputes that touch on gender issues have focused on Twain and women, especially on whether or not he created interesting female characters or whether he had deleterious effects on the female family members and women writers with whom he came in contact.[1] Recent criticism—by Fishkin, Laura Skandera-Trombley, John Cooley, Peter Stoneley, J. D. Stahl, Susan Harris, and others[2]—has addressed these issues in a variety of ways, using examples that have ranged from Twain's early life and best known writings to his late years and unpublished manuscripts. In the process, these scholars have begun producing a substantial body of information about Mark Twain and women.

However we still have seen little consideration of Mark Twain and his writings within a wider gender context. With the exception of Guy Cardwell's *The Man Who Was Mark Twain: Images and Ideologies,*[3] and more recently, Leland Krauth's *Proper Mark Twain,*[4] few scholars have juxtaposed Twain's ideas about women to his ideas about men, to "map," as it were, his gender assumptions. To look at Twain's treatment of women without a sense of the way he mapped gender generally is to blind ourselves to the ways that ideas about one sex reflect assumptions about the other. By the same token, to ignore sexuality is to miss an important element of the investigation into gender, since concepts of sexuality grow out of beliefs about the sexes. However determining an individual's gender map depends on knowing something about his or her culture's gender topography, and determining that topography for a historical period is difficult because we rarely have much to go on other than public dogmas, which often reflect fantasy as much as fact.

Because it is so difficult to chart nineteenth-century gender, and because I am not convinced of the usefulness of creating a map and then showing how an individual writer conforms to or deviates from it, I begin this essay with a story Twain wrote with the intention of upsetting his contemporaries' gender assumptions. By looking at the places that he clearly created to startle his audience, we can "read" cultural norms in their apparent absence. Rather than assuming normative stability, this enables us to see how Twain himself perceived his culture's ideas about gender, and how he responded to their strictures.

"1002nd Arabian Night" is one of Mark Twain's lesser-known stories, unpublished during his lifetime. Appropriating the storyteller Scheherazade for his own purposes, Twain turns her into a prolix yarn-spinner, who tells a tale so long that the king dies before she finishes. Like *The Prince and the Pauper* and *Puddn'head Wilson*, the story's plot involves switched children. Rather than focusing on class or race, as he did in these other works, however, in "1002nd Arabian Night" Twain focuses on gender. "Now at the very moment of the births a wicked witch had come . . . and by parting the hair of the Sultan's boy-babe in the middle had made it seem to be a girl, and by parting the hair of the grand Vizier's girl-babe on the side, had thus caused it to seem to be a boy," Scheherazade tells the king.[5] "In this manner had the inscrutable fates ordained that the boy should be named and reared as a girl, and the girl be named and reared as a boy."[6] The girl-reared-as-a-boy is named Selim; the boy-reared-as-a-girl is named Fatima, and throughout the story, Twain revels in the absurdity he has constructed; the children grow, doted on by parents apparently so blinded by gender labels that they never discover the deception: "When the babies took their bath, nothing pleased the doting Vizier and the loving Sultana so much as to be themselves near by, and witness their healthful pastime."[7]

Twain is not overtly suggesting here that gender characteristics are socially constructed; part of his fun comes from knowing that his readers assumed that girls and boys would (or should) demonstrate fixed, inherent behaviors. To this end he makes it clear that both children engage in activities "proper" to their "natural" sex. Because their sexes have been exchanged, however, they seem transgendered, and their behavior disturbs the other characters. When "Fatima . . . showed interest in none but matters proper to the manly sex, and Selim cared for nothing but matters proper to the womanly sex," Selim is called a "milksop" and Fatima is regarded as "defective."[8] As the story proceeds, Twain increasingly plays with the possibilities of sexual blurring, a strategy made especially effective by his insistence on referring to the biological female as "she," despite her masculine name (Selim), and to the biological male as "he," despite his feminine name (Fatima). Hence, when "Selim" matures sexually, "All in one little moment Selim had been changed from a girl . . . to a woman . . . All her dream was Fatima. In her memory of her one vision of Fatima she lived, and moved, and had her being. Hour after hour would she lie, with closed eyes, . . . communing in spirit with her loved one."[9]

As if this evocation of same-sex love were not sufficiently confusing for his audience, Twain takes his young couple into marriage, blessing them with fertility and passing off the reproductive confusion as an exercise in mass gullibility. When Selim gives birth, Fatima bursts into her father's room, crying, "the miracle of miracles is come to pass . . . not I but my husband is the child's mother!"[10] and the people rejoice, "saying, one to another: 'To think that the father, and not the mother, should be the mother of the babes! Now of a truth are all things possible with God—whose name be exalted, whose perfections be extolled!' "[11]

"1002nd Arabian Night" was written in 1883, during the same summer that Twain was finishing *Adventures of Huckleberry Finn*. It's not only "about" gender-crossing, it's also "about" language, frequently parodying romantic or pretentious diction. Some of the parodies work; many don't. Twain's friend William Dean Howells, to whom he submitted the story for critique, wisely told him that it was more tedious than funny and that he shouldn't attempt to publish it. Twain shifted his attention to other manuscripts and permanently pigeonholed this one.

Still, "1002nd Arabian Night" is of interest to us because it shows Twain investigating gender much as he investigated other social categories that most people took for granted. In this story, as he would later do with race in *Pudd'nhead Wilson*, Twain struggles, largely unsuccessfully, to free himself from the sex / gender assumptions of his age. Most of the time, he suggests that feminine and masculine traits are inborn, what later generations would categorize as genetically linked; still, there are moments when he evades these categories, especially when he juxtaposes gendered names and pronouns. Twain's playful reassignment of gendered pronouns indicates that on some level he perceived that the words themselves produce the gender; that femininity or masculinity are constituted by the language employed to evoke them.[12] The story, written at the apex of his literary career and at the time when his own children were very young, suggests that Twain was questioning an entrenched cultural assumption that to be male or female meant to have a predetermined set of behaviors as well as a particular genital organization.

The nineteenth century was deeply interested in such issues, as it was about defining essences of all kinds. Prior to the Civil War, much public attention was given to categorizing groups of people—by sex, by race, by ethnicity, by class—and describing each group's essential characteristics. After the war, shifts in behavioral patterns led to increasing public uneasiness about moral standards, but they also fueled intellectual inquiry into the nature of humankind, which in turn led to the birth of the social sciences. The breakdown of gender categories was of primary importance in most of these new areas of inquiry.

The nineteenth century's legacy to the twentieth century was an increasing preoccupation with distinctions between sex and gender; the differences between reproductive functions and social behaviors that Twain perceived have come to occupy the center of our stage and have given us the means to look back at our progenitors' own assumptions. Sex—a biological phenomenon manifested in X or Y chromosomes and evidenced by the possession of male or female reproductive organs—is, we are coming to understand, different from gender—a culturally assigned set of behaviors often associated with male or female sexual traits but not biologically sex-linked. For some investigators, gender is culture mapped onto sex; for others, most notably Judith Butler, whose investigations into the philosophical and linguistic presentations of sex and gender have made her central to the field, not even sex is a stable category. In either case, teasing out the differences between sex and gender is a complex process, often requiring intensive self-reflection on the observer's part.[13] For historians, the investigation carries the added challenge of unpacking layers of cultural assumptions forgotten by subsequent generations. Still, we are beginning to assemble a framework for examining gender issues in historical periods, a framework that Mark Twain clearly sought. Twain's noted ambivalences about women's behavior and his fraught relationships with powerful men, his adulation of prepubescent girls and his cross-dressing characters, are signs of his engagement in a society that was disturbed about changing behaviors and looking for ways to talk about the differences between sex and gender. Like his contemporaries, his shifting and often contradictory attitudes reflect his movements through the sex/gender debates of his era.

Twain and Sexuality

Sex is not gender, and sexuality is neither sex nor gender, but sexuality—the production and regulation of physical desire—is directly related to both. Most important, it is deeply disruptive on individual and group levels, and all cultures evolve systems to control it. The public policing of private sexuality has been a major concern in American life for at least one hundred and fifty years, with everyone, from dieticians to politicians, noisily contributing to the national debate about how to determine and enforce a healthy, normative, "American" sexuality. Examination of figures like Mark Twain is a good way to explore some of the terms of that debate and some of the systems by which the society attempted to regulate activities that originate in biology but are expressed through culture.

The mature Mark Twain was a sexual conservative, most especially in regard to women's sexuality. As Margaret Sanborn and Andrew Hoffman[14] both note, he probably had had ample sexual experience during his early years on Mississippi steamboats, in the Nevada Territory, and in San Francisco. However, in later life, he was quick to insist on the highest standards of chastity, at least for white, middle-class women. "Your purity is your most uncommon & most precious ornament," he told his fiancée Olivia Langdon in 1869, as they recommended books to each other shortly before they were married. "Preserve it, Livy. Read nothing that is not *perfectly* pure."[15] Twain's vigilance in regard to his wife's chastity—mental as well as physical—was representative of mainstream attitudes of his time, when both women and men were urged to maintain an inner as well as outer "cleanliness" that precluded sexual appetite and even sexual curiosity.

One way to look at this facet of Twain's character is within the health reform movement of the nineteenth century. The national concern for personal purity that marked Sylvester Graham's campaign for control of dietary and sexual appetites in the 1830s and 1840s and the whole health reform movement of the 1840s and 1850s was a significant backdrop to Mark Twain's young manhood, especially to the small-town, aspiring middle-class environment in which he was reared. These reformers were especially concerned about young male sexuality and urged the inculcation of self-control and self-regulation as an antidote to the breakdown of small communities and local control.[16] For health reformers, the body was the location, or site, where the forces of disorder—conceived of as the uncensored quest for personal, often sensory, pleasures—did battle with the forces of order—conceived of as self-regulated boundaries on the sensory self.[17] Men, no less than women, were victims of their reproductive organs, and the future of a healthy society depended on their exercising strict control over themselves and, by extension, over the women who depended on them. These strictures applied to all sexual activity; while masturbation and extramarital sex were forbidden, marital sex was also strictly controlled. In this context Twain's strictures on sexual adventuring of any kind were well within the pathology of his age.

Another way to look at Twain's sexual conservatism is within the role sexuality played in the economic exchange of women in the nineteenth century.[18] For Marxist critics, marriage is as much an exchange system as any other contract, and societies that position women as objects of exchange (as, for instance, from parents to husbands) tend first, to construct a set of characteristics that they value as particularly feminine and then, to conflate social values and biological categories and assume that the values describe qualities intrinsic to the sex itself. Meekness, for instance, was a valuable asset for women living in rigidly hierarchical societies such as colonial New England, and parents who could advertise a daughter who would never defy her husband had a valuable asset on the marriage market. Eventually, humility became associated with the female sex, and the woman who was not meek was said to be unwomanly—"unsexed." In the nineteenth century, highly valued properties for women particularly focused on issues of sexual purity, and women fetching the highest price were those whose families could demonstrate that they had never engaged, imaginatively as well as physically, in anything smacking of sexuality.

It is clear from Clemens's letters to Livy that he cherished her purity in large part because it raised her value on the marriage market. Both Twain and Olivia's parents referred to her in economic terms: they as their "pearl without price" and he as their "treasure." Although both these terms have their roots in New Testament images of the good wife, by the nineteenth century, they had become a code marking women who were highly valued on the marriage market. As Twain and the Langdons negotiated Livy's exchange it was evident that her purity was a premium, and after the deal was struck, Twain marvelled that he had become the owner of such a rare commodity. "I have stolen away the brightest jewel that ever adorned an earthly home," he boasted in 1869.[19]

The economic exchange of women is also the basis of Twain's

1903 article "Why Not Abolish It?", which argues that the age of consent (the age under which a woman could not be said to have "freely consented" to sexual relations) should be abolished because seduction at any age damaged the reputation of the woman's family, and that therefore any extramarital sexual activity by a woman should bring punishment on the man who convinces her to engage in it. "There is *no* age at which the good name of a member of a family ceases to be a part of the *property* of that family—an asset, and worth more than all its bonds and moneys," Twain asserted.[20]

Twain's concerns here are not about sexuality itself but about the roles that sexuality plays in the maintenance of family reputations, that is, the social and economic, not the individual, ramifications of sexual activity. If we remember, too, the weight given family purity in southern culture, Twain's anxieties about Livy's purity assume an even greater dimension. Although Hannibal, Missouri, where Samuel Clemens passed his childhood, resembled the midwestern frontier more than the Deep South, it was sufficiently permeated by southern culture to have absorbed many of its codes of honor. In *Southern Honor*, Bertram Wyatt-Brown singles out the Colonel Sherburn episode in *Adventures of Huckleberry Finn* as a sign of the charivari (or carnival) and lynch law typical of southern forms of community control.[21] To maintain honor, a man had to be backed by a family whose reputation was irreproachable. Women were central to this reputation—the family harboring an unchaste woman was publically humiliated. Between the codes of his childhood, the Grahamite ideologies ubiquitous in the popular press, and the definitions of femininity most valued in his social milieu, it would have been difficult for Mark Twain to avoid absorbing the sexual formations of his environment.

Cultural formations are complex mechanisms, however, often allowing for large disparities between public norms and private behaviors. Moreover, in American life at least, strident public prohibitions tend to spawn private oppositions. In *Intimate Matters*, John D'Emilio and Estelle Freedman note that during the same years that the reformers were rampant, Americans also came to value sexuality for its physical gratifications.[22] Certainly, neither the reformers' strictures nor Clemens's fastidiousness prevented Olivia and Sam Clemens from having a thoroughly gratifying sexual relationship; both their letters to each other and the record of her pregnancies testify to mutual fulfillment. Moreover, the public strictures on sexuality, like almost any public strictures on anything, provoked Mark Twain's rebellion as much as they elicited his consent, giving impulse to subterranean writings that exhibit tensions generated by the social codes.

At the same time that he played the sexual conservative, however, Twain was writing clandestine pieces revealing his fascination with the sexuality, both male and female, that public representations of acceptable behavior sought to deny. This is especially evident in "[Date, 1601] Conversation, as It Was by the Social Fireside, in the Time of the Tudors."[23] Delivered orally to male friends in 1876, privately printed in 1883, and until recently rarely found in standard collections of Mark Twain's works, this short sketch shows the flip side of the sexual conservative; the man who is fascinated by sexual desire. As always in his work, Twain's major focus here is on language; as a writer, especially one who played with multiple dialects, he was engrossed in the exploration of linguistic variation. With this, he was sufficient social historian to know that cultures recognize different phenomena at different times, and that consequently what can be said in any given society varies across era, place, and class.

Polite nineteenth-century Americans did not discuss sex; they also preferred not to recognize biological functions such as flatulence. "1601" is about both. In order to write it, Twain sets it in the English Renaissance and uses Queen Elizabeth I, Francis Bacon, William Shakespeare, and other historical personages as characters. He does this because he imagines Renaissance Englishmen as having far more freedom to discuss biological processes than nineteenth-century Americans, so he uses his skill with dialect (here, "Shakespearean"—English spoken as Shakespeare's contemporaries spoke it) to create a sketch pandering to nineteenth-century repressions. Most interesting for our purposes, "1601" represents men and women taking equal interest in sexual intercourse. After an argument about the spelling of the word "bollocks," for instance, one older dame expostulates:

"Gentles, what mattereth it how ye shall spell the word? I warrent ye when ye use your bollocks ye shall not think of it; and my Lady . . . be ye content; let the spelling be; ye shall enjoy the beating of them on your buttocks just the same, I trow. Before I had gained my fourteenth year I had learnt that them that would explore a cunt stop'd not to consider the spelling o't."[24]

Both the enthusiasm for sexuality and the specificity of the language in "1601" expose the fissures in nineteenth-century public representations of acceptable sexuality. The fact that the piece was originally written for a highly respectable, all-male writing group[25] suggests the roles that "Otherness" (here, as the English Renaissance) played in giving nineteenth-century Americans a way to talk about physical functions that the offical culture refused to recognize.[26]

Twain's other fugitive pieces, often written for specific occasions at single-sex events, demonstrate the popularity of such topics at the very moment of their official repression. During the same decade in which he produced "1601," Twain gave an after-dinner speech to the Paris Stomach Club, in which he expatiated on the "science" of onanism.[27] Again, his framework is "literary"; part of the fun of these pieces is the juxtaposition of highly revered cultural figures and forbidden bodily desire; the resulting disruption is an example of what Freud calls unmasking.[28] In "Some thoughts on the Science of Onanism" Twain marshals his authorities and has them debate the pros and cons of masturbation: for instance, "Caesar, in his *Commentaries*," argues for the question, claiming that "to the lonely [onanism] is company; to the forsaken it is a friend; to the aged and impotent it is a benefactor"; Benjamin Franklin celebrates it as "the mother of invention," and Robinson Crusoe laments that he "cannot describe what I owe to this gentle art."[29] Voices for the negative include Solomon, who finds "nothing to recommend it but its cheapness," and Brigham Young, who comments that "as compared with the other thing, it is the difference between the lightning bug and the lightning."

Since the dangers of masturbation were one of the health reformers' greatest fixations, Twain's speech clearly engages their obsessions. Parodying the almost universal assumptions of advice books of his day, his Speaker solemnly declares that "the signs of excessive indulgence in this destructive pastime are easily detectable. They are these: A disposition to eat, to drink, to smoke, to meet together convivially, to laugh, to joke, and tell indelicate stories—and mainly, a yearning to paint pictures."[30] Interestingly, Twain's speech does not present a moral argument against onanism. Rather, in satirizing the reformers, Twain exposes their real fears, that male sociality and sexuality are always in danger of veering beyond social bounds. Masturbation is dangerous not, as the reformers insisted, because it depletes the body, but because it is intensely pleasurable and because it encourages homosocial conviviality. Moreover if "painting pictures" is metonymic for homosexuality, it may lead to forbidden sexualities as well.

In the end, Mark Twain senses, sexuality, both male and female, is a universal biological imperative that all cultures find dangerous and that they control through a variety of social networks. Recongizing this, however, does not prevent him from participating in the sexual formations of his era: as a private individual, he ensures that the economic and social ramifications of uncontrolled sexuality will not harm him or his family, and publically, too, he thinks and speaks about sexuality as a drive needing constant social monitoring. At the same time, he enjoyed sex, knew that others did so as well, and delighted in disrupting his contemporaries' complacencies. With sexuality as with most other issues, Mark Twain managed to participate in more than one side of his culture's debates.

Twain and Gender

Twain's interests in sex are connected to his interests in gender, but they are not the same thing. As we saw in "Why Not Abolish It?," what has often been read as Twain's anxieties over sexuality has as much to do with his anxieties over the instability of the family as about sexuality itself. One way of characterizing nineteenth-century America is as a society panicked by the apparent dissolution of controls and boundaries of all kinds.

Within that framework, the health reformers' focus on the body as the site of regulated power presented only one set of solutions. Another response to the perceived emergency was to celebrate the family, defined as a heterosexual nuclear unit. In addition to its function as an economic agent, the nineteenth-century family became a cultural symbol, an icon of order in a disorderly world. Paintings and photographs, public entertainments, and mass media of all kinds celebrated the family unit. By the late Victorian period, the integrity of the family had accrued sufficient social power to become a primary means of reinforcing social boundaries, and culturally defined gender roles were central to the family profile. Yet, like the public pronouncements on sexual purity, this formulation was under seige even as it was being constructed. Flux—geographical, social, and economic—characterized American society, and gender roles were no more fixed than other socially ascribed behaviors. Moreover, death, divorce, and abandonment were commonplace in a landscape where individuals were constantly on the move. Both women and men during this period were finding that the roles they had been reared to play were not necessarily operative in the world in which they found themselves, and they were searching for new ways of being in that world.

Men

For men, this often resulted in a marked ambivalence about the gender models presented to them. Although the twentieth century has tended to view nineteenth-century manhood, especially before the war, through the myth of the solitary individual, in fact, the majority of men were closely knit into family, business, and community life. The Leatherstockings, Thoreaus, and Andrew Jacksons, all of whom achieved iconic stature in the antebellum period or soon after, may well be signs of an escape fantasy rather than the norm, and the cultural anxieties about bachelors suggest how important it was for men to be tied into heterosexual networks rather than enjoying solitary pleasures, whether in the wilderness or comfortable urban "digs."[31]

In his influential study of antebellum America, *Manhood and*

the American Renaissance, David Leverenz synposizes some of
the dominant paradigms historians have employed to examine
nineteenth-century gender and social structure.[32] Most relevant
for Mark Twain are the models of the patrician and the entrepreneur—the first defining manhood "through property, patriarchy,
and citizenship"[33] and the second as "an ideology of dominance."[34] More recently, E. Anthony Rotundo has examined
American manhood from the late eighteenth into the twentieth
centuries, and demarcated three models: communal manhood,
which he associates with colonial New England; self-made manhood, which he sees emerging with the new nation; and passionate manhood, evolving at the end of the nineteenth century.[35]
While both these writers temporalize and spatialize their paradigms, and while it is certainly true that the entrepreneurial paradigm came to dominate popular culture, it may be more useful
to see them existing simultaneously, throughout the century, and
in both the North and the South. Using Leverenz's model because it more accurately describes Mark Twain's movements
through both southern and northern environments, we can see
Twain positioned between dominant paradigms, simultaneously
influenced by and resisting both.

In the patrician model of American manhood, the ideal man
was settled, fiscally sound, and socially responsible, and he moved
through life-stages that progressively positioned him as head of
his family, his business, and his community. Masculinity was enacted as patriarchy, and true men were fathers—of children, countries, ideas. Benevolent, secure in their positions, patricians ruled
by virtue of an inherited order. In contrast, the entrepreneur embodied the intense competition that marked emerging capitalism.
Rarely benevolent, often insecure, he was ruthless in his business
methods and judged other men by their willingness to return his
violence. He created his own economic and social positions and
presented himself as the best man to fill them, and he imposed
provisional order on chaos rather than embodied traditional authority. If the patrician represented the manly ideal of an orderly
society, the entrepreneur represented the ideal of a society on
the make. Most important, both paradigms rested on a shame
culture; men who did not succeed within their definitions were

humiliated by other men.[36] In Rotundo's schema, this is the moment when "passionate manhood" came to the fore; the competition that was a necessary adjunct to the self-made man became the very definition of maleness for passionate men. As with meekness in women, the use-value of the male was fetichized as competition and aggression; as Rotundo notes, these qualities were "exalted as ends in themselves."[37]

Paradigms are models, ideal abstractions; few actual people reflect them in their entirety. If the patrician and the entrepreneur were the dominant male paradigms in nineteenth-century America, it's clear that many men—probably most—were uncomfortably wedged between them, and overt aggression has always been a troubled value in male culture. Much of the literature of manhood in the late nineteenth century suggests male ambivalence about masculine roles. Howells's Silas Lapham, Dreiser's Frank Cowperwood and George Hurstwood, and Henry Adams's autobiographical self were all literary representatives of American men for whom the models did not provide sufficient flexibility; all felt themselves failures in a society that had mutated beyond their control.

Mark Twain's life and writings suggest the influence of patrician, entrepreneurial, and even "passionate" models on his sense of the masculine, but neither he nor his characters can be defined within any of these paradigms. Like his contemporaries, he was ambivalent about the masculine roles his culture offered, and many of his apparent contradictions are comprehensible within that ambivalence. Happy to play the paterfamilias to his wife and three daughters, he was also happy to be called to the lecture circuit, where, despite slow trains and grubby hotels, he was free from the constraints of Victorian gentility and the demands of property ownership. Always eager to be regarded as a successful businessman, in fact, he was a poor competitor; he was emotionally repelled by ruthlessness and his forays into venture capitalism were undermined by his talent for backing the wrong invention. Politically he was an outsider, a critic rather than a leader. Although he constructed his own and his characters' masculinities in the reflection of dominant images, they remained marginal to dominant paradigms of any type.

One way to examine Twain's ambivalence about prevailing male roles is to examine the men in his life and representations of men in his writings. The patrician ideal is usually represented by fathers, but in Twain's work, fathers are problematic. In *Cradle of the Middle Class*, Mary Ryan notes how changing gender expectations in the first half of the nineteenth century caused breaches between fathers and sons, a reality certainly reflected in Twain's life and writings.[38] His own father, John Marshall Clemens, by most accounts a stern and undemonstrative man, died when he was twelve, and he grew up in a household run by his mother, an active woman certainly equal to the task; his older brother, Orion, whose own lack of visible success always disturbed Clemens; and, until she married, his older sister Pamela. As I noted earlier, death, divorce, and abandonment were common in nineteenth-century America, and young Samuel Clemens's was not the only broken family in Hannibal, Missouri, in the 1840s and 1850s.

This cultural phenomenon was reflected in Twain's writing, where absent fathers and ineffectual father-surrogates are the norm, especially in the novels most centrally concerned with young boys. *Tom Sawyer*, *Huck Finn*, and *The Prince and the Pauper*, all feature fathers who are either dead or dysfunctional. In their place Twain creates father-substitutes such as Jim or Miles Hendon. However Twain's father-surrogates are often of a less hegemonic class or race than his young protagonists, a strategy Twain uses to diffuse the direct authority of the mentor to the mentee. The most obvious case here is Jim, in *Adventures of Huckleberry Finn*, whose status as black and slave undermines his status as older male, thus making even his moral power over Huck tenuous. In *The Prince and the Pauper*, Miles Hendon's ability to control the young prince is similarly diffused by his position first, as non-royalty and second, as a man displaced within his own family by his younger brother. Again, the normative authority of older to younger male is undermined by class, leaving the mentor with only moral affect. Even Judge Thatcher and Colonel Grangerford, images of traditional patrician authority, are minor characters in the novels in which they appear, and they are clearly representative of a dying order. For Twain the patrician ideal was untenable in life and imagination.

If the patrician is a marginal and unlamented figure in Twain's work, the entrepreneur and the passionate man—mostly conflated in Twain's writings—fare little better. The character most exemplary of the aggressive male is, of course, Hank Morgan, from *A Connecticut Yankee in King Arthur's Court*; the portrait of the self-made man, Hank's violence makes him less a celebration of manhood than an entrepreneurial machine in the patrician garden. More important, although Hank speaks in the voice of the American inventor and therefore evokes some of the cultural authority granted the entrepreneur, his political ideologies are so unstable that he cannot maintain the system of universal uplift that he has instituted in the society he hopes to reform. When they are not violent, Twain's entrepreneurs are failures; especially in the late fiction, they tend to be men who have gambled and lost on the commercial front. Humiliated, they stand by helplessly as both family and fortune disappear. Neither patrician nor entrepreneur, Twain's adult males negotiate gender roles nervously, never quite sure where they stand in the hierarchy of masculinity.

Rejecting both patrician and entrepreneurial models in his writings, in his life Twain attempted, as did many of his contemporaries, to carve out a territory, where he could enact masculinity without entangling himself in the kinds of power relationships those models entailed. Fiercely independent, miserable in work situations requiring him to acknowledge subservience to other men (one of the reasons why he rarely held a steady job and why he quarreled with most of the men with whom he had professional relationships), he nevertheless maintained many successful friendships with men during his lifetime. The minister Joseph Twichell and the writer and editor William Dean Howells are only two of the best known of the many men with whom he smoked, drank, joked, and played over the years.

Additionally, Twain's resistance to male power relations did not prevent him from seeking the friendship of powerful men. Beginning with Anson Burlingame, the U.S. minister to China whom he met in Hawaii in 1866, Twain proceeded, throughout his life, to form close friendships with such figures as President Ulysses S. Grant; Henry Huttleston Rogers, the vice-president of

Standard Oil; and Andrew Carnegie, the steel magnate. In part, because as a nineteenth-century American he admired business success even if he could not achieve it himself, and in part, because the relationships were not predicated on legal or contractual bonds, Twain valued his contacts with these men. All advised him and even arranged important deals for him; for instance Rogers took over management of Twain's finances after his publishing company's bankruptcy in 1894. Like Twichell and Howells, these were men with whom he played and on whom he often depended—in fact, critics have often noted the almost childlike demands he made on Rogers and his staff, as he "allowed" them to straighten out his finances.

These dependencies are most appropriately categorized as sentimental, affective; they are ties based on emotional affinities rather than on legal or contractual relations. Twain's preference for sentimental ties over contractual ones is a sign both of his own personality and of his generation's search for alternatives to existing male power relations. Emerging from the dissolution of the antebellum social structure without a clear hierarchy of social relationships, many Victorian-American men rejected purely business models, instead creating new affiliations based on friendship in the hope that affective ties would help usher in a different, and better, order. Recognizing his own weaknesses as an entrepreneur, but also knowing that he needed help from business minds, Twain configured his business mentors as fathers and himself as son, a relationship that held only because no legal contract enforced it. For Twain and his generation, voluntary bonds posited the possibility of homosociality existing outside of either patrician or entrepreneurial models. Within this framework, Twain's relationships with his male mentors reflect the dynamics of his age.

Women

Twain's relationships with women, both private and public, also reflect his generation's sex/gender debates. While relatively little has yet been written about nineteenth-century manhood, nineteenth-century women have received a fair amount of scholarly attention. Here the dichotomy historians model is between what Twain's contemporaries labeled the "True Woman" and the "New Woman," the "True" living roughly before the Civil War and the "New" evolving after it. As with any gender paradigm, these categories were constructed by a society with particular needs for certain kinds of people; the public image of the "True" woman satisfied a need for a domestic adjunct to the American man, whose own role was increasingly played out in the public arena. Positioned as head of the domestic sphere, the "True" woman was capable, cultured, and selfless. Always calm and organized, she lived for others, especially her family; in particular, she was her husband's helpmate and moral guide. She was in fact defined by the private sphere; true women did not enter the public as workers, performers, or citizens.

In contrast, the "New" woman ventured into the world, exploring it, and herself, and seeking new relationships between self and world. "New" women left home, getting jobs and supporting themselves; they lived alone or in groups in the absence of male authority; they explored their own desires and acted on them; they pressed for the right to vote, demanded respect from their husbands, performed in the public arena. "New" women entered the twentieth century looking for equality both in the home and the world.

Both Samuel Clemens and Olivia Langdon grew up between these generations. Born ten years apart—in 1835 and 1845—they were reared in a culture permeated with images of "True" women but lived to see their daughters come of age in the era of the "New." The Clemenses' lifespans saw the transformation both of women's public images and their private sense of self, and Mark Twain's writings about women, as well as his relationships with specific women, illustrate the ways he negotiated those transformations.

Some of the least palatable of Mark Twain's writings (for women, at any rate) are his two essays on female suffrage, both written for newspapers in 1867.[39] The first is composed as a series of letters to the editor on the suffrage question and positions an irascible, misogynistic "Mark Twain" at the center of several female voices, all of whom he attacks unrelentingly. Arguing that "it is inexpedient to extend the suffrage to women"[40] because it would enable "mediocrity and dishonesty [to be] appointed to conduct the affairs of government more surely than ever before,"[41] the Editor-narrator constantly belittles both his correspondents and women in general. His covert violence becomes overt when he vows to "touch off a keg of powder" under the parlour, where his wife has called a prosuffrage meeting of "seditious old maids."[42] Alternately sneering, sarcastic, and condescending, in "Female Suffrage" the Mark Twain persona is calculated to enrage any reader sympathetic to the women's cause.

Much of this essay is as satirical of male arguments against female suffrage (and of men in general) as it is of women, and it is unlikely that Mark Twain meant it to be taken entirely seriously. In fact, I have argued elsewhere that the sketch is more an attack on political ideology in general than it is on women, and that it actually deconstructs all its ideological positions.[43] Still, combined with his subsequent article about female suffrage, which imagines a session of the Missouri legislature run by women that legislates dress styles instead of aid to railroad construction, "Female Suffrage" shows that prior to about 1870, Twain participated fairly comfortably in a general cultural assumption that women were too frivolous to participate in the public sphere and that "True" women should stay in the home and meddle neither with politics nor other affairs that rightfully belonged to men.

The seeds for reconsideration (if not exactly conversion) were already planted, however, in part by Clemens's feisty mother, Jane Lampton Clemens, and in part by his private observation that intellectually, women were as capable as men. When women themselves began to change, Mark Twain had to take their demands more seriously. Although scholars of the late twentieth century have tended to assume that Twain preferred passive to active women, in fact, he enjoyed the company of spirited women—at least when they were not telling him what to do. During his San Francisco years, for instance, he was friendly with young Lillie Hitchcock, the honorary fireman, sharpshooter, horsewoman, and Paris correspondent to the *San Francisco Evening Bulletin*. Though he never sanctioned Hitchcock's activities, he genuinely enjoyed talking with her, remembering

her as "as generous and warm-hearted a girl as you ever saw.
. . . It always seemed funny to me, that she and I could be
friends, but we *were*—I suppose it was because under all her wild
and repulsive foolery, that warm heart of hers *would* show."[44]
Clemens's response to Hitchcock is telling; he liked her in large
part because her liveliness made her a good conversationalist, but
he felt compelled to label her activities "repulsive," especially because they trespassed so far onto male terrain. In later years he
would celebrate Hitchcock in a sketch titled "Hellfire Hotchkiss"
(c. 1897), about a fiery young heroine who rode swift horses, rescued stranded men, and had more courage than anyone else in
her village. Twain's secret admiration for spirited women such as
Hitchcock was one of the factors enabling him to slowly evolve
toward a more liberal position regarding women's activities in
the public sphere.

After Clemens and Olivia Langdon married, Olivia was a
major influence in helping him rethink his assumption that
gender-appropriate behavior was a sure indicator of moral character. Though she herself conformed to the image of a True
rather than New woman, Olivia Langdon was sympathetic to the
suffrage movement and had many women friends who were actively involved in public life. One influence, certainly, was Isabella
Beecher Hooker, a distant relative of the Langdons, who became
the Clemenses' neighbor when the young couple moved to Hartford. Far more radical in her feminism than her more famous sisters, Harriet Beecher Stowe and Catharine Beecher, Isabella
Beecher Hooker was a fairly constant presence in the Clemens's
household. Twain's own relations with her were uneven—they
were not compatible personalities—but through her, feminism
entered the Clemens household, making an impact even where it
was not welcome.

More powerfully, Anna Dickinson, who lectured publicly for
both abolitionism and feminism, influenced both Mark Twain
and the Langdon family. The latter's acquaintanceship with her
predated their meeting Clemens, and he was inexorably, if un-
happily, drawn into Dickinson's orbit when he began courting
Olivia. Although he admired her oratorical skills, he did not like
her, and she returned the sentiment, referring to him in a letter

to a friend as a "vulgar bore."[45] Nevertheless, her feminism, like Hooker's, came to Twain through his family and, combined with his other experiences, moved him toward more liberal views.[46] In addition to women such as Hooker and Dickinson, whose friendship with Livy put them in a special category, Twain knew, respected, and mentored at least two women whose publications were known and appreciated in their time. Both Fishkin and Skandera-Trombley discuss Twain's assistance to southern writer Grace King, and Fishkin notes that he also encouraged Charlotte Teller, another writer published in the early twentieth century.[47] Twain's willingness to work closely with these writers is a sign that despite his generally misogynist environment (at least as regarded intellectual women) and his own reflection of that environment in many of his speeches and writings, he respected bright, capable women, especially those who were doing creditable literary work. As Skandera-Trombley notes, he maintained correspondences with over one hundred women writers during his lifetime, doing some of them the ultimate homage of publishing their work as well.[48]

In 1882, Twain gave an after-dinner toast to the New England Society of New York. Titled "Woman—God Bless Her," it was a typical specimen of its genre—proposing to "consider" women's "ways" but in fact characterizing women synecdochically in terms of dress—or more precisely, undress. What is of interest is not the general tenor of the toast but one line, just before the conclusion, where Twain lists women's roles. In addition to "mother," "wife," "widow," "hired girl," and other traditional roles, Twain also lists "telephone operator," "telephone helloer," "book agent," and "boss." Though they are all milked for comic effect (he also lists "wet nurse," "queen," and "professional fat woman"), the fact that these jobs even occurred to him suggests the gender changes taking place in the labor environment.

In 1895, Twain wrote a passage in his notebook declaring that "no civilization can be perfect until exact equality between man and woman is included."[49] Like other men of the nineteenth century, Twain had come to this slowly, over time. In private life especially, he had difficulty accepting his daughters' budding sexuality and their wish to live their own lives. In the 1880s and

1890s, he played the role of the overbearing paterfamilias, who would not allow his girls to be alone with young men and who broke up their friendships with women if he thought their companions inappropriate.[50] By the early twentieth century, however, he capitulated. As the New Woman assumed prominence in the 1890s and 1910s, he came to accept—if not to embrace—the fact that a woman was not unfeminine if she was publically active and politically engaged. When his daughter Clara insisted on a career as a singer, he must have realized that his desire to "protect" her by confining her talents to the domestic sphere was antiquated. When the daughter demonstrated that she, like her father, could be a performer, it was a signal that by the turn into the twentieth century, gender had come to matter far less than environment and will in determining an individual's objectives, and the father who opposed a daughter's career was condemned as a recidivist curmudgeon. Perhaps to compensate for the loss of parental control over his adult child, in his last decade, Clemens emotionally adopted a series of prepubescent girls, whom he courted and petted and to whom he wrote letters that were alternately flirtatious and admonitory.[51] Although he was willing to admit women to adult equality on a rational level, on an emotional level, Samuel Clemens needed the reassurance that women loved and needed him as much as he loved and needed them.

Twain's ambivalence about women's changing roles may be the reason that his fictional women tend to be less interesting than his men. His "good" female characters—the Wilks girls in *Adventures of Huckleberry Finn*, for instance, or the goodhearted if flustery Aunt Polly from *The Adventures of Tom Sawyer*, or Sandy from *A Connecticut Yankee in King Arthur's Court*—tend to conform to one or another facet of True Womanhood. Expertly executed stereotypes, they primarily exist as backdrops for masculine activity, part of the setup Twain constructs to display the antics of his iconoclastic males. Two of his fictional women, however, expose some of the social tensions of postbellum debates about women's roles: Laura Hawkins, from *The Gilded Age* (coauthored with Charles

Dudley Warner in 1873), and Joan, from *Personal Recollections of Joan of Arc, by the Sieur Louis de Conte* (1896).

Written more than twenty years apart, both *The Gilded Age* and *Joan of Arc* show Twain working within standard definitions of white femininity, especially the model of the True Woman. Within that convention, for instance, Laura Hawkins his heroine in *The Gilded Age*,[52] is a female villain—she is ambitious, holds herself in high esteem, is complicit in her own sexual fall, and manipulates men for political gain. At the same time, however, Twain recognizes that she is emotionally faithful to her friends and family and that her energies, if wisely guided, might have made her a grand example of a new kind of woman. Like Lillie Hitchcock, Laura is trapped by gender conventions. Her ambitions—"to go to Washington and find out what I am"[53]— are, in gender terms, far more suitable to a budding self-made man than to a virtuous woman. Like many male American heroes, she struggles to escape both her small town and her victimization by an unscrupulous man. Anticipating Hank Morgan, she tries to create and control her own life. This was not the way the culture defined the role of True Women, however, and Laura's desire to shape the course of her own life becomes, in the cultural model that equates female aggression with impurity, a fallen angel, doomed to a tragic end. After conspiring with a corrupt politician to get a bill passed through Congress, Laura encounters the man who had trapped her in a false marriage and shoots him in a "crime of passion." She is acquitted of murder but compounds her affront to the social order by going on the lecture circuit to address The Woman Question.

At that point, Twain had taken her beyond his own capacity to imagine a woman who could have Laura's experiences of the world and still remain a heroine, and his only recourse was to make his heroine disappear. Or, as he wrote his friend Mary Fairbanks on April 16, 1873, "I killed my heroine dead as a mackerel yesterday (but Livy don't know it yet)."[54] In 1873, when the woman's rights movement was just resuming momentum after the hiatus of the Civil War, Twain could play with the possibility that a woman could operate successfully in the male arena and still be, at least at heart, good, but Laura's evolution threatened

his own tolerance for gender bending. Since the genre convention that he engaged was melodrama, in which both character
and plot follow predictable formulas, it was easy for him to ter-
minate his character when she threatened to evolve beyond
imaginative and generic control.

As we saw in his notebook entry for 1895, by the 1890s, Twain
had accepted the idea of equality intellectually. He had not, however, embraced it emotionally. If the 1870s had seen him experi-
menting with cross-gendering and self-creating women, the
1890s saw him settling for female characters whose courage consists of exemplary obedience to male authority. *Personal Recollections of Joan of Arc, by the Sieur Louis de Conte* (1896),[55] which
Twain believed was his best book, shows him resolving his struggles in the direction in which he was most comfortable. Rather
than positioning Joan as an active, self-fashioning character, a
model, as George Bernard Shaw would make her, for New Womanhood, Twain portrays her as willingly subject to male authority of all kinds—from God to the French king to her personal lieutenants—and undertaking her mission as an act of
self-sacrifice rather than as an adventure into a new mode of
being. Despite her air of authority and proficiency on the battle-
field, Twain's Joan is a domestic angel; in her private moments
she confesses that she would rather be home, spinning, than
leading the armies of France. Or at least so we are told; in fact,
Joan is so overshadowed by an intrusive narrator that her own
voice is rarely heard. Twain's rendering of his heroine's exploits
makes her a more suitable character for the 1850s than the 1890s
(a fact reflected in its poor sales and reviews) and is for us most
useful as an illustration of his discomfort with the direction in
which young women were headed by the end of the nineteenth
century. Joan may ride astride her warhorse and wear a suit of
armor, but she only usurps male perogatives because God commands her to do so, and she never enjoys the role. For Twain, her
self-sacrifice makes her the truest of True Women, the "spirit
which in one regard has had no peer and will have none—this; its
purity from all alloy of self-seeking, self-interest, personal ambition."[56] It does not, however, suggest a viable model for women
of the new century.

As always with Mark Twain, however, it is too easy to make blanket statements about characters, themes, or social consciousness. Additionally, it is generally a mistake in American society to discuss gender issues as if they existed apart from issues of ethnicity and class. I have already noted how Twain uses class and/or race to undermine the authority of his father-surrogates in *Adventures of Huckleberry Finn* and *The Prince and the Pauper.* These factors also skew his presentation of women of color. Because he was born and reared in a racially charged environment, Twain was not immune to his society's racializing of gender and sexuality. This is especially evident in his construction of Roxanna, his female protagonist in *Pudd'nhead Wilson* (1894).[57] Decisive, active, sexual, and dominating, Roxanna is neither the soiled lady of a melodrama, like Laura Hawkins, nor a rehearsal for canonization, like Joan of Arc. Mother of a child whose father is glaringly absent, active intervener in her own and her son's destinies, capable of maternal sacrifice but also vengeful when she discovers her son has betrayed her, Roxy demonstrates that Mark Twain could construct a female figure that escaped white female stereotypes. But only because, in the end, she is *not* white; Roxy is a mulatta, and despite her fair skin and soft brown hair "by a fiction of law and custom," "the one-sixteenth of her which was black outvoted the other fifteen parts and made her a negro."[58]

Throughout *Pudd'nhead Wilson,* Twain consciously struggles with these "fictions of law and custom"—fictions that create cultural narratives about the nature of specific groups of people—in racial terms. In the end, he loses his battle to see through race as socially constructed; his male protagonists, switched in their cradles, demonstrate racially marked behaviors despite their rearing. What he doesn't quite understand is that Roxanna's gender is also a "fiction of law and custom." When Roxy, angry over her son's betrayal of her generosity, shows up in his room dressed as a man and threatens to take her knife and "jam it right into you"[59] if he does not get her the money she needs, Twain almost affirms a new kind of American hero—a multiracial American woman who can act in her own defense. However, he was unable to see beyond Roxy's race and gender, using race to explain away her unwomanly actions and bringing in a smart white male to sort out the racial tangle she has created. At the conclusion of *Pudd'nhead Wilson*, this most aggressive of heroines is relegated to a minor role—not killed, as was the fate of Laura Hawkins, but reduced to an aging churchwoman, a threat neither to white hegemony nor to male dominance. Uneasily balanced between black and white, male and female spheres, Roxanna is the figure on whose body Twain writes his own and his culture's conflicts about both gender and race.

Let us return briefly to "1002nd Arabian Night" and the sex/gender system. At the heart of this convoluted tale, there is a boy baby and a girl baby and two sets of parents who can't see the sex for the gender. But Mark Twain can, and for all his experiments with pronouns, his suggestions of same-sex love, and his fondness for disrupting his contemporaries' complacencies, this author always knows not only which character is male and which is female, but also which is masculine and which is feminine. As he would do with race in *Puddn'head Wilson*, Twain sets up a potentially radical reading of one of his culture's most explosive issues, only to undermine his overt stance by his basic assumptions. This was not his only experiment with cross-dressing; other published sketches, most notably "An Awful – – – – Terrible Medieval Romance" (1870) and "Wapping Alice" (final version 1907), also play with the practice and consequences of transvestism. Even though Twain was fascinated by the possibilities of gender-bending, however, in the end he retreated from their implications. In "1002nd Arabian Night," the male baby demonstrates culturally sanctioned masculine behaviors and the female baby demonstrates culturally sanctioned feminine behaviors. Twain may "know," rationally, that gender is constructed through language and culture, but emotionally he does not want to believe it. When he abandoned "1002nd Arabian Night" in order to finish *Adventures of Huckleberry Finn*, he was choosing, more than he realized, to stay within the parameters of the sex/gender system of his time.

Despite everything his experience as a writer taught him

about the relationship between language and the construction of reality, Mark Twain was a man of the nineteenth century: he wanted to believe that the family was a bulwark against chaos and needed women to be at the family's core; he sought the voluntary friendship of powerful men but resisted the idea of institutionalized authority; he saw men's status undermined by changing economic and material technologies but could not envision a new man who would function as an effective model for the twentieth century. Perhaps more than most of us, he understood that social life is a series of overlapping performances, but he sought, as we do, the illusion of stability to shield himself from the chaos behind the mask.

NOTES

1. Shelley Fisher Fishkin, "Mark Twain and Women," in *The Cambridge Companion to Mark Twain*, ed. Forrest G. Robinson (Cambridge: Cambridge University Press, 1995), 52–73.

2. See Fishkin, "Mark Twain and Women"; Laura E. Skandera-Trombley, *Mark Twain in the Company of Women* (Philadelphia: University of Pennsylvania Press, 1994); Peter Stoneley, *Mark Twain and the Femine Aesthetic* (Cambridge: Cambridge University Press, 1991); J. D. Stahl, *Mark Twain, Culture and Gender* (Athens: University of Georgia Press, 1994); John Cooley, *Mark Twain's Aquarium: The Samuel Clemens–Angelfish Correspondence, 1905–1910* (Athens: University of Georgia Press, 1991); Susan K. Harris, *The Courtship of Olivia Langdon and Mark Twain* (Cambridge: Cambridge University Press, 1997). These represent a few of the many books and articles focusing on Twain and women that were produced in the 1990s.

3. Guy A. Cardwell, *The Man Who Was Mark Twain: Images and Ideologies* (New Haven: Yale University Press, 1991).

4. Leland Krauth, *Proper Mark Twain* (Athens: University of Georgia Press, 1999)

5. Franklin R. Rogers, ed., *Mark Twain's Satires and Burlesques* (Berkeley: University of California Press, 1968).

6. Ibid., 101.

7. Ibid., 105.

8. Ibid., 107–8.

9. Ibid., 114

10. Ibid., 131.

11. Ibid., 132.

12. For a philosophical investigation into the sex/gender system see Judith Butler, *Gender Trouble: Feminism and the Subversion of Identity* (New York: Routledge, 1990), especially pp. 24–25 of the preface "Subjects of Sex/Gender/Desire." Ultimately, Butler employs performance theory to question the reality of sex as well as gender.

13. For discussion of the evolution of gender studies, see Elaine Showalter, *Speaking of Gender* (New York and London: Routledge, 1989).

14. Margaret Sanborn, *Mark Twain: The Bachelor Years* (New York: Doubleday Dell, 1990), especially ch. 15, "Wild Oats"; and Andrew Hoffman, *Inventing Mark Twain: The Lives of Samuel Langhorne Clemens* (New York: William Morrow, 1997). Also see Hoffman's "Mark Twain and Homosexuality," *American Literature* 67, no. 1 (March, 1995), 23–50.

15. Victor Fischer, Michael Frank, and Dahlia Armon, eds., *Mark Twain's Letters, Vol. 3, 1869* (Berkeley: University of California Press, 1992), 132–33.

16. Jayme A. Sokolow, *Eros and Modernization: Sylvester Graham, Health Reform, and the Origins of Victorian Sexuality in America* (Rutherford, N.J.: Fairleigh Dickinson University Press; London and Toronto: Associated University Presses, 1983), 72–73.

17. Ibid., 92.

18. Luce Irigaray and Claude Lévi-Strauss are the major voices in the discussion about the exchange of women. See Irigaray, *This Sex Which Is Not One*, trans. Catherine Porter, with Carolyn Burke (Ithaca: Cornell University Press, 1985), especially ch. 8, "Women on the Market." Irigaray bases her work in this chapter on Lévi-Strauss's *The Elementary Structures of Kinship*, trans. James Haile Bell, John Richard von Sturmer, and Rodney Needham (Boston: 1969).

19. Victor Fischer, Michael Frank, and Dahlia Armon, eds., *Mark Twain's Letters, Vol 3, 1869*, 137.

20. "Why Not Abolish It?" in Louis J. Budd, ed., *Mark Twain: Collected Tales, Sketches, Speeches, and Essays, 1891–1910* (New York: Library of America, 1992), 551.

21. Bertram Wyatt-Brown, *Southern Honor: Ethics and Behavior in the Old South* (New York: Oxford University Press, 1982), 435–36.

22. John D'Emilio and Estelle B. Freedman, *Intimate Matters: A History of Sexuality in America* (New York: Harper & Row, 1988), 56–57.

23. See [Date, 1601], in Budd, ed., *Mark Twain: Collected Tales, Sketches, Speeches, and Essays, 1891–1910*, 127–33.

24. Ibid., 131.

25. "1601" was first presented to the Monday Evening Club, an informal but institutionalized gathering of some of Hartford's leading male intellectuals. The Club met in members' homes on alternate Mondays, and members read and discussed papers they had written. It became a first venue for several of Twain's short works, including "The Facts Concerning the Recent Carnival of Crime in Connecticut" and "Universal Suffrage."

26. See Mikhail Bakhtin, *Rabelais and His World*, trans. Helene Iswolsky (Bloomington, Indiana University Press, 1984), especially ch. 6, "Images of the Material Bodily Lower Stratum," for a discussion of the role of bodily functions in the imaginative release from cultural restraints.

27. See "The Science of Onanism" in Budd, ed., *Mark Twain: Collected Tales, Sketches, Speeches, and Essays, 1852–1890*, 722–24.

28. See Sigmund Freud, *Jokes and Their Relation to the Unconscious* (New York: W. W. Norton and Co., 1960).

29. Budd, ed., *Mark Twain: Collected Tales, Sketches, Speeches, and Essays, 1852–1890*, 722.

30. Ibid., 723.

31. In "Fireside Chastity: The Erotics of Sentimental Bachelorhood in the 1850s," *American Literature* 68, no. 4 (December 1996), 707–38, Vincent J. Bertolini charts the threat bachelors represented to nineteenth-century sexual ideologies among the middle class: "the appearance of a codified male subject position that could respectably host non-normative sexual subjectivity and alternative erotic practice" (708).

32. David Leverenz, *Manhood and the American Renaissance* (Ithaca, N.Y.: Cornell University Press, 1989).

33. Ibid., 78

34. Ibid., 90

35. E. Anthony Rotundo, *American Manhood: Transformations in Masculinity from the Revolution to the Modern Era* (New York: Basic Books, 1993).

36. Leverenz, *Manhood and the American Renaissance*, 73.

37. Ibid., 6.

38. Mary Ryan, *Cradle of the Middle Class: The Family in Oneida County, New York, 1790–1865* (New York: Cambridge University Press, 1981), 113–64.

39. Budd, ed., *Mark Twain: Collected Tales, Sketches, Speeches, and Essays, 1852–1890*, 214–27.

40. Ibid., 220.

41. Ibid., 221.

42. Ibid., 223.

43. Susan K. Harris, *The Courtship of Olivia Langdon and Mark Twain* (New York: Cambridge University Press, 1996), 131–33.

44. Fischer, Frank, and Armon, eds., *Mark Twain's Letters*, Vol. *3, 1869*, 32. Lillie Hitchcock eventually became Lillie Coit, after a long and at times outrageous life, bequeathing money to her beloved city that eventuated in the observation tower named after her—Coit Tower. For an account of the relationship between Hitchock and Twain, see Sanborn, *Mark Twain: The Bachelor Years*, 244–45.

45. Fischer, Frank, and Armon, eds., *Mark Twain's Letters*, Vol. 3, 66, n2.

46. See Laura E. Skandera-Trombley's *Mark Twain in the Company of Women* for additional information on Isabella Beecher Hooker and Anna Dickinson.

47. For Clemens's relationship with Grace King, see Skandera-Trombley, *Mark Twain in the Company of Women*, 150–53; and Fishkin, "Mark Twain and Women," 68. For Charlotte Teller, see Fishkin, 68.

48. Skandera-Trombley, *Mark Twain in the Company of Women*, 3.

49. Albert Bigelow Paine, ed., *Mark Twain's Notebook* (New York: Harper & Brothers, 1935), 256.

50. See Hamlin Hill, *Mark Twain: God's Fool* (New York: Harper & Row, 1973), Skandera-Trombley, and Cardwell, *The Man Who Was Mark Twain*, for assessments of Twain's relationship with his daughters.

51. Although Hamlin Hill's *Mark Twain: God's Fool* was one of the first studies to seriously grapple with the question of Twain's "Angel-Fish," as the writer called his "aquarium" of young girls, John Cooley has been responsible for the most recent research. See *Mark Twain's Aquarium*, and "Mark Twain's Aquarium: Editing the Samuel Clemens–Angelfish Correspondence," *Mark Twain Journal* 27, no. 1 (Spring 1989), 18–25.

52. Shelley Fisher Fishkin, ed., *The Gilded Age*, by Mark Twain and Charles Dudley Warner (New York: Oxford University Press, 1996). For an expanded argument on Laura Hawkins see Susan K. Harris, "Four Ways to Inscribe a Mackerel: Mark Twain and Laura Hawkins," *Studies in the Novel* 21, no. 2 (Summer 1989), 138–53.

53. Fishkin, ed., *The Gilded Age*, 275.

54. Lin Salamo and Harriet Elinor Smith, eds., *Mark Twain's Letters, Vol. 5, 1872–73* (Berkeley: University of California Press, 1997), 339.

55. Shelley Fisher Fishkin, ed., *Personal Recollections of Joan of Arc*, by Mark Twain (New York: Oxford University Press, 1996). For an expanded argument on this novel, see the Afterward by Susan K. Harris.

56. Ibid., 461.

57. Shelley Fisher Fishkin, ed., *The Tragedy of Pudd'nhead Wilson and the Comedy Those Extraordinary Twins*, by Mark Twain (New York: Oxford University Press, 1996). For an expanded argument on Roxy, see Susan K. Harris, "Mark Twain's Bad Women," *Studies in American Fiction* 13, no. 2 (Autumn 1985), 157–68.

58. Fishkin, ed., *The Tragedy of Pudd'nhead Wilson*, 33.

59. Ibid., 244.

Mark Twain and Social Class

Robert E. Weir

In *A Connecticut Yankee in King Arthur's Court*, Mark Twain wrote, "The master minds of all nations, in all ages, have sprung in afflu-ent multitude from the mass of the nation, and from the mass of the nation only—not from its privileged classes."[1] It was one of Twain's many blistering comments attacking the rich and power-ful, all of which are ironic coming from a man who supped with and depended upon the patronage of the very privileged classes he so forcibly denounced. But irony is cut from different cloth than contradiction. Twain's views and behaviors—though fre-quently inconsistent—are consonant with those of other mem-bers of the late-Victorian middle class. Like his contemporaries, Twain saw himself as a man of the middle, sandwiched between the potentially corrupting influences of unfettered power and privilege from above and debilitating poverty from below. Hav-ing risen from the ranks of the humble, Twain was envious of the rich but more sympathetic to common folk.

Two homes that sheltered Twain reflect the social, intellec-tual, and material worlds that he sought his entire life to recon-cile. The white clapboard two-story frame house at 208 Hill Street, Hannibal, Missouri—Twain's boyhood home—bespeaks modesty. Though comfortably furnished and a cut above the domiciles of both Hannibal's poor and destitute urban dwellers,

208 Hill Street is vastly more modest than the balloon-frame hulks of Victorian America's emergent bourgeoisie. Hill Street is a fitting monument to Twain's father, John Marshall Clemens, a man with middle-class pretensions, but whose financial ineptitude condemned the future author to a childhood of poverty.[2]

By contrast, Twain's house at 351 Farmington Avenue, Hartford, Connecticut, is a quirky nineteen-room mansion, dubbed by Justin Kaplan "part steamboat, part medieval stronghold, and part cuckoo clock."[3] It contains the trappings of bourgeois life: a billiards room, five bathrooms, ornate furniture, a solarium, chandeliers, overstuffed Victorian furnishings, and six servants to attend to creature comforts.

The Farmington Avenue home also contrasts markedly with the rough-and-tumble steamboat berths, flop houses, and tents of Twain's young adulthood, as chronicled in *Roughing It* and *Life on the Mississippi*. Kaplan argues that Twain's 1870 marriage to Olivia Langdon made him conservative: "within five years of their marriage, Sam Clemens the bohemian and vagabond had undergone a thorough transformation. He embraced upper-middle-class values. He became a gentleman, and for a while . . . despised the raw democracy which bred him."[4] Kaplan concedes that Twain's "monomania subsided," but argues that "all his life [Twain] had plutocratic ambitions. . . . As a writer he stood outside American society of the Gilded Age, but as a businessman he embraced its business values."[5]

During his lifetime, Mark Twain assumed many personnae: playful eccentric, nomad, crusading journalist, misanthrope, social climber, literary lion. His daughter, Clara Clemens Gabrilowitsch, added to the list. In a 1924 tribute to her late father, she connected his childhood and his social vision, while downplaying his attachments to wealth and power. She wrote:

In many ways he remained a boy to the year of his death. With the keenness of youth his responsive nature bloomed and blossomed with each fresh cause. The contemplation of injustice in the world, whether from individual toward individual or country toward country, gradually modified his capacity to enjoy the bright side of life, and more and more he fell into brooding until his voice came to be a "wail for the world's wrong."[6]

By the time of his death in 1910, many hailed Twain as a moral philosopher and social reformer. Among his eulogists was Samuel Gompers, president of the American Federation of Labor, who declared the author a friend of labor. That sentiment was echoed by Twain's good friend and mentor William Dean Howells, who wrote that Twain believed in the "glorious gospel of equality" outlined in *A Connecticut Yankee* and was an ally of working people "in life as he was in literature."[7] Subsequent Twain biographers agreed; in 1958, historian Philip Foner analyzed Twain's writings and speeches on politics, religion, and labor and dubbed the author a "social critic." Foner's views confirmed those of Paul Carter made a year earlier and presaged those of Maxwell Geismar who, in 1970, proclaimed Twain "an American prophet."[8]

Twain was a public man whose quips and observations have become part of American popular culture. As a literary figure, he is so firmly entrenched in the literary canon that his life has been scrutinized in minute detail and his work subjected to multiple analyses. Indeed, he is such an endlessly fascinating individual that it's a Herculean task to separate the man from his reputation.[9] Yet this is precisely what we must do if we wish to understand Twain's views on social class. Twain was neither a plutocrat nor a laborer; he was part of a rising middle class in the process of defining itself. But the middle-class literary world to which he belonged was an inchoate one that drew from both privileged ranks of society and the humbler ranks of society from which men like Twain had risen. Gregg Camfield (in this volume) notes Twain's deep ambivalence toward industrial and venture capitalism; the same ambivalence appears in his views of social class.

How could it have been otherwise given the nature of both his personal journey and the historical trajectory of the class into which he rose? Twain's rise was neither swift nor even. "The Celebrated Jumping Frog of Calaveras County" (1865) brought the writer minor acclaim, but not enough to staunch rumors that Charles Dudley Warner wrote most of *The Gilded Age* (1873). *Tom*

Sawyer (1876) and *Huckleberry Finn* (1884) generated mostly nega-tive reviews when first published, and Twain often prevailed on both William Dean Howells and Bret Harte, whose literary repu-tations eclipsed his, to write positive reviews of his novels.[10]

Much to Twain's chagrin, he was known more as a humorist and minor bon vivant—often lumped with Josh Billings, Petro-leum Nasby, Sut Lovingood, and Artemus Ward—than as a seri-ous writer. In his lifetime, Twain's greatest literary success was with what might be called a "middle-brow" reading audience.[11] Stung by critics and the public's slow acceptance of his work, Twain often exaggerated his successes. He claimed that an initial two-month sale of *The Gilded Age* was the "largest . . . sale any American book has ever achieved . . . except the cheaper edi-tions of *Uncle Tom's Cabin*."[12]

In truth, none of Twain's sales approached those of Harriet Beecher Stowe, though his play *Colonel Sellers* generated healthy royalties. Like many middle-class men, Twain was aware of his precarious status. This made him touchy, driven, protective, and insecure. As Karen Halttunen notes, "members of the middle class imagined themselves on a social escalator to greater wealth and prestige."[13]

Halttunen's use of the word *imagined* is crucial for under-standing Twain's place in the Gilded Age middle class. The Gilded Age produced wealthy tycoons like John Rockefeller and Jay Gould, but they were by no means typical of middle-class achievement. Like many members of the middle class, Twain dreamed of great wealth and managed to accrue (and lose) large sums of money. But relatively few from the middle class com-pletely broke from the need to *earn* a livelihood. Even when they aped the material and cultural tastes of elites, the middle class worked for compensation, be it in the form of wages, salaries, or royalties. To be middle class was to feel imperiled by both those above and below on the social scale.

Sociologists building on the pioneering work of Max Weber's *Economy and Society* (1920) have stressed the links between class identity and values, with members of a given class tending to share lifestyles with one another while holding in disdain those not in their class.[14] Wealth, power, and prestige are crucial identifiers of social class. By the 1820s, in the United States neither the working nor the middle class fit traditional class hierarchy classifications; that is, they were not elites, yeoman farmers, agrarian poor, or even "middling sorts."[15]

Both the middle and working class sensed themselves as breeds apart. As Stuart Blumin observes, crucial to middle-class awareness were nonmanual labor, suburban or urban living, a focus on "character" as opposed to "honor," and distinct social, economic, and cultural styles.[16] But middle-class awareness was also grounded in the reality of "wage" labor. That socioeconomic fact led some members of the middle class to view manual laborers with disdain. Alan Trachtenberg noted that the middle class stereotyped the working class as "foreign, alien, in need of Americanization," while David Montgomery asserts that Gilded Age labor strife so alarmed the middle class that, more often than not, it involved "itself in labor controversies on business's side."[17]

The working class and middle class were not in constant opposition to one another, however. Skilled artisans often identified more with the middle class than with manual laborers. Moreover, the boundaries between working-class respectability and an appropriation of bourgeois culture that Marxists dubbed "false consciousness" were razor thin.[18]

Both workers and members of the middle class demonized plutocracy. Thus, in terms of social values, the middle class gazed downward as well as upward. Halttunen notes that though middle-class Americans feared mob rule, they also condemned speculators, political demagogues, and amoral wealth-seekers who blocked access to the "social escalator."[19]

Mark Twain epitomized middle-class attitudes. He both praised workers and lectured them like a schoolmaster. In similar fashion, he rubbed elbows with workers at one moment, and the next donned black tie to attend gala balls. He was not completely comfortable in either world. Like many men of moderate wealth, Twain's ideal society synthesized the best traits of those above and below him. To paraphrase one of his novels, it was a world in which there was neither "prince nor pauper."

The synthesis that Twain called the "middle ground" necessarily involved critiquing other groups.[20] Twain echoed workers and social reformers in his views of pretense, practicality, the exploitation of labor, the need for labor unions, the hypocrisy of organized religion, a dislike of social parasites (like bankers, crooked politicians, and Pinkerton detectives), and attitudes concerning personal debt. In addition, he shared ambivalence about the machine age, civilization, and progress.

For many Americans, the term "aristocrat" was used to slander the arrogant, the greedy, the self-interested, and the pretentious, with the Russian czar a frequent nonflattering comparison. When the Knights of Labor struck Austin Corbin's Reading Railroad combine in 1889, the *Journal of United Labor* labeled him "Czar Corbin." Editorialist Merlinda Sisins noted she was "unable to learn anything in [Corbin's] career which entitles him to respectful consideration from the law-abiding citizens of this State [Pennsylvania]." She labeled him a "conceited egotist, an "idle sharper," and a "tyrant" exercising "imperial authority."[21]

Twain had little use for those who put on royal airs. In *A Connecticut Yankee in King Arthur's Court*, protagonist Hank Morgan concluded of the Knights of the Round Table, "There did not seem to be brains enough . . . to bait a fish-hook with." In still another passage he writes that "I had inherited the idea that human daws who can consent to masquerade in peacock-shams of inherited dignities and unearned titles, are of no good but to be laughed at."[22]

Twain's lampoon of "A Royal Banquet" in *Connecticut Yankee* bears striking resemblance to Gilded Age fests held at upper-crust restaurants like Delmonico's or Murray's Roman Gardens, in which the pompous and powerful donned laurel crowns and dined amid faux antiquities.[23] In his review for *Harpers' Monthly*, William Dean Howells correctly notes the book was "an object lesson in democracy. . . . [T]here are passages in which we see that the noble of Arthur's day . . . is one in essence with the capitalist . . . who grows rich on the labor of his underpaid wagemen."[24]

Twain railed against hypocrisy and pretense his entire career. In an unfinished of parody of Victorian social forms, he wrote a scathingly funny satire on the proper forms of address to be used when a gentleman escorts an unknown young lady from a burning building. He should bow, offer his arm, and state:

> Although through the fiat of a cruel fate, I have been debarred the gracious privilege of your acquaintance, permit me, Miss [here insert name, if known] the inestimable honor of offering you the aid of a true and loyal arm against the fiery doom which now o'ershadows you with its crimson wing.

His parody included a twenty-seven-level hierarchy of the order in which a gentleman should rescue those encircled by fire. Later, he added the suggestion that calling cards be printed on playing cards, with the face values denoting one's net worth in hundreds of thousands of dollars, the ace having "no limit."[25] Writings like "The Facts Concerning the Recent Carnival of Crime in Connecticut," "The Man that Corrupted Hadleyburg," and "The £1,000,000 Bank-note" are veritable lectures on the hypocrisy of elevating social custom over deep-seated principles.[26]

Labor delighted in attacking elites for their utter lack of common sense. In 1840, Sarah Hale, editor of *Godey's Lady's Book*, foolishly complained that working-class women aped the fashions of the rich, right down to their gold watches:

> O, the times. O, the manners. Alas! how very sadly the world has changed! The time was when the *lady* could be distinguished by the *no-lady* by her dress. . . . But now you might stand in the same room, and, judging from their outward appearance, you could not tell which was which.[27]

Female factory operatives in Lowell, Massachusetts, were aghast at Hale's shallowness. An editorialist in *The Lowell Offering* sneered,

> I pity the girl who cannot take pleasure wearing the new bonnet which her father has presented her, because, forsooth, she sees some factory girl has, with her hard-won earnings, procured one just like it. I said I pitied the girl; but I fear there is too much contempt and indignation . . . to render it wor-

thy of the gentle name of pity. . . . Factory Girls shine forth
in ornaments more valuable than *Gold Watches.*[28]

More than four decades later, female factory hands continued
to bristle with anger at callow ignorance. A female Knights of
Labor stitcher in a Lynn, Massachusetts, shoe factory hurled this
rhetorical challenge: "Has it ever occurred to you, careless
wearer of . . . boots, how many hands every pair went through
before they reached you? Well at least thirty. . . . Women with
just the same womanly instincts and desires that you have." The
writer went on to inform *Boston Herald* readers that the women
of Lynn were any woman's equal in family pedigree, intellect,
dress, and manners.[29]

Like the factory women of Lowell and Lynn, Twain's humble
characters had an easier time negotiating upper-class life than aristocrats had of adjusting to life as commoners. In both *Connecticut
Yankee* and *The Prince and the Pauper*, low-born protagonists learn
to manipulate customs to their advantage, given that courtliness
was more style than substance. Hank Morgan kowtowed when
necessary, then went outside the channels of official power to un-
seat Merlin as King Arthur's chief advisor. As "The Boss," Morgan
headed a sprawling industrial and commercial complex. In *The
Prince and the Pauper*, Tom Canty, the doppelganger who changes
places with Edward VI, has a tough time at first and was thought
insane for forgetting court manners, Greek, and Latin, but he
quickly staves off disaster and promulgates progressive laws.

By contrast, Kings Arthur and Edward VI are devoid of common sense. Though dressed in commoner garb and desirous of
circulating among their subjects, neither can lay aside claims to
special privilege, even when asserting those rights endanger their
lives. Were it not for their protectors—Hank Morgan in Arthur's
case and the pragmatic knight Miles Hendon in Edward's—both
royals would have met a sorry fate. Edward was a particularly
spoiled fop. Even though Hendon's intervention saved his life
several times, Edward continues to order him about.

Twain also decried the way common people were used as if
disposable. Humphrey, the official court whipping boy, appears in
The Prince and the Pauper. The king's tutors beat Humphrey each

time Canty/Edward makes a mistake in his lessons. When the good-hearted Canty threatens to discontinue his studies to stop the thrashings, Humphrey pleads: "My back is my bread, o my gracious liege. If it go idle, I starve. An' thou cease from study, mine office is gone, thou'lt need no whipping boy. Do not turn me away!"[30]

Both Joe Fulton and Andrew Hoffman note that writing *The Prince and the Pauper* temporarily radicalized Twain. Indeed, as Hoffman notes, Twain briefly considered himself a revolutionary after reading Thomas Carlyle's *French Revolution,* and his novel perhaps reflects a touch of romantic fancy on Twain's part.[31] Nonetheless, Twain's take on the potential of poverty to crush the human spirit resonated with the working class. Terence V. Powderly, former head of the Knights of Labor, recalled similar degradation on the part of Gilded-Age laborers: "I wondered why strong, skilled, and apparently independent workingmen approached the man of prominence, the clergyman, and the petty foreman with an air of abject servility, hat in hand, with faltering voice, and, in many cases, trembling in every limb." His explanation was much like Twain's: poverty reduced workers to servant mentality.[32]

Other members of the middle class agreed with Powderly and Twain. In his testimony before the U.S. Senate in 1883, Dr. Timothy Stow, a physician from Fall River, Massachusetts, accused greedy factory owners of forcing workers "to live hand to mouth" and of pushing some into theft from the "desire to relieve some physical want." The Rev. Heber Newton, an Episcopal minister, added, "It is open to ask how well for *public* good most of the gigantic private fortunes are administered. They seek investments solely with reference to dividends, and with an almost sublime indifference to every consideration of what . . . people most need. . . . It is not a question of A's having $2,000,000 or the State having it. It is a question of A's having it and the rest of the alphabet having it."[33]

Twain was more sympathetic to labor unions than is often appreciated. In *Life on the Mississippi,* Twain relates the story of his own experience with the Western Boatman's Benevolent Association. When pilots first unionized in 1860, association organizers were fired. Improved economic conditions allowed pilots to even the score. They used their superior knowledge of the river, set up networks that communicated channel changes only to union men, and increased the pressure on boat captains. Twain wrote, "Every day . . . a new victim fell, every day some outraged captain discharged a nonassociation pet, with tears and profanity and installed a hated association man in his berth."[34]

Boat underwriters, troubled by the number of accidents involving untrained pilots, ordered intransigent captains to hire only association men. Nonunion scabs were forced to seek association membership to find employment and had to pay dues retroactively to the founding of the pilots' union. One by one, "repentant sinners . . . were added to the fold" until, by 1861, the Mississippi River was a closed shop.[35]

During Twain's tenure in Hartford, the American labor movement grew by leaps and bounds. The "Great Upheaval" of 1885–1887 was marked by boycotts, protests, and strike-related violence. Trade unions grew, with the Knights of Labor mushrooming to as many as 1 million members by 1886.[36] Twain saw unions as the solution to, not the cause of, social ills. In an 1886 speech before Hartford's Monday Evening Club, Twain dubbed the Knights of Labor "the New Dynasty," and challenged the fearful to "read their manifesto; read it . . . and ponder it." Twain assured his listeners,

> We need not fear this king. All the kings that have ruled the world hitherto were born the protectors . . . of cliques and classes and clans of gilded idlers, selfish pap-hunters, restless schemers, [and] troublers of the State in the interest of their private advantage. But this king is born the enemy of them that scheme and talk and do not work. . . . He will see to it that there is fair play, fair working hours, [and] fair wages. . . . He will be strenuous, firm, sometimes hard . . . for a while, till all his craftsmen be gathered into his citadel and his throne be established.[37]

Never known for effusive compliments, Twain heaped praise on defenders of labor like poet and editor John Boyle O'Reilly;

Peter Cooper, the one-time Greenback candidate for president; Episcopalian Bishop Henry Codman Potter, a strong advocate of the Social Gospel movement; and William Swinton, brother of radical labor editor John Swinton.[38] According to Howells, Twain's unflinching support for organized labor deepened upon reading Edward Bellamy's *Looking Backward*. He came to see "that in the Unions was the working-man's only present hope in standing like a man against money and the power of it."[39] Howells exaggerated; Twain was well on his way to such conclusions long before his encounter with Bellamy. In an 1867 letter to the *Alta California* he wrote, "Prosperity is the surest breeder of insolence I know of." Twelve years later he told the *New York Evening Post*, "I regard the poor man in his present condition as so much wasted raw material."[40]

Twain was an indefatigable foe of anything that stood in the way of human progress and individual potential. Thus, he also shared labor's abhorrence of religious hypocrisy and of clerics who denounced unions. The Knights' Terence Powderly charged that most Gilded Age denominations had lapsed into ritualist "Churchianity," that "largely supplanted" morality-based Christianity.[41] He was scornful of Social Darwinist clergymen, who betrayed "the Christ they professed to represent in proclaiming that God had ordained that certain men should be born and remain hewers of wood and drawers of water and that certain other men had been . . . commissioned by the Almighty to be their masters by divine right." Powderly charged, "I never heard a prominent churchman defend organized labor until . . . labor had won recognition another way."[42]

Twain shared Powderly's distrust of organized religion, even though the Rev. Joseph Twichell was one of his closest friends. Twain's next-door neighbor was Harriet Beecher Stowe, but he was deeply troubled by the adultery scandal involving her brother, the Rev. Henry Ward Beecher. He attended the famed Beecher-Tilton trial in 1875, and his notes indicate that he thought Beecher guilty, despite the hung jury verdict.[43] Twain certainly had clerical cant in mind when he penned his wicked "The Facts Concerning the Recent Carnival of Crime in Connecticut" (1876). The work is a cynical encomium to amorality, in which a man slays his own conscience and gains license to kill, spoil, swindle, and steal without the burden of guilt or remorse. The story lumps cabinet members, editors, and clergymen among those with shrunken consciences![44]

Twain mercilessly skewered Catholicism in his writings. An 1878 visit to The Vatican spawned the remark, "This brutal superstition squeezes and robs the poor of the whole world of millions annually . . . but when a priest gives 15 cents worth of bread to the starving they make a five thousand dollar picture of it and put a dob [sic] of whitewash around his head to stand for 'glory'."[45] Howells notes that Twain harbored the view that "Christianity had done nothing to improve morals and conditions."[46] Twain brought to bear his anti-Catholic biases and his animus toward organized religion, in general, in *A Connecticut Yankee*. The church is placed in league with magicians and reactionary nobles in opposing Hank Morgan's innovations. One illustration depicts a cleric kicking a king, kicking an aristocrat who, in turn, boots a commoner.[47] As Fulton notes, Twain thought his own novel of more use to workers than the Bible or political tomes. He considered offering it to labor groups at a discount as they "have no Gospels thus far except very serious ones and sometimes dreary."[48]

Like Powderly, Twain deplored "Churchianity." Both men were moralists more interested in demonstrable behavior than Social Darwinist platitudes or clerical titles. Twain admired individual clergymen, like Joe Twichell, whom he felt practiced what they preached, but did not shrink from denouncing hypocrisy. The essay "Letters to the Earth" records a mock exchange between a Recording Angel and a Buffalo coal dealer named Abner Scofield, whose public prayers could not be granted because "certain sorts of Public Prayers of Professional Christians are forbidden to take precedence over Secret Supplications of the Heart." Scofield's open prayer for "better times and plentier food for the hard-handed sons of toil" was contradicted by his "Secret Supplication . . . for [an] influx of laborers to reduce wages 10 percent," as well as his request "for deportation to Sheol of annoying swarms of persons who appear daily for work, for favors of one sort or another."[49]

Twain also disliked bankers, sharing the working class's distrust of those who did not do "productive" labor. The Knights of Labor opened their ranks to sympathetic employers, but "parasitical" professions were banned, including lawyers, gamblers, land speculators, liquor tradesmen, and bankers. Twain often used bankers as satirical foils. Banker Pinkerton in "The Man that Corrupted Hadleyburg" is described as a "mean, smirking, oily" man, who worked his clerk Edward Richards until 11 PM.[50] The protagonist of "Making a Fortune" is a lowly bank watchman whose request for a raise is rejected by haughty officials until the watchman exacts revenge by robbing the bank and finagling a deal, involving immunity, a share of the booty, and marriage to the cashier's daughter. Twain's not-so-subtle moral is "how, by industry, and perseverance, and frugality, and nitroglycerine, and monkey wrenches, and cross-cut saws, and familiarity with the detective system, even the poor may rise to affluence and respectability."[51]

Twain held special scorn for those who preached frugality, hard work, and humility to common laborers but advanced themselves through insider trading, graft, and pretense. In an 1873 speech in London, he caustically lampooned,

> a great and glorious land . . . that has developed a Washington, a Franklin, a William Tweed, a Longfellow, a Motley, a Jay Gould, a Samuel C. Pomeroy, a recent Congress which has never had its equal. . . . I think I can say with pride, that we have some legislatures that bring higher prices than any in the world.[52]

Such themes informed *The Gilded Age*, a novel whose catalogue of inequities includes land swindles, political corruption, bribery, shoddy public works construction, sexual seduction, murder, and speculative fever. Its preface broils with withering sarcasm:

> It will be seen that [the book] deals with an entirely ideal state of society; and the chief embarrassment of the writers in this realm of imagination has been the want of illustrative exam-

ples. In this State where there is no speculation, no inflamed desire for sudden wealth, where the poor are all simple-minded and contented, and the rich are all honest and generous, where society is in a condition of primitive purity and politics is the occupation of only the capable and the patriotic, there are necessarily no materials for a history as we have constructed.[53]

Later, the authors caution readers traveling to Washington, D.C., not to pose as a member of Congress when seeking a room in the city's crowded housing market. When a willing renter is finally located, "she makes you pay in advance. That's what you get for pretending to be a member of Congress. If you had been content to be merely a private citizen, your trunk would have been sufficient security for your board." Capitol Hill is a veritable den of political intrigue, in which "you cannot get an employment of the most trivial nature in Washington. Mere merit, fitness, and capability are useless baggage to you without 'influence.' "[54]

Lost in the brutal world of *The Gilded Age* are simple virtues like honesty, hard work, trust, character, and the sacredness of one's word and reputation. The novel chronicles the Hawkins family as it abandons those virtues, reaps misfortune, then rekindles dignity, family bonds, and morality.

Although some have found the novel's ending mawkish, Twain and Warner echoed working-class values. The Knights of Labor's preamble to its statement of principles pledged to make "moral and social worth—not wealth—the true standard of individual and national greatness."[55] Knights and other laborers upheld exacting codes of personal morality, respectability, and honor. Indeed, many labor organizations, including the Knights, expelled members who lied, abused spouses, drank too much, defrauded landlords, or defaulted on debts.

When investments in the ill-fated Paige typesetting machine bankrupted Twain, his response to debt was more in line with working-class morality than ruthless business logic. Although Twain relied heavily on loans advanced by industrialist Henry Huttleston Rogers, he utterly rejected the advice of friends and well-wishers to turn over his assets to creditors and cut his losses.

Reneging on debt was so common and so open to abuse in the days of laissez-faire capitalism that the Knights of Labor and other unions advocated the passage of mechanics' lien laws to force employers seeking bankruptcy protection to pay wages from seized assets. A favored dodge was for companies to close their doors before payday, organize a phantom board of directors, and reopen under a new name.

Twain's financial plight was real, but he saw responsibility, not opportunity. As he put it, "I was morally bound for the debts, though not legally."[56] Twain rented the family's Hartford home, moved to Europe to economize, and, at the age of sixty, put himself through a grueling schedule of lecturing and writing. Twain persevered even though the Panic of 1893 ruined his publishing house and exacerbated his debt. In 1898, Twain paid off the last of his creditors and returned home humbled, but with his dignity and conscience intact. Howells thought Twain's attitude noble and singular in a Gilded Age climate "so wrapped in commerce and so little used to honor among its many thieves."[57]

A final parallel between Twain and the working class can be seen in their shared ambivalence about civilization and progress. Middle-class society feared "over-civilization," while the working class worried about overpauperization, but editorials on the discontents of modern society were staple fare in the journals of both classes. Twain lamented humanity's progress to the point of misanthropy, see Janet Smith's *Mark Twain on the Damned Human Race*.[58] And, despite his extensive and obsessive investments in technology, Twain in his more sanguine moments agreed with workers that machines could destroy as well as liberate. The denouement to *A Connecticut Yankee* finds Hank Morgan besieged by an alliance of clergymen, nobles, and magicians. He retreats to an electrified compound and electrocutes an attacking army of 25,000, but the weight and bulk of armor-encased knights entombs Morgan and his followers. They sit in their compound to await their demise by foul disease, starvation, and thirst. Kaplan insists that "Hank Morgan *is* Mark Twain." He notes that despite his expressed enthusiasm for "machine culture," Twain "nursed the covert belief that the machine was a destructive force."[59]

Mark Twain thus sought social redemption within a set of values that embraced hard work, practicality, and fair play. Such a worldview had no place for frippery, pretense, or hypocrisy. Twain found consonance in the attitudes of labor unions and social reformers, while the demeanor of the upper crust offended his sense of moral justice.

In many ways, though, Twain was far removed from the world of toil. Twain's support for the working class was tempered by opinions that were at odds with those of laborers. Like many middle-class observers, who rose from humble stock through personal effort, Twain often viewed social problems through the lens of individuals, not systems. It was not capitalism, unequal wealth, or machines per se that caused injustice, rather their misuse by the unworthy or the amoral.

Despite his sympathy toward labor and his biting critiques of power and society, Twain exhibited middle-class traits by never gazing too far below himself. His advocacy of self-reliance and his distrust of radicals were more at home in the Victorian parlor than on the shop floor. He also betrayed his middle-class sympathies in his conspicuous consumption, his placement in well-defined social networks, his preference for nonmanual labor, and his concern for social order.[60]

For all of his professed admiration for labor unions, Twain's formula for reforming society sometimes lay more in asserting middle-class self-reliance than in collective action. Consider Twain's naive scheme for alleviating unemployment. Twain advised an unemployed Calvin Higbie go to a mine superintendent and announce he desired "the refreshment of work and require[d] nothing in return." Twain predicted, "It would be difficult to find [a foreman] who could stand out a whole fortnight without getting ashamed of himself and offering you wages." Within three weeks, he assured, Higbie would either have high wages or himself be foreman. Twain alleged this same advice also worked for an aspiring St. Louis journalist and for his nephew.[61]

This is little more than a bourgeois platitude, as Twain himself must have realized in more reflective moments. Robber barons like Jay Gould felt little compulsion to reward hard work or enterprise, which is why Twain himself cast Gould as a slave driver. Charles Harding, a woolen-mill president in Dedham, Massachusetts, stated bluntly, "When [workers] get starved down to it, then they will go to work at just what you can afford to pay."[62] But, like many in the middle class, Twain paid lip-service to the elevating possibilities of hard work and pluck.

Twain was also a materialist. In *What Is Man?* he wrote, "Any so-called material thing that you want is merely a symbol: you want it not for *itself*, but because it will content your spirit for the moment."[63] Twain spent considerable time and money in symbolically indulging momentary desires. His Hartford home— though not as indulgent as many homes of the period—was an idiosyncratic and playful place, where he frolicked in the conservatory and whiled away the hours in his billiards room. When William Dean Howells first visited, he wrote to his father of the "splendors of the Twain mansion" and catalogued its wonders.[64]

Throughout his life, Twain was drawn to that which was modern and conspicuous. (A notable exception was the telephone, which he allowed in his homes, but hated.) His garb made him instantly recognizable: a sealskin hat and coat for winter, trademark white suits for milder temperatures, and top hat and well-tailored dark suits for other occasions. He enjoyed being photographed on boats and in automobiles. So great was his love of novelty that he invested in everything from marine telegraphy to "plasmon," a ludicrous scheme for developing synthetic food.[65]

Middle-class status also allowed Twain to exploit social networks unavailable to humbler Americans, including Hartford's Monday Evening Club, a gathering of city luminaries. Membership was limited to twenty men who held meetings in private homes. Each gathering featured a twenty-minute essay (assigned to members in alphabetical order), followed by discussion limited to ten minutes per member. Supper, cigars, and chat followed.[66] The Monday Evening Club provided Twain with social contacts as well as a forum. Regular attendees included Hartford socialites like professor J. H. Trumbull, *Hartford Courant* editor Charles Dudley Warner, and the Rev. Horace Bushnell.

Society contacts literally paid off when Twain fell into financial ruin. The knight who rescued him was not a toiler, but rather industrialist Henry Huttleston Rogers, who headed John Rockefeller's Standard Oil trust. Rogers also invested extensively in the stock market and offered no apologies for his singular pursuit of profit. Even among fellow robber barons, Rogers's reputation for ruthlessness gained him the nickname "Hell-Hound Rogers."[67]

Rogers took charge of Twain's finances as if overseeing a merger. He worked out a payment schedule with Twain's creditors, negotiated a Harper contract for his books, and forestalled efforts to put a lien on his home. Not surprisingly, Twain was thankful. He referred to Rogers as "a great man" and his best friend.[68] Later he recalled, "I am grateful to his memory for many a kindness and many a good service he did me, but gratefulest [sic] of all for the saving of my copyrights—a service that saved me and my family from want and assured us of permanent comfort and prosperity."[69]

Twain had few qualms about swallowing his personal pride to aid his family. Contact with Rogers came initially through Twain's Hartford society contacts via his wife. As the daughter of a coal magnate, Olivia ("Livy") was more comfortable in society than her husband. Twain was devoted to her and worried about the effects of financial ruin on Livy's delicate health. It was as much for her sake as his own that Twain entered into dealings with Rogers. He knew what he was getting into and remarked, "He's a pirate all right, but he owns up to it and enjoys being a pirate."[70] In his *Autobiography*, Twain inserted this curious remark while praising Rogers: "gratitude is a debt which usually goes on accumulating, like blackmail."[71]

Still, there is no denying that Twain enjoyed his association with Rogers. He also occasionally hobnobbed with Andrew Carnegie and John Rockefeller, both of whom overlooked Twain's earlier harsh comments about them. Twain admired their business acumen, which stood in marked contrast to his ineptitude on that score. Other powerful family social contacts included ambassador Joseph Choate, Harvard president Charles William Eliot, former president Ulysses S. Grant, financier J. P. Morgan, and publishers Charles Dana and Whitelaw Reid.

As he aged, Twain's ardor for manual laborers cooled. This is reflected in his writings. Early works, like *Roughing It* (1872), *The Gilded Age* (1873), *The Adventures of Tom Sawyer* (1876), and *Life on the Mississippi* (1883) presented heroes who were humble personally and financially. Later protagonists retain humility and a folksy, pragmatic charm but are no longer commoners. *A Connecticut Yankee's* Hank Morgan (1889) is the superintendent of an arms factory; David Wilson, hero of *The Tragedy of Pudd'nhead Wilson* (1894), is a lawyer; and the seldom-read *The American Claimant* (1892) reduxes Colonel Beriah Sellers from *The Gilded Age*, but as an inventor and heir to an earldom.

Other projects found Twain far removed from the hoary hands of toil. He published the memoirs of Ulysses S. Grant in 1885, the *Personal Recollections of Joan of Arc* in 1896, and the sardonic travelogue *Following the Equator* in 1897. Twain's autobiography makes it clear that both the Grant and Joan of Arc projects were near-obsessions. Many critics found Twain's later works to be meandering and uninspired.[72] Twain's final works may well explain why his literary reputation foundered shortly after his death.[73]

Nonetheless, Twain's late writings contain attitudes typical among the middle class. Blumin notes that despite the glamorization of hard work and craft labor gushing from bourgeois pens, the middle class frowned upon manual labor and accorded it ever-diminishing prestige.[74] By the 1890s, mechanization, expansion of factory production, and new methods of management control had thoroughly routinized, homogenized, and de-skilled labor. It is no accident that few roustabouts or riverboat pilots appear in Twain's later works. By century's end, such colorful characters evoked nostalgia but were hardly representative of the toiling masses. Twain preferred wily, proactive individualists to factory drones. It is tempting to conflate Twain with Grant and Joan of Arc, for in each lies the middle-class hope that plucky determination, inner resolve, and morality will lead to earthly success and posthumous glory.

Like many of his middle-class contemporaries, Twain ultimately opted for a world of social order that led him to reject radicalism. As early as 1879, Twain denounced communism as "idiocy" and lampooned its desire to abolish private property.[75]

He remained troubled by extremist views. While his friend William Dean Howells immersed himself in the appeals for the eight anarchists condemned for an 1886 bomb-throwing incident in Chicago's Haymarket Square, Twain remained relatively silent on their fate. Similarly, he confessed to being baffled by commentaries on Tolstoy and socialism forwarded by Howells. Nor did Twain embrace the theories of Henry George, though some in his circle found them fashionable. He admired Edward Bellamy's *Looking Backward*, but did not follow the lead of his friend Sylvester Baxter and declare himself a Nationalist.[76]

Guy Cardwell notes that Twain "was never a consistent social rebel; like the most bourgeois of the bourgeois, he delighted in money and higher living, and he frequently wished to become a member of the eastern establishment."[77] More deftly, Shelley Fisher Fishkin suggests that Twain was in the grand American tradition of inventing and reinventing oneself and thus both a "poor man's pal [and a] rich man's pet."[78] In other words, Twain selected personal values from both Gilded Age workers and plutocrats. His repudiation of radicalism and embrace of industrialists like Rogers, Carnegie, and Rockefeller never prevented Twain from criticizing business practices that he felt were unfair or ignored the public good. Nor did he shy away from mocking the ceaseless lust for wealth (including his own), which he dubbed "a madness."[79] Cavorting with the rich no more made Twain a plutocrat than friendship with William Swinton made him a radical. Twain waived off both groups: "The radical invents the views. When he has worn them out the conservative adopts them."[80]

Twain spent his productive years during one of America's most chaotic periods. The war between labor and capital raged with great intensity, and it was not until after World War I that the hallmarks of a class-bound society were made manifest: accumulation of capital among a select few, inheritable wealth, a permanent wage-earning class, mass production, a deskilled work force, the destruction of radical reform movements, and ever-widening wealth gaps between the rich, the poor, and the middle.

In Twain's lifetime the middle class could still reasonably pose as an alternative to plutocracy or penury. Like contemporaries such as Jane Addams, Edward Bellamy, John Dewey, Richard Ely, William James, and Henry Demarest Lloyd, Twain longed for social evolution, not revolution. This dream sustained Twain's seeming contradictions of praising labor unions while lambasting mass democracy, or heaping scorn upon Jay Gould yet sharing cigars and quips with Henry Huttleston Rogers.

Twain and Charles Dudley Warner championed the middle class in *The Gilded Age.* They noted that Washington society contained "three distinct aristocracies," two of which were corrupt. The "Antiques" were the "cultivated, high-bred old families . . . [and] into this select circle it was difficult to gain admission." They were essentially outmoded aristocrats concerned with form, who long ago outlived their usefulness. More reprehensible still were the "Parvenus," in which "official position, no matter how obtained, entitled a man to a place in it and carried his family with him, no matter whence they sprang. Great wealth gave a man a still greater and nobler place. . . . If the wealth had been acquired by conspicuous ingenuity, with just a pleasant little spice of illegality about it, all the better."[81]

The group Twain and Warner championed was the aristocracy of "the middle ground," who were "blemishless . . . educated and refined." They "had no troublesome appearances to keep up, no rivalries which they cared to distress themselves about, no jealousies to fret over. . . . They were people who were beyond reproach, and this was sufficient."[82] This is the group that eventually rescues morality and virtue from the corruption and greed that is the dramatic crux of the novel. It is also Twain's view of the idealized middle class: serious, honest, productive, and without pretense. Twain romping with Gilded Age Antiques and Parvenus is a real-life parallel to the literary discomfort of Hank Morgan at King Arthur's court or of noble Miles Hendon bowing before young King Edward.

In a symbolic sense, Mark Twain never really left Hannibal, Missouri. Within that community, the Clemens family homestead was neither rude nor grand. Twain's move to Hartford represented his own ideal of social mobility. What he attempted was to dwell intellectually in both Hannibal and Hartford. Perhaps it was a misguided desire, but it was typical of American leveling impulses. Terence Powderly, who spent most of his vital years in the labor movement and never achieved financial security, said of social class: "I have always refused to admit that we have classes in our country. . . . I have always refused to be labeled as belonging to a class, and objected to being classified."[83]

Both Twain and Powderly held increasingly antiquated beliefs in an organic society, in which mutual economic interests bound social classes in a web of interdependence. Both hoped that eventually enlightened entrepreneurs and their employees would come to link individual wealth to social progress, and thus mediate disputes instead of letting them reach bloody impasse. Society would reach its idyllic balance when neither princes nor paupers roamed the land.

Twain's writings reveal the drama of a man suspended between childhood pauperism and adult prosperity. He fits into classic patterns of social mobility, in which one ascends the social ladder in small increments, not large strides to the top.[84] Such small steps often leave the individual with one foot in the world he is entering and the other in the world he leaves behind. Twain's cross-class loyalties, values, and friendships reflect this.

Twain's personal rise exemplifies the fluidity of late-nineteenth-century American society. Elites held inordinate power, the working class struggled, and writers like Twain articulated the social values of the middle class that he and his circle thought represented the social ideal. Twain could thus consistently be neither a plutocrat nor an uncritical friend of organized labor. He was, above all, an apologist for the emergent middle class. Only the "middle ground" could ensure that future "master minds" could, like Twain himself, rise from the masses.[85]

NOTES

1. Mark Twain, *A Connecticut Yankee in King Arthur's Court*, ed. Shelley Fisher Fishkin (New York: Oxford University Press, 1996), 320.

2. For more on Twain's childhood see Ron Powers, *Dangerous Water: A Biography of the Boy Who Became Mark Twain* (New York: Basic Books, 1999).

3. Justin Kaplan, *Mr. Clemens and Mark Twain: A Biography* (New York: Touchstone, 1966), 181.

4. Ibid., 80–81.

5. Ibid., 322.

6. Gabrilowitsch's remarks are contained in a Mark Twain tribute issue of *The Mentor*, vol. 12, no. 4 (May 1924), 22.

7. William Dean Howells, *My Mark Twain* (reprint, Mineola, N.Y.; Dover, 1997), 44.

8. Philip S. Foner, *Mark Twain: Social Critic* (New York: International Publishers, 1958); Paul Carter, "Mark Twain and the American Labor Movement," *The New England Quarterly* (September 1957): 352–58; Maxwell Geismar, *Mark Twain: An American Prophet* (New York: McGraw-Hill, 1970). More recent work has hailed Twain for his progressive views on race and gender, as well as social class. The best of these works is Shelley Fisher Fishkin, *Lighting Out for the Territory: Reflections on Mark Twain and American Culture* (New York: Oxford University Press, 1997). This work is a continuation of her pathbreaking *Was Huck Finn Black? Mark Twain and African-American Voices* (New York: Oxford University Press, 1993). Another fine study is Joe B. Fulton, *Mark Twain's Ethical Realism: The Aesthetics of Race, Class, and Gender* (Columbia: University of Missouri Press, 1997). Numerous Twain biographers emphasize his complexity and multiple personnae. For a sampling see Kaplan, *Mr. Clemens and Mark Twain*; Everett Emerson, *The Authentic Mark Twain: A Literary Biography of Samuel L. Clemens* (Philadelphia: University of Pennsylvania Press, 1984); Andrew Hoffman, *Inventing Mark Twain: The Lives of Samuel Langhorne Clemens* (New York: Morrow, 1997), Guy Caldwell, *The Man Who Was Mark Twain* (New Haven, Conn.: Yale University Press, 1991).

9. Shelley Fisher Fishkin discusses this problem in more detail in *Lighting Out for the Territory*. See especially chap. 1, "The Matter of Hannibal."

10. Foner, *Mark Twain*, 52; Henry Nash Smith, *Mark Twain: The Development of a Writer* (Cambridge, Mass.: Belknap Press, 1962); Kaplan, *Mr. Clemens and Mark Twain*, 148–49, also ch. 10. See also Frederick Anderson, William Gibson, Henry Nash Smith, eds. *Selected Mark Twain-Howells Letters* (New York: Atheneum, 1968), especially chaps. 1–3.

11. For more on Twain's popularity as a speaker see Foner, *Mark*

Twain: Social Critic. See also Marlene B. Vallin, *Mark Twain: Protagonist for the Popular Culture* (Westport, Conn.: Greenwood Press, 1992). For Twain's reaction to the charge that Warner wrote *The Gilded Age,* see Twain to Dr. John Brown, 28 February 1874, Albert Paine, ed., *Mark Twain's Letters* (New York: Harper and Brothers, 1917), 203.

12. Twain to Brown, *Mark Twain's Letters,* 28 February 1874.

13. Karen Halttunen, *Confidence Men and Painted Women: A Study of Middle-Class Culture in America, 1830–1870* (New Haven, Conn.: Yale University Press, 1982), 29.

14. For a brief discussion of Weber and others on the processes of class identification see Leonard Beeghley, *The Structure of Social Stratification in the United States* (Boston: Allyn and Bacon, 2000), especially ch. 2. See also Max Weber, *Economy and Society* (Totowa, N.J.: Bedminster, 1920).

15. "Middling sorts" was a term much used by eighteenth-century commentators. It was a catchall group that included shopkeepers, merchants, landlords, and professionals, who lacked the status and wealth of elites, and were neither self-sufficient producers nor living hand-to-mouth. Mostly, it was viewed as a temporary and transitional category for families on the rise. As Karen Halttunen and Stuart Blumin note, few middling sorts possessed even rudimentary class consciousness. See Halttunen, *Confidence Men and Painted Women,* and Stuart Blumin, *The Emergence of the Middle Class: Social Experience in the American City, 1760–1900* (Cambridge: Cambridge University Press, 1989). A superior study of the entire question of class development is Martin Burke, *The Conundrum of Class: Public Discourse on the Social Order in America* (Chicago: University of Chicago Press, 1995). Burke's introduction contains an excellent overview of shifting debates within the sociological community of how to construe social class.

16. Blumin, *The Emergence of the Middle Class,* quoted from p. 13. See also chaps. 4–8.

17. Alan Trachentenberg, *The Incorporation of America: Culture and Society in the Gilded Age* (New York: Hill and Wang, 1982), 87; David Montgomery, *The Fall of the House of Labor: The Workplace, the State, and American Labor Activism, 1865–1925* (Cambridge: Cambridge University Press, 1989), 318.

18. See Robert Gray, *The Labour Aristocracy in Victorian England* (Oxford: Oxford University Press, 1976). Gray coined the phrase "labour aristocrats" to distinguish the consciousness of skilled artisans from that of manual laborers. I discuss expressions of working-class respectability in my own work. For more see Robert Weir, *Beyond Labor's Veil: The Culture of the Knights of Labor* (University Park: Pennsylvania State University Press, 1996), especially chapters 2, 4, 5, and 7.

19. Halttunen, *Confidence Men and Painted Women*, 29.

20. The term "middle ground" appears in *The Gilded Age*. Mark Twain and Charles Dudley Warner, *The Gilded Age: A Tale of Today* (Garden City, N.Y.: Doubleday, 1969), 244–45.

21. *Journal of United Labor*, 10 October 1889, University Microfilms.

22. Mark Twain, *A Connecticut Yankee in King Arthur's Court*. Quotes (in order) come from pp. 43, 218.

23. For more on the opulence and conspicuous consumption of wealthy Americans see Lewis Erenberg, *Steppin' Out: New York Nightlife and the Transformation of American Culture, 1890–1930* (Westport, Conn.: Greenwood Press, 1981). See also Lawrence Levine, *Highbrow/Lowbrow: The Emergence of Cultural Hierarchy in America* (Cambridge, Mass.: Harvard University Press, 1988). Ironically, Twain's 70th birthday party was held at Delmonico's.

24. Howells's review is found in Louis J. Budd, ed., *Mark Twain: The Contemporary Reviews* (Cambridge: Cambridge University Press, 1999), 292–95.

25. Mark Twain, *Letters From the Earth*, ed., Bernard DeVoto, (Greenwich, Conn.: Crest, 1963), 153–56, 161.

26. Mark Twain, *The Mysterious Stranger and Other Stories* (New York: Signet, 1962). "The Facts Concerning the Recent Carnival of Crime in Connecticut" (1876) is found on pp. 24–41, and "The £1,000,000 Bank-Note" (1893) on pp. 68–88.

27. The Sarah Hale papers are located in the Sophia Smith Collection at Smith College, Northampton, Massachusetts. This quote was taken from Benita Eisler, ed., *The Lowell Offering: Writings by New England Mill Women (1840–1845)* (New York: Harper Colophon, 1962), 185.

28. Eisler, *The Lowell Offering*, 186–87.

29. The *Boston Herald* quote is dated 8 August 1888 and is quoted

from Mary Blewett, ed., *We Will Rise in Our Might: Workingwomen's Voices from Nineteenth-Century New England* (Ithaca, N.Y.: Cornell University Press, 1991), 167–70.

30. Twain, *The Prince and the Pauper* (New York: A Tom Doherty Associates Book, 1988), 88.

31. Fulton, *Mark Twain's Ethical Realism*, 44–45; Hoffman, *Inventing Mark Twain*, 240.

32. Terence V. Powderly, *The Path I Trod*, ed. Harry Carman, Henry David, and Paul Guthrie (New York: AMS, 1968), 390. See also p. 38.

33. John Garraty, ed. *Labor and Capital in the Gilded Age: Testimony Taken by the Senate Committee upon the Relations between Labor and Capital—1883* (Boston: Little, Brown, 1968), 31, 173–74.

34. Mark Twain, *Life on the Mississippi* (New York: Signet, 1961), 103.

35. Ibid., 103, 106. Andrew Hoffman correctly adds that the pilots' association had "one foot in bourgeois prosperity and another in bohemian sensationalism." See Hoffman, *Inventing Mark Twain*, 57. This is in keeping with Twain's subsequent middle-class status and ambivalence. See n. 18 above.

36. For an overview of the Great Upheaval, union activity, and the growth of the Knights of Labor during the Great Upheaval, see Weir, *Beyond Labor's Veil*, introduction.

37. "The New Dynasty," speech delivered before the Monday Evening Club, Hartford, Conn., 22 March 1886.

38. Paul Fatout, ed., *Mark Twain Speaks for Himself* (West Lafayette, Ind.: Purdue University Press, 1978). Also see Mark Twain, *Mark Twain's Autobiography: Volume 2*, (New York: Gabriel Wells, 1925), 256–68.

39. Howells, *My Mark Twain*, 43.

40. R. Kent Rasmussen, ed., *The Quotable Mark Twain: His Essential Aphorisms, Witticisms, and Concise Opinions* (Chicago: Contemporary Books, 1997), 225, 218.

41. Powderly, *The Path I Trod*, 265.

42. Ibid., 60, 342.

43. R. Kent Rasmussen, *Mark Twain A to Z: The Essential Reference to His Life and Works* (New York: Facts on File, 1995). The Rev. Beecher was accused of seducing a prominent parishioner's wife, a charge of which he was surely guilty. During the trial, however,

Beecher's lawyers argued that the Rev. Beecher was counseling an abused woman. His trial ended in a hung jury, though most labor papers convicted Beecher of hypocrisy and denounced him bitterly. See also Kaplan, *Mr. Clemens and Mark Twain*, chap. 8.

Both Terence Powderly and Mark Twain spoke kindly of the Rev. Beecher when he passed away in 1887. By then, some of the anger against Beecher had subsided. Twain's remarks were probably also influenced by the fact that his good friend, the Rev. Joseph Twichell, delivered one of the eulogies. Perhaps just as tellingly, Twain did not attend the funeral.

Powderly's comments were even more generous than Twain's. Among workers, only the industrialist Jay Gould was a greater symbol of arrogance. During the 1877 railroad strikes, Beecher condemned strikers demanding higher pay and impetuously remarked, "Water cost nothing; and a man who can't live on bread and water is not fit to live." Many never forgave him for that remark and when Powderly eulogized Beecher, many fellow Knights of Labor skewered Powderly. See Weir, *Beyond Labor's Veil*, 75–77.

44. Twain, *Great Short Works* (New York: Perennial Classic, 1967), 113–28.

45. Frederick Anderson, Lin Salamo, and Bernard Stein, eds., *Mark Twain's Notebooks and Journals, Volume 2 (1877–1883)* (Berkeley: University of California Press, 1975), 241–42.

46. Howells, *My Mark Twain*, 31.

47. Twain, *A Connecticut Yankee*. See p. 218 for said illustration.

48. Fulton, *Mark Twain's Ethical Realism*, 92

49. *Letters from the Earth*, 103–5.

50. Twain, *The Mysterious Stranger*, p. 102. Twain's use of the name "Pinkerton" could not have been a coincidence. Among members of the Gilded Age working class, "Pinkerton" evoked fear and hatred. The Pinkerton Detective Agency had considerable success in spying on behalf of the Union during the Civil War. After the war, however, the agency turned to industrial espionage, security, and union busting to sustain itself. Employers contracted with the Pinkerton agency to infiltrate union ranks to fire and blacklist union activists. During labor strife, the agency provided guards and paramilitary forces that constituted de facto private armies. So widespread were documented abuses by the Pinkertons that unions called for legislation to control them. Several states enacted such laws.

51. Fatout, *Mark Twain Speaks for Himself,* 78–79.

52. Paul Fatout, ed., *Mark Twain Speaking* (Iowa City: University of Iowa Press, 1976), 75. In this passage, Twain juxtaposes those he finds admirable with those he detests. The names Washington, Franklin, and Longfellow speak for themselves. The other favored name on the list is that of John Lothrop Motley, a noted diplomat and historian of the Dutch Republic who served as U.S. ambassador to Austria

Jay Gould and William Marcy Tweed head the cast of miscreants. The latter was the infamous boss of New York City's corrupt Tammany Hall Democratic political machine. Estimates of the Tweed Ring's plunder of city coffers range from $30 million to as much as $200 million. Tweed was finally jailed in 1873, the year Twain gave his speech.

Also in the news that year was Samuel C. Pomeroy. In Twain's mind, Pomeroy was an example of politics' ability to corrupt. Pomeroy was appointed to the U.S. Senate, where he made a reputation as a Radical Republican during Reconstruction. In 1867, however, Pomeroy was charged with bribery. The charges were not sustained, but Pomeroy was widely suspected of dishonesty. He was not returned to the Senate in 1873, a development that no doubt delighted Twain. Pomeroy ran for president on the National Prohibition ticket in 1884, but fared poorly.

53. Twain and Warner, *The Gilded Age,* 1.

54. Ibid., 181–82. For a discussion of how Twain and Warner based characters in their novel on real-life examples see Bryant French, *Mark Twain and 'The Gilded Age': The Book That Named an Era* (Dallas, Tex.: Southern Methodist University Press, 1965).

55. The Knights of Labor preamble and platform can be found in most issues of *The Journal of United Labor,* available from University Microfilms.

56. Twain, *Autobiography: Volume 2,* 258.

57. Howells, *My Mark Twain,* 55.

58. Among the works dealing with the middle-class fear of "overcivilization" are Elliott Gorn, *The Manly Art: Bare-Knuckle Prize Fighting in America* (Ithaca, N.Y.: Cornell University Press, 1986); Donald J. Mrozek, *Sport and American Mentality 1880–1910* (Knoxville: University of Tennessee Press, 1985); and T. Jackson Lears, *No Place of Grace: Antimodernism and the Transformation of American Culture 1880–1920*

(New York: Pantheon, 1981). One is also reminded of Twain's own youthful embrace of the strenuous life as expressed in works like *Life on the Mississippi* and *Roughing It.*

Twain's misanthropy and pessimism are expressed clearly in his mature works. For example, see Janet Smith, ed., *Mark Twain on the Damned Human Race* (New York: Hill and Wang, 1962).

Working-class papers took up themes of over-civilization. For example, see the editorial "Is Civilization a Failure?" in *The Journal of United Labor,* 28 November 1889.

Among those working-class champions warning of over-pauperization was the Rev. Jesse Jones. See Irwin Yellowitz, ed., *The Position of the Worker in American Society, 1865–1896* (Englewood Cliffs, N.J.: Prentice-Hall, 1969), 103. Jones's comments were originally printed in the May 1875 issue of *Equity.*

The Yellowitz volume also includes Charles Litchman's comments on how mechanization ruined the shoemaking trade. Others taking up the issue include Terence Powderly and Edward Hall of the machinists' union. Powderly's comments are found in Powderly, *The Path I Trod,* p. 54. See *The Journal of United Labor,* 25 November 1886, for remarks by Hall.

59. Kaplan, *Mr. Clemens and Mark Twain,* 297, 300. It should be noted that in *A Connecticut Yankee* Hank Morgan escapes the horrid fate awaiting his comrades. Morgan sleeps until he is returned to his own time, courtesy of a sleeping potion that Merlin tricked him into drinking.

60. Blumin, *The Emergence of the Middle Class.* Blumin sees all these as middle-class "markers."

61. Twain, *Autobiography: Volume 2,* 256–68. The quotes are taken from p. 261.

62. Leon Litwack, ed., *The American Labor Movement* (Englewood Cliffs, N.J.: Prentice-Hall, 1962), 58.

63. The quote was located on *Microsoft Bookshelf 98* CD-ROM.

64. Anderson, Gibson, and Smith, *Selected Mark Twain-Howells Letters,* 71.

65. Samuel Webster, *Mark Twain, Business Man* (Boston: Little, Brown, 1946). See also Fishkin, *Lighting Out for the Territory,* 172–74.

66. Twain, *Autobiography, Volume 1* (New York: Gabriel Wells, 1925), 294–95; Rasmussen, *Mark Twain A to Z* .

67. Kaplan, *Mr. Clemens and Mark Twain,* 321–22.

68. Twain, *Autobiography, Volume 1*, 258.

69. Ibid., 262.

70. Kaplan, *Mr. Clemens and Mark Twain*, 323.

71. Twain, *Autobiography, Volume 1*, 257.

72. For examples of tepid reviews of Twain's works see Budd, *Mark Twain: The Contemporary Reviews*, especially 364, 368–69, 384-85. In 1896, Andrew Lang raised questions about the very wisdom of Twain's Joan of Arc project, while a 1904 *Bookman* review by Peck slammed *Extracts from Adam's Diary* as "pathetic" and "pitiable."

73. Ibid., 648–50. One particularly brutal assessment was a posthumous look at the Twain oeuvre in the *Athenaeum:* "it seems clear that Mark Twain was not a genius, and that only the desire to irritate the worshippers of William Dean Howells . . . could ever induce a man to say he was."

74. Blumin, *The Emergence of the Middle Class*, chap. 4.

75. Anderson et al., *Mark Twain's Notebooks*, 302.

76. For more details on the correspondence alluded to in this section see Anderson et al., *Selected Mark Twain-Howells Letters*, chap. 9.

Henry George's *Progress and Poverty* created a stir with its notion of the "single-tax" that would replace all other revenues and tariffs. George proposed a 100% tax on unimproved lands to which value accrued through no effort on the part of its owner. Although George's ideas did not gain a foothold among the middle class, they were frequent subjects of parlor discussion.

Sylvester Baxter was a Boston reporter who became an ardent Nationalist. This group formed in response to Edward Bellamy's utopian novel *Looking Backward* and was dedicated to realizing through peaceful means the vaguely socialist commonwealth described by Bellamy.

77. Guy Cardwell, *The Man Who Was Mark Twain* (New Haven: Yale University Press, 1991), 47.

78. Fishkin, *Lighting Out for the Territory*, 127.

79. Bernard DeVoto, ed., *Mark Twain in Eruption* (New York: Harper and Brothers, 1940), 65.

80. Twain made this remark in 1898. The quote was located on the *Microsoft Bookshelf 98* CD-ROM. It comes from Twain's *Notebook*, a work edited by Albert Bigelow Paine and published in 1935.

81. Twain and Warner, *The Gilded Age*, 244–45. Admittedly, "Parvenus" are technically members of the middle class. It is a mistake,

though, to view the middle class as monolithic. European scholars often distinguish between the humbler *petite bourgeoisie* (of which Twain would be a member) and the *haute bourgeoisie* of financiers, venture capitalists, and captains of industry.

Modern visitors to Twain's Hartford home might be uncomfortable with locating Twain amid the humbler *petite bourgeoisie*. In classic Marxist terms, the *petite* (or "petty") *bourgeoisie* is a reactionary group of small manufacturers, shopkeepers, artisans, and landowning peasants, who ally themselves with the rich for fear of losing their status and property. In *The Communist Manifesto*, Marx and Engels referred to this group as "social scum." Subsequent writers have used the term *petite bourgeoisie* to refer to professionals, owners of small businesses, shopkeepers, and property owners of modest means. For many, the term is purely descriptive and is stripped of Marx's ideological value judgments.

Still other scholars find too much range in status, wealth, and prestige within the *haute/petite bourgeoisie* breakdown. In addition, the term "bourgeoisie" evokes European social and historical contexts that do not apply directly to North American reality. Mark Twain's material circumstances elevated him above the level of *petite bourgeoisie* as it is currently considered. In modern terms, Twain was part of what is considered—in W. Lloyd Warner's classification— "middle middle class." That, however, is a term neither Twain nor his contemporaries would have recognized. This highlights a terminology conundrum for the Gilded Age. Objectively and materially a middle middle class existed, but if rudimentary consciousness is necessary for class formulation, there was no such group. As we see in Twain's writings, he saw a bifurcated middle class. That alone made him more insightful than many of his contemporaries.

82. Ibid., 258.

83. Powderly, *The Path I Trod*, 424–25.

84. For example, see Peter M. Blau and Otis Dudley Duncan, *The American Occupational Structure* (New York: Wiley, 1967).

85. Twain and Warner, *The Gilded Age*, 258; Twain, *A Connecticut Yankee*, 320.

Mark Twain and Imperialism

Jim Zwick

Mark Twain had direct experience with two major periods in the history of imperialism. He was born on the frontier in 1835, ten years before the phrase "manifest destiny" was used to claim that "Providence" gave the United States a right to spread across the continent. Both in the Americas and worldwide, it was a period of colonial consolidation marked by migrations of European populations into areas that had previously been claimed but not fully controlled. In 1861, Sam Clemens and his brother Orion followed the westward path to Nevada Territory after Orion was appointed territorial secretary. Twain's experiences there and in California provided material for two of his early books, *The Celebrated Jumping Frog of Calaveras County, and Other Sketches* (1867) and *Roughing It* (1872). Both books conclude with sections drawn from letters he wrote for the *Sacramento Union* during an 1866 trip to the Sandwich Islands (Hawaii). That trip provided a personal introduction to the issues of overseas expansion that would become one of his fundamental concerns during the early 1900s. By then a new imperialist surge was underway in which the United States, the European powers, and Japan were in competition for control of markets in China; the United States had acquired an overseas empire spanning from the Caribbean to Asia; and Africa was being divided among the European powers.[1] In 1867, Twain claimed that "civilization and several other diseases" were killing off the native population of Hawaii; in 1901, the "Blessings-of-Civilization Trust" was the culprit, robbing colonized peoples of their land, liberty, and lives.

There is a popular view of America's rise to world power at the beginning of the twentieth century that sees it as a smooth and logical transition from the westward expansion across the continent that preceded it. Adventurers and pioneers reached California and kept going, crossing the Pacific to Hawaii, Guam, and the Philippines. The idea of continuity was promoted after the Spanish-American War by proponents of imperialism to justify annexation of Spain's former colonies, and it was popularized in books such as H. Addington Bruce's *The Romance of American Expansion* (1909). Bruce portrayed a continuous "romance" of expansion from Daniel Boone scouting the western frontier to William McKinley's annexation of Puerto Rico, Hawaii, Guam, and the Philippines.[2] The actual course of events and the ideas behind them were much more complex. During the decades leading up to the Civil War, annexation of territory was viewed within the context of the debate about slavery. No anti-imperialist organization was formed to oppose the Mexican War or the annexation of territory that resulted from it because it was seen primarily as a war for the extension of slavery and opposition was channeled through abolitionist organizations.[3] Throughout the period from the Civil War to the 1890s, proposals for annexation of overseas territories were repeatedly brought before the U.S. Congress. It reluctantly approved the purchase of Alaska in 1867. In the early 1870s, it rejected two treaties for control of a small part of Samoa for use as a naval base before accepting a third proposal in 1878. Treaties to annex the Danish West Indies, Santo Domingo, and Hawaii were all rejected.[4] If the hand of "Providence" was guiding the United States toward world dominion, it was slapped by Congress more often than it was accepted. Although a consensus was achieved after the Civil War in favor of a continental empire, efforts to annex overseas territories continued to face strong opposition even after the Spanish-American War. The treaty that brought that war to a close and ceded Spain's colonies to the United States was ratified by the U.S. Senate by a slim one-vote margin. The debate about imperialism involved interpretations of progress, civilization, and national mission that Mark Twain began to address from the lecture platform more than thirty years before.

The Disease of Civilization

Mark Twain's opposition to imperialism found its most significant literary and organizational expressions from 1900 until his death in 1910, but it can be traced back to a lecture tour on the Sandwich Islands that he started before his first book was published. Twain's 1866 trip to Hawaii was a significant turning point in his career. The Jumping Frog story was published the year before, but he was still struggling to make a living as a writer. When the first steamship line between California and Hawaii was about to open, he proposed to the *Sacramento Union* that they send him there to write a series of letters, assessing conditions in the islands and prospects for future commerce. The opening of the steamship line presented opportunities for expanded trade relations, and there was strong sentiment on the West Coast and among American residents of Hawaii in favor of U.S. annexation of the islands. They feared that if the United States did not annex the islands, Hawaii would fall into British hands, and opportunities for American commerce would be reduced.

In his letters from Hawaii, Mark Twain played into the debate about annexation by providing considerable detail about the Hawaiian sugar industry and its relation to California. In one of his letters he gave a glowing report on the productivity of the industry and suggested that Hawaiian planters were interested in establishing a monopoly in California to sell their product throughout the Pacific coast. He closed the letter with a sweeping vision of California's place in the broader trade with Asia that the new steamship line would facilitate. "We have found the true Northwest Passage. . . . The gateway of this path is the Golden Gate of San Francisco; its depot, its distributing house, is California; her customers are the nations of the earth;

her transportation wagons will be the freight cars of the Pacific Railroad, and they will take up these Indian treasures at San Francisco and flash them across the continent."[5]

Containing a mixture of humor, vivid descriptions of people and scenery, and geographic and economic facts and projections, Twain's letters from Hawaii generated considerable interest in California. After his return from the islands, he took advantage of his new-found fame to start a career as a professional lecturer with "The Sandwich Islands" as his topic. He made his debut on October 2, 1866, at Maguire's Academy of Music in San Francisco, and followed it with a whirlwind three-month tour of other cities and mining towns in California and Nevada. He then brought the lecture through the East and Midwest in 1867 and continued to revise the lecture for later tours through December 1873. Paul Fatout points out that "he used the Islands as a lecture topic more often than any other: almost one hundred times in the United States and England, usually announcing the title as 'Our Fellow Savages of the Sandwich Islands.'"[6]

During the first western tour, Twain undoubtedly knew that he was speaking on a topic of great importance to his local audiences, but his performances were also watched from Hawaii. The *Daily Hawaiian Herald*, established in Honolulu by former *San Francisco Call* editor James J. Ayres, reprinted the *San Francisco Bulletin's* review of Twain's first lecture and later expressed anxiety because Twain would not allow the lecture to be published in full. Ayres founded the *Herald* to advocate U.S. annexation of the islands and was obviously concerned about the influence Twain's speeches might have on public opinion regarding that issue. Available texts and reviews indicate that Twain's western lectures supported the annexationist position by repeating the material about the sugar industry and California trade from his earlier letter for the *Sacramento Union*. When he took the lecture east, however, that material was apparently dropped, and he placed more emphasis on the destruction of the Hawaiian people by the "disease" of civilization.[7]

On March 25, 1867, Twain gave his lecture on "The Sandwich Islands" before an audience in St. Louis, Missouri. The *St. Louis Daily Missouri Democrat's* review provides one of the earliest texts

of the lecture that includes his criticism of the devastating impact of "civilization" on the native Hawaiians: "The white men
came, brought civilization and several other diseases, and now
the race is fast dying out, and will be extinct in about fifty years
hence." He suggested that the islands would then pass to the
United States as "lawful heirs," but he does not seem to have re-
peated his celebration of California's new role in world trade.[8]
After a January 1870 lecture in Jamestown, New York, a member
of the audience wrote a letter to the local paper claiming that
Twain's "intimation that *civilization* was responsible for the de-
crease of population there is another insult to America."[9] Some
appreciated his comments, though. Reviewing his lecture the
month before, the *Philadelphia Evening Bulletin* commented favorably on Mark Twain as a reformer: "Like all men of his temperament he has a hearty hatred of sham, hypocrisy and cant,
whether in religion, social life or politics. Some of his sturdiest
blows have been aimed at the follies of the times; and we believe
that he may, if he chooses, exercise a very considerable influence
as a reformer."[10] Assessments like that were common later in his
life, but it was unusual in 1869 when many people across the
country were laughing at the jokes and comic images in *The Innocents Abroad*.

The death of King Kamehameha V at the end of 1872 revived
the debate about U.S. annexation of Hawaii. The *New York Tribune* solicited an article on the subject from Mark Twain, and he
sent them two long letters that were published on January 6 and
9, 1873. Before the end of the month, Twain had also revised his
lecture on Hawaii and toured with it that year in both the United
States and England. In his letters to the *Tribune*, he expressed a
still more critical view of what was happening in the islands. The
decimation of the native population was no longer an accident of
history:

The traders brought labor and fancy diseases—in other
words, long, deliberate, infallible destruction; and the missionaries brought the means of grace and got them ready. So
the two forces are working along harmoniously, and anybody
who knows anything about figures can tell you exactly when

the last Kanaka will be in Abraham's bosom and his islands in the hands of the whites.

In his second letter, Twain addressed the issue of annexation, writing sarcastically:

> We *must* annex those people. We can afflict them with our wise and beneficent government. We can introduce the novelty of thieves, all the way up from street-car pickpockets to municipal robbers and Government defaulters, and show them how amusing it is to arrest them and try them and then turn them loose—some for cash and some for "political influence."[11]

Here he undermined the idea of a civilizing mission by focusing on corruption at home. He would repeat this argument nearly thirty years later in his writings about the "Blessings-of-Civilization Trust" and its operations in the Philippines, China, and South Africa. In the 1873 letter, Twain continued by using financier Jay Gould, the model for Dan Beard's illustration of the Slave Driver in *A Connecticut Yankee,* and Boss Tweed of Tammany Hall as examples of the baseness of American economic and political "civilization." In his anti-imperialist writings of the early 1900s, the Trusts and Richard Croker of Tammany Hall served the same purpose.

Getting Organized

Mark Twain's January 1873 letters about Hawaii were published in the same month that he and his Hartford neighbor Charles D. Warner began work on *The Gilded Age.* Their novel named an era that was marked by widespread political corruption, the accumulation of great wealth by a few while most lived in poverty, of rapid industrialization and urbanization, and expansion of national networks of railroads and cable lines. In the late 1860s and early 1870s, Mark Twain expressed his opposition to the annexation of Hawaii as an individual. Before the issue of U.S. imperialism reemerged at the end of the century, a national network of reform organizations was established that facilitated the creation of the Anti-Imperialist League, the country's first national anti-imperialist organization. Widespread concern about the social, political, and economic problems of the era gave strength to new movements for reform. Improvements in transportation and communications facilitated coordination among reformers, and many local efforts quickly became national models. For example, Hull House, the country's first urban settlement house, was founded in Chicago in 1889. In 1900, there were more than one hundred settlement houses in cities across the country.[12] The 1880s and 1890s also saw the formation of the Indian Rights Association, the national single tax and social gospel movements, the American Anti-Lynching League, and numerous other reform organizations and clubs. The country was emerging from the Gilded Age and entering the Progressive Era.

Published in 1879, Henry George's *Progress and Poverty* and the single tax movement it inspired had a profound influence on efforts for reform and on the anti-imperialist movement that emerged in the late 1890s. It focused attention on the growing disparities of wealth and poverty taking place in the United States after the Civil War. Like Twain's earlier criticism of the devastating impact that "civilization" had on the population of Hawaii, George's *Progress and Poverty* undermined conventional concepts of unilinear progress by arguing that progress *caused* poverty. Noting that the great advances in technology made during the nineteenth century had not eliminated poverty and a host of related problems, he argued that "poverty deepens as wealth increases, and wages are forced down while productive power grows, because land, which is the source of all wealth and the field of all labor, is monopolized."[13] As long as private monopolies in land ownership continued, increases in the capacity for production would be met by increases in the fees land owners charged for its use. He proposed a natural rights view of land as common property that should be taxed by the state. Private ownership of land could continue, but taxes on land values should increase so the unearned wealth generated by technological and material progress could be used to benefit the community as a whole. At the same time that he argued for increased taxation on land values, George proposed that all other taxes should be eliminated, and his proposal became popularly known as the "single tax." Especially after his *Protection or Free Trade* was published in 1886, free trade became an international corollary to the single tax. George argued that protective tariffs failed to raise the living standards of workers for the same reason technological and other material progress had failed: any increase in their incomes was met with an increase in the "tribute which those who own the land can demand for its use." He proposed a "true free trade" based on abolition of monopolies in land ownership and elimination of all other taxes levied on economic transactions.[14]

George and many of his followers presented the single tax as a comprehensive panacea for society's ills. They expected that it would end speculation in land and make parcels of previously unused land available for housing, farming, and other productive uses. It would increase employment, raise wages, end poverty, and reduce urban crowding. In *Progress and Poverty*, George carried the argument even further, writing that it would "afford free scope to human powers, lessen crime, elevate morals, and taste, and intelligence, purify government and carry civilization to yet nobler heights." In an 1895 speech before the Universal Peace Union, William Lloyd Garrison, son of the famous abolitionist, argued that the single-tax was "the fundamental reform of the present generation, as slavery was of the past."[15]

During the late 1800s and early 1900s, the single tax movement was a home-grown rival of the socialist movement in the United States. Because it advocated radical tax reform instead of a more revolutionary transformation of society, it gained support from many middle-class reformers as well as workers and farmers. Twain developed at least a brief interest in the single tax in the late 1880s. An article on monopoly of land ownership, entitled "Archimedes," appeared under the byline "Twark Main" in the *Australian Standard* in 1889, and single-taxer Dan Beard's illustrations for *A Connecticut Yankee in King Arthur's Court*, also published that year, were read by the *Standard* as pointing out "the fundamental cause and radical cure for wrongs" described in the text. Twain later endorsed Beard's interpretation of the book as his own: "Beard got everything that I put into that book and a little more besides. . . . Beard put it all in that book. I meant it to be there. I put a lot of it there and Beard put the rest."[16] By early 1893, Mark Twain's publishing company, Charles L. Webster & Co., had published four of Henry George's books and was preparing a complete set. Besides any appreciation Twain may have had for George's works, this was a good business decision because of their immense popularity. In 1905, George's son claimed that more than two million copies of *Progress and Poverty* were in circulation and that as many as three million copies of his other books had been published.[17]

Along with the formation of new movements for domestic reforms, national organizations were also created in the 1890s to address international concerns. In April 1891, Mark Twain was a founding member of the American Friends of Russian Freedom, a national solidarity organization created in Boston to support the Russian Revolution. Its stated goal was "to aid by all moral and legal means the Russian patriots in their efforts to obtain for their country Political Freedom and Self-Government." A diverse group of intellectuals was brought together under its banner, including many who would later join the Anti-Imperialist League. Among them were Thomas Wentworth Higginson, William Lloyd Garrison, Jr., Charles G. Ames, Frank B. Sanborn, E. Winchester Donald, Frederic D. Huntington, John W. Chadwick, W. N. McVickar, and Francis J. Garrison.[18] Two months after the formation of the American Friends of Russian Freedom, Mark Twain closed his Hartford residence and moved his family to Europe to reduce their living expenses. Although the family did not return to live in the United States again until 1900, Twain's support for the Russian Revolution was far from over. He included a section about the plight of Siberian exiles in *The American Claimant* (1892) and finally fulfilled an 1890 promise to write an essay for the cause with "The Czar's Soliloquy," published in 1905. He agreed to chair a benefit dinner for Maxim Gorky the following year, and his name was probably included in the list of officers of the American Friends of Russian Freedom until he died.

An Old Empire and the New Imperialism

During his overseas sojourn of the 1890s, Mark Twain had a remarkably diverse range of experiences related to both the colonial
consolidation that had taken place earlier in the century and the
escalating international belligerency that marked the "new imperialism" of the late 1800s and early 1900s. His 1895–1896 speaking
tour of the British Empire, recorded in *Following the Equator* (1897),
took him through India, Sri Lanka, Australia, New Zealand, and
South Africa, all areas where he could see European encroach-
ments on native territories. In 1895, when President Grover Cleveland threatened war with Great Britain to enforce the Monroe
Doctrine during a border dispute between British Guiana and
Venezuela, Twain was in Australia. In the uncomfortable position
of being a guest of an empire with which his own country might
soon be at war, he opened his next speech by stating that "blood is
thicker than water, and there must be no bloodshed between England and America."[19] During the South African leg of the tour,
he witnessed the expansion of British interests there that would
lead to the Boer War three years after his visit.

Twain was living in Europe during the Spanish-American
War, the start of the Philippine-American War, and the Boxer
Uprising in China. Believing that the war with Spain was being
fought by the United States solely to liberate Cuba from Spanish
oppression, he was offended by European commentaries on the
war that portrayed the United States as having imperial ambitions. "Brutal, base, dishonest? We? Land thieves? Shedders of innocent blood? We? Traitors to our official word? We?" he wrote
rhetorically in "A Word of Encouragement for Our Blushing
Exiles," an essay addressed to Americans in Europe he wrote in
1898 but decided not publish. That Twain clearly believed his
country was none of those things highlights the antiseptic view
of westward expansion across the North American continent
that allowed him to accept that form of imperialism while opposing annexation of overseas territories. He expressed unreserved
enthusiasm about the Spanish-American War in private correspondence. "I have never enjoyed a war—even in written
history—as I am enjoying this one," he wrote to his friend Joseph

H. Twichell in June 1898. "For this is the worthiest one that was ever fought, so far as my knowledge goes. It is a worthy thing to fight for one's freedom; it is another sight finer to fight for another man's. And I think this is the first time it has been done."[20]

After enthusiastically endorsing the war to "free Cuba" while it was being fought, Twain was sorely disappointed with the Treaty of Paris that brought it to a close. Had he revised "A Word of Encouragement for Our Blushing Exiles" after reading the treaty, he might have replaced each rhetorical "We?" with "Yes!" Under its terms, the United States gained control of Cuba, Puerto Rico, Guam, and the Philippines. Only Cuba was promised eventual independence. The United States agreed to pay Spain $20 million for the Philippines. Twain later described that payment as "the stupendous joke of the century" because Spain had already lost control of the islands to the Filipinos before selling them to the United States. The payment was the United States' "entrance fee into society—the Society of Sceptred Thieves," he commented. "We are now on a par with the rest of them."[21]

The Anti-Imperialist League

Twain was far from alone in his opposition to American imperialism. On June 15, 1898, two days before he wrote his enthusiastic letter to Twichell about the Spanish-American War, a mass meeting was held in Boston to "protest against the adoption of a so-called Imperial Policy by the United States."[22] Anti-Imperialist Committees of Correspondence were organized that used contacts in reform organizations throughout the United States to form a national movement in opposition to the annexation of Spain's colonies at the conclusion of the war. The creation of the Anti-Imperialist League was formally announced on November 19, 1898. "We are in full sympathy with the heroic struggles for liberty of the people in the Spanish Islands," its first appeal for membership declared, "and therefore we protest against depriving them of their rights by an exchange of masters." Its first action was to circulate a petition "against any extension of the sovereignty of the United States over the Philippine Islands, in any event, or other foreign territory, without the free consent of the people thereof, believing such action would be dangerous to the Republic, wasteful of its resources, in violation of constitutional principles, and fraught with moral and physical evils to our people."[23] After narrowly failing in its attempt to block ratification of the Treaty of Paris in February 1899, the League turned its attention to broader national mobilization aimed at defeating the policy of imperialism at the polls during the 1900 presidential election. In October 1899, a national conference of anti-imperialists was held in Chicago in an attempt to shift the center of the movement away from Boston. A new Chicago-based American Anti-Imperialist League was formed to facilitate organization of local branches and coordinate an anti-imperialist electoral strategy. Local branches were formed in cities across the country and an expanded national slate of officers was developed with prominent representatives from states and territories from coast to coast.

Single-taxers formed and served as presidents and/or secretaries of most of the Anti-Imperialist League's local branches, including the Anti-Imperialist League of New York in which Twain would serve as a vice president. The issue of imperialism divided nearly every other reform movement in the United States, including the peace movement, but single-taxers were essentially unanimous in their opposition. They saw imperialism as yet another consequence of monopolies in land ownership and as a poor excuse for avoiding the root causes of social problems. Joseph Fels, a vice president of the Anti-Imperialist League and a major financier of the single tax movement, argued, for example, that it would be unnecessary to have foreign markets to sell surplus goods if the single tax was established: "The unemployed and partially employed population and the underpaid workers form a potential market far greater than any war of conquest could secure. To secure this new market, labor need but be given access to the natural resources now withheld by private monopolists."[24] The introduction of modern commercial enterprises and political practices in the colonies would add to the wealth of a few at home, while bringing poverty and moral and physical destruction to the native populations.

Among the League's other officers were many people whose names are still widely known today, including former president Grover Cleveland; philosophers William James and John Dewey; American Federation of Labor President Samuel Gompers; urban reformers Jane Addams and Josephine Shaw Lowell; Society for Ethical Culture founder Felix Adler; and Rabbi David Philipson, a leading figure in American Reform Judaism during the first half of the twentieth century. Many of Twain's friends were also officers of the League, among them William Dean Howells, Andrew Carnegie, Henry Van Dyke, Thomas Wentworth Higginson, C. E. S. Wood, and Carl Schurz.[25] With a platform stating that imperialism was "the paramount issue" of the day, the League was able to bring together a remarkably diverse group of officers, many of whom took opposing sides on other issues. Ernest Crosby, a single-taxer and president of the Anti-Imperialist League of New York, once used Andrew Carnegie, one of its vice presidents, as an example of a rich man engaging in "orgies of charity" that were "just a drop in the bucket" compared with the wealth he had amassed at the expense of workers. "The attempt of Mr. Carnegie to die poor will remain one of the magnificent failures of history," he concluded sarcastically.[26] The League also included people who took opposing sides on domestic racial issues. Many opposed the annexation of foreign territories because they thought the "colored" peoples of the colonies would eventually become citizens with a voice in the U.S. government. Others who were critical of domestic racism opposed the annexation of colonies because they feared that racially diverse peoples located thousands of miles away would receive even worse treatment. Leaders of the movement to establish Jim Crow laws in the South, like Benjamin R. Tillman and Josephus Daniels, were officers of the Anti-Imperialist League right along with abolitionists George S. Boutwell and Thomas Wentworth Higginson; two of the most militant "neoabolitionists" who defended the rights of African Americans at the turn of the century, Herbert S. Bigelow and Charles B. Spahr; and Moorfield Storey, first president of the National Association for the Advancement of Colored People (NAACP). The League's official position, as stated in its platform, was that "all men, of whatever race or color, are entitled to life, liberty, and the pursuit of happiness."[27]

During a time when African Americans were being disfranchised in the South and women had not yet gained the right to vote, the practical politics of forming a broad coalition with an electoral strategy initially restricted the League's slate of officers to white males. In 1899, both a "Colored Auxiliary" and a "Women's Auxiliary" of the Anti-Imperialist League were formed in Boston, and an Illinois Women's Anti-Imperialist League was formed in 1900. In February 1900, Rev. Henry L. Phillips of the Church of the Crucifixion in Philadelphia broke the League's color line when he became a vice president of its Philadelphia branch. In January of the following year, after the presidential election, Josephine Shaw Lowell became the first female officer of one of the League's major urban branches when she was made a vice president of the Anti-Imperialist League of New York.[28]

Mark Twain returned to the United States on October 15, 1900, during the height of the debate about imperialism leading up to the presidential election in November. He immediately announced his opposition to imperialism in interviews given at the docks in New York City. "I am an anti-imperialist," he declared. "I am opposed to having the eagle put its talons on any other land." His initial statements also highlighted the anti-imperialist movement's inability to make imperialism the "paramount issue" of the presidential campaign. When asked by a reporter if he was going to vote for the anti-imperialist candidate, Democrat William Jennings Bryan, Twain replied, "I guess not. I'm rather inclined toward McKinley, even if he is an imperialist." In a January 4, 1901, speech, he explained that his opposition to both Bryan's Free Silver financial policies and William McKinley's imperialism kept him from voting for either candidate. Bryan's insistence on including Free Silver in the Democratic Platform for the 1900 presidential campaign alienated many anti-imperialists who supported the Gold Standard for currency and it, along with his close relationships with Southern Democrats and the corrupt Tammany Hall political machine in New York, was enough to split the anti-imperialist coalition on election day.[29]

After focusing on the presidential election for almost two

years, its defeat at the polls left the anti-imperialist movement without a clear strategy. Splits developed within the movement, and the Anti-Imperialist League entered a period of relative quiet as its officers assessed their options. It was during this period that Mark Twain emerged as the country's most prominent and outspoken opponent of imperialism. He raised the issue of imperialism repeatedly in speeches, interviews, and writings from November through February, addressing conditions in the Philippines, China, and South Africa and producing two of the anti-imperialist movement's most widely disseminated publications: "A Salutation Speech from the Nineteenth Century to the Twentieth" and "To the Person Sitting in Darkness." In January 1901, *The Public*, a Chicago-based weekly, reprinted Twain's "Salutation Speech" along with new century greetings by William McKinley, Theodore Roosevelt, and William Jennings Bryan. Twain held no public office, but he was grouped with the president, the vice president-elect, and their opponent in the recently concluded presidential election. The following month, while "To the Person Sitting in Darkness" was creating controversy throughout the country, the *Springfield Republican* (Mass.) editorialized that "Mark Twain has suddenly become the most influential anti-imperialist and the most dreaded critic of the sacrosanct person in the White House that the country contains."[30] In January, Twain agreed to serve as a vice president of the Anti-Imperialist League of New York, and in February he gave it permission to reprint "To the Person Sitting in Darkness" in pamphlet form. By bringing a new and widely accessible voice to the cause at a critical juncture, Mark Twain helped to revive the anti-imperialist movement after the presidential election. For both Twain and the movement as a whole, however, the battle was just beginning. Warfare in the Philippines would continue throughout the rest of Mark Twain's life.

The Philippine-American War

Although the Spanish-American War is still usually thought of as centering on Cuba, George Dewey's defeat of the Spanish fleet in

Manila Bay on May 1, 1898, was the first major battle of the war and the surrender of Manila to the Americans in a mock battle staged August 13th was its last, occurring a day after terms of peace were agreed upon on the Caribbean front. Filipinos had been fighting for their country's independence since 1896. Believing that the United States would grant the country independence at the end of the Spanish-American War, they cooperated with the U.S. military to defeat the Spanish at Manila, surrounding the city on the land while the U.S. navy controlled the Bay and waited for additional troops to arrive from San Francisco. With the Spanish confined to Manila and a few other garrisoned towns, Philippine independence was declared on June 12 and the government of the Philippine Republic was organized under the leadership of General Emilio Aguinaldo. The Philippine Republic is notable in world history as the first republic formed in Asia through an anti-colonial revolution. The United States refused to recognize the new republic however, and negotiated the purchase of the Philippines from Spain at the end of the Spanish-American War. It claimed legal title to the entire archipelago, but the United States actually controlled only Manila and its immediate suburbs. With the exception of a few scattered Spanish garrisons, Filipinos controlled the rest of the country. On December 21, 1898, President William McKinley issued the Benevolent Assimilation Proclamation, stating the government's intention to retain control of the Philippines and to maintain "the strong arm of authority, to repress disturbance and to overcome all obstacles to the bestowal of the blessings of good and stable government upon the people of the Philippine Islands under the free flag of the United States."[31] On February 4, 1899, two days before the U.S. Senate ratified the treaty giving the United States possession of the Philippines, it became the site of a new war of conquest as U.S. troops tried to extend their control beyond Manila. Opposition to the Philippine-American War became a major focus of Mark Twain's organizational and literary efforts throughout the remainder of his life.[32]

The Philippine-American War was the United States's first protracted war in Asia, and it was arguably the longest war in U.S. history. When it is mentioned in American history texts, it is usually dated from 1899 to July 4, 1902, when President Theodore Roo-sevelt issued a proclamation that the "insurrection" was over.[33] Roosevelt's declaration was made less than a week after the U.S. Senate concluded embarrassing hearings on army atrocities in the Philippines, and it had more symbolic meaning and domestic po-litical influence than anything else. Warfare continued in the northern provinces of the Philippines through 1906, but in No-vember 1902, the U.S. Philippine Commission passed the Bando-lerismo Statute or Brigandage Act, which defined all further armed resistance to U.S. rule as banditry. Although the war con-tinued, it was essentially defined away. Before the northern provinces were fully "pacified," the United States opened the war's second front against the Muslim Filipinos of the southern Philippines. Using a "divide and conquer" strategy, General John C. Bates negotiated a controversial treaty with the Muslim Filipinos in 1899 that forestalled warfare by promising them au-tonomy. Mark Twain and other anti-imperialists were outraged by this treaty on religious grounds, viewing it as an endorsement of polygamy and slavery while U.S. troops were fighting Christian Filipinos in the northern provinces. In the same year the treaty was negotiated, more then seven million Americans petitioned Congress protesting the seating of Brigham H. Roberts, the elected representative from Utah, because he had once been con-victed of polygamy. George Ade later used the treaty with the Muslim Filipinos to create a musical comedy, *The Sultan of Sulu*, that had a successful run on Broadway in 1902 and 1903. In early 1903, U.S. troops were ordered to occupy the southern islands. Moro Province was formed under U.S. military rule in September, and in March 1904, the U.S. unilaterally abrogated the Bates Agree-ment. One of the worst massacres of the war occurred in the south in March 1906, and it provided Twain with a subject for two days of scathing autobiographical dictations. United States troops under the command of General Leonard Wood trapped a group of 900 Muslim Filipinos-men, women, and children—in the ex-tinct volcanic crater of Bud Dajo and fired down at them from the heights above for four days until all were reported dead. That chil-dren were killed in the massacre helped Twain to overcome his earlier religious antipathy toward the Muslim Filipinos. "They were mere naked savages, and yet there is a sort of pathos about it when that word *children* falls under your eye," he commented, "for it always brings before us our perfectest symbol of innocence and helplessness; and by help of its deathless eloquence color, creed and nationality vanish away and we see only that they are children—merely children." Wood's order to "kill or capture" the Filipinos provided steam for one of Twain's angriest assessments of the conduct of the U.S. army in the Philippines: "Apparently our little army considered that the 'or' left them authorized to kill *or* capture according to taste, and that their taste had remained what it has been for eight years, in our army out there—the taste of Christian butchers."[34] In June 1913, a similar massacre, led by General John J. Pershing, resulted in the deaths of about 500 Muslim Filipinos at Bud Bagsak. United States military government of Moro Province was not lifted until December of that year, more than three years after Mark Twain's death.

Biographical Consequences and Legacies

For Mark Twain and many other anti-imperialists, the conquest of the Philippines represented a betrayal of American traditions. They were quick to draw comparisons between the revolutions of 1776 and 1896, with General Emilio Aguinaldo, first president of the Philippine Republic, portrayed as a "Filipino George Washington." In a biographical review essay written in 1901, Mark Twain gave Aguinaldo even higher praise, comparing him with Joan of Arc, the liberator of France. Twain later described Joan of Arc as "easily and by far the most extraordinary person the human race has ever produced."[35] Aguinaldo was one of a select few, including Helen Keller and Émile Zola, that Twain honored with such a comparison.

Twain had great sympathy for Aguinaldo and his cause, but he also feared what the reversal of traditions meant for his own country. In a series of historical fantasies written in 1901 and 1902, he projected the fall of the American republic and its replacement by either a despotic monarchy or a repressive military dictatorship. "Lust of conquest had long ago done its work," he wrote; "trampling upon the helpless abroad had taught her, by a natural process, to endure with apathy the like at home; multitudes who had applauded the crushing of other people's liberties, lived to suffer for their mistake in their own persons."[36] Such writings have often been interpreted as a product of a personal despair and cynicism that developed after the death of his daughter Susy in 1896, but he was far from alone in expressing such views in the early 1900s. He was an officer of an organization that routinely presented the country's options in stark dichotomies such as "democracy or militarism," "republic or empire," and "liberty or despotism." His critical views of imperialism and its impact on American society were widely shared by other prominent men and women of the time.

Nor were his anti-imperialist writings and activities merely part of an optimistic public persona (Mark Twain) that was put forward by a deeply pessimistic author (Samuel Clemens).[37] At the same time that "Mark Twain" was making public pronouncements against imperialism, "Samuel L. Clemens" was listed on the letterheads and in the annual reports of the Anti-Imperialist League. He also frequently discussed the issues with his friends, both privately and publicly. After his Hartford friend and pastor, Joseph Twichell, advised him not to make public statements against imperialism, Twain replied, "if you teach your people— as you teach me—to hide their opinions when they believe the flag is being abused and dishonored, lest the utterance do them and a publisher a damage, how do you answer for it to your conscience?"[38] Other friends supported his efforts. William Dean Howells, his close friend and literary advisor, encouraged publication of "To the Person Sitting in Darkness" in the *North American Review*, and Andrew Carnegie offered to finance its publication in pamphlet form. Carl Schurz sent him some of the Anti-Imperialist League's publications in December 1900, and Twain seconded a motion put forward by Schurz at a meeting of the officers of the Anti-Imperialist League of New York the following year. His participation in the anti-imperialist movement strengthened those and other friendships and led to new acquaintances and political involvements. In December 1902, he dined with the prominent British anti-imperialist, John A. Hobson, author of *Imperialism: A Study* (1902), and in 1904, he was invited by Edmund D. Morel, founder of the Congo Reform Association, to support his effort to form an American branch.

In 1905, some of Mark Twain's fears about the fate of democracy in the United States seemed to be confirmed when Harper and Brothers, his exclusive publisher, refused to publish two of his best polemical writings. On March 22, "The War Prayer" was rejected by *Harper's Bazaar* as "not quite suited to a woman's magazine." A few days later, Twain wrote to his friend Dan Beard, to whom he had read the story, "I don't think the prayer will be published in my time. None but the dead are permitted to tell the truth."[39] The following month, "King Leopold's Soliloquy," Twain's major essay about the Belgian king's brutal rule of the Congo Free State, was similarly rejected. Harper and Brothers was "doubtful about the commercial wisdom of dipping into Leopold's stinkpot," Twain explained in a letter to Edmund D. Morel of the English Congo Reform Association. Because of his exclusive contract with Harper and Brothers, Twain had to obtain its permission to allow the American Congo Reform Association to publish the essay in pamphlet form. His frustration was exacerbated by a misunderstanding that delayed release of the manuscript until the end of June.[40] While still waiting for the pamphlet to be published, he protested his treatment by Harper and Brothers by contributing an article on "Christian Citizenship" for anonymous publication in the September 2, 1905, issue of *Collier's* magazine and challenging his editor at Harper and Brothers to locate the breach of contract. After those experiences with his publisher, Twain stopped writing about imperialism for publication, and four months later, in January 1906, he turned his attention to his autobiography, a project he planned for publication after his death. He continued to speak out against imperialism in public speeches, interviews, and letters to the press that did not have to be channeled through his publisher, but he set aside such literary works as "The War Prayer," his 1906 comments on the Moro Massacre, and the anti-imperialist chapter in *Captain Stormfield's Visit to Heaven* for posthumous publication. "In America—as elsewhere—free speech is confined to the dead," he wrote in his private notebook in 1905.[41]

Ironically, after Mark Twain's death, his anti-imperialist writings fell victim to a denial of empire similar to that which he and other anti-imperialists had maintained in relation to the conquest of the North American continent. In American history texts, it is not unusual to find the fifteen-year Philippine-American War treated in a few paragraphs at the end of a chapter on the three-month Spanish-American War. The nearly fifty years of U.S. colonial rule of the Philippines is often masked by euphemisms about the countries' "shared history." Of the colonies acquired in 1898 and 1899, only Cuba and the Philippines were granted independence, but mention of an American empire can provoke an outcry like Twain's concerning the Spanish-American War: "Brutal, base, dishonest? We? Land thieves? Shedders of innocent blood? We?" Although the denial of empire became most acute after World War II, when the word "imperialism" became part of the verbal ammunition deployed during the Cold War, censorship of Twain's anti-imperialist writings began decades earlier. Hoping to preserve what he described as "the traditional Mark Twain" and the "Harper Mark Twain property," Albert Bigelow Paine, his biographer and first literary executor, silently edited many writings to remove passages about the Philippine-American War before including them in posthumous editions.[42] After literary scholars in the Soviet Union accused the United States of official censorship of Twain's social and political writings in 1959, many of Twain's anti-imperialist writings were reprinted in the United States for the first time in more than fifty years. Since then they have been reprinted and quoted as antiwar literature relevant to the war in Vietnam, interventions in Central America, and the Gulf War of the early 1990s.

Although most of Twain's anti-imperialist writings have now been published in full, Paine's vision of "the traditional Mark Twain" has endured. Public celebrations of the author held in the United States typically feature jumping frogs, river rafting, and avoiding work by getting other people to whitewash fences. Most Americans had little context for understanding the announcement made in April 2000 that a monument to Mark Twain would be constructed in a new José Martí Anti-Imperialist Square opposite the U.S. diplomatic mission in Havana, Cuba. Along with a statue of Martí, the square will house monuments to other socialist and national heroes from around the world. The United States will be represented by monuments to Abraham Lincoln, Twain, and Martin Luther King, Jr.[43] Twain liked to joke that he was a "statesman without salary," but even he would be surprised to find himself being honored alongside the "Great Emancipator" and one of the most influential civil rights leaders of the twentieth century. To understand how Twain could deserve such an honor, we need to recognize the historical significance of his organizational affiliations. The American Friends of Russian Freedom was one of the first modern solidarity organizations formed in the United States. The Anti-Imperialist League was the country's first national anti-imperialist organization. The American Congo Reform Association was the American branch of what Adam Hochschild describes as "the first great international human rights movement of the twentieth century."[44] After Twain's death, those organizations were followed by a succession of other anti-imperialist, noninterventionist, solidarity, and human rights organizations. Especially since 1960, when the Fair Play for Cuba Committee was formed, they have become a major force in foreign policy debates within the United States. Thus, Mark Twain's roles in the historical development of the movements reflect a different significance today than he and his contemporaries might have assigned to them one hundred years ago, when they were more concerned with the limits of their ability to influence policy than the legacy of dissent they were leaving to posterity.

NOTES

1. In *Imperialism: From the Colonial Age to the Present* (New York: Monthly Review Press, 1978), 29, 35, Harry Magdoff estimates that European colonial powers and their descendants in the Americas controlled 35 percent of the world's surface in 1800, 67 percent in 1878, and 85 percent by 1914. Although he dates the shift from the period of colonial consolidation to the "new imperialism" in the mid-1870s, 1893 is a more significant date in U.S. history. In that year the western frontier

was declared closed, and American residents of Hawaii overthrew its monarchy and presented a petition for U.S. annexation.

2. H. Addington Bruce, *The Romance of American Expansion* (New York: Moffat, Yard & Co., 1909).

3. See Philip S. Foner and Richard C. Winchester, eds., *The Anti-Imperialist Reader: A Documentary History of Anti-Imperialism in the United States*, vol. 1, *From the Mexican War to the Election of 1900* (New York: Holmes & Meier, 1984), xvii, 3–40.

4. Hawaii was finally annexed in July 1898, when its location between San Francisco and the Philippines increased its strategic importance during the Spanish-American War. The Danish West Indies (now the U.S. Virgin Islands) were annexed during World War I, when they were seen as crucial bases for defense of the Panama Canal Zone.

5. A. Grove Day, ed., *Mark Twain's Letters from Hawaii* (New York: Appleton-Century, 1966), 274. Brian Collins, "Presidential Reconstructions: Mark Twain's Letters from Hawaii and the Integration of Civil Society," *American Studies* 37 (Spring 1996): 51–62, highlights other relevant aspects of Twain's writings from Hawaii, including how his portrayals of "savage" and "civilized" played into contemporary debates about imperialism.

6. Paul Fatout, ed., *Mark Twain Speaking* (Iowa City: University of Iowa Press, 1976), 4.

7. See chapter 22, "'Mark Twain' Doing the Islands," in James J. Ayres, *Gold and Sunshine: Reminiscences of Early California* (Boston: Richard G. Badger, 1922), 223–33; and the articles collected in Barbara Schmidt, ed., *Mark Twain in the Daily Hawaiian Herald*, http://www.twainquotes.com/dhhindex.html (Nov. 18, 2000). Twain constantly revised the lecture and it is impossible to know exactly what was included at different times because he did not allow the full text to be published. The discussion here is based largely on a comparison of the reviews published in newspapers across the country. It is possible that the shift in emphasis seen in the reviews is a reflection of the reviewers' interests rather than changes in the lecture. It seems more likely, though, that Twain was catering to his audiences. There was little support for the annexation of Hawaii in the East and Midwest, and although Twain's celebration of California trade was very relevant to audiences there, it might not have interested people in New York and St. Louis.

8. "Mark Twain at the Mercantile Library Hall," *St. Louis Daily Missouri Democrat* (March 26, 1867) http://etext.virginia.edu/railton/onstage/stldemo.html, in Stephen Railton, ed., *Mark Twain in His Times*, http://etext.virginia.edu/railton/index2.html (Nov. 18, 2000). Later in 1867, Mark Twain published "Information Wanted," a comic sketch satirizing the government's plan to purchase the island of St. Thomas. In *Mark Twain: Social Critic* (New York: International Publishers, 1958), 240, Philip S. Foner notes that "Twain's satire attracted wide attention" and "had a devastating effect on the move to annex St. Thomas." "Information Wanted" was first published in the *New York Tribune* (Dec. 18, 1867) and later collected in *Sketches, New and Old* in 1875 (reprint, New York: Oxford University Press, 1996), 123–25.

9. "Mark Twain Criticised—An Indignant Spectator," *Jamestown Journal* (Jan. 28, 1870), http://etext.virginia.edu/railton/onstage/sandrev4.html, in Railton, *Mark Twain in His Times* (Nov. 18, 2000).

10. "Mark Twain," *Philadelphia Daily Evening Bulletin* (Dec. 8, 1869), http://etext.virginia.edu/railton/onstage/sandrev2.html, in Railton, *Mark Twain in His Times* (April 23, 2000).

11. "The Sandwich Islands," in Charles Neider, ed., *The Complete Essays of Mark Twain* (Garden City, N.Y.: Doubleday, 1963), 16, 27.

12. Allen F. Davis, *Spearheads for Reform: The Social Settlements and the Progressive Movement, 1890–1914* (New York: Oxford University Press, 1967), 12.

13. Henry George, *Progress and Poverty* (New York: Robert Schalkenbach Foundation, 1937), 328.

14. Henry George, *Protection or Free Trade* (New York: Robert Schalkenbach Foundation, 1962), 278.

15. George, *Progress and Poverty*, 405–6; William Lloyd Garrison, "The Things That Make for Peace," *The Sterling Library* 2 (Oct. 21, 1895): 3.

16. Henry Nash Smith, *Mark Twain's Fable of Progress: Political and Economic Ideas in* A Connecticut Yankee (New Brunswick, N.J.: Rutgers University Press, 1964), 80; "Joan of Arc," in *Mark Twain's Speeches* (New York: Harper and Brothers, 1910), 243. "Archimedes" was reprinted in *The Twainian* 12 (Nov.–Dec. 1953): 2–3. For more on Twain's interest in the movement, see Jim Zwick, "Mark Twain and the Single Tax Movement," http://www.boondocksnet.com/twainwww/essays/twain-single-tax9706.html (Dec 1, 2000). For an excellent examination of anti-imperialist thought in *A Connecticut*

Yankee, see "Mark Twain's Rediscovery of America in *A Connecticut Yankee in King Arthur's Court*," in John Carlos Rowe, *Literary Culture and U.S. Imperialism* (New York: Oxford Univiersity Press, 2000), 121–39.

17. See the list of "Books by Henry George" in the Charles L. Webster & Co. catalog printed in the back pages of Mark Twain, *The $1,000,000 Bank Note and Other New Stories* (New York: Oxford University Press, 1996), 7–8; Henry George, Jr., "How the Book Came to Be Written," in George, *Progress and Poverty*, xii. Charles L. Webster & Co. must have printed only a small portion of the five million copies of George's works in print by 1905. It went into bankruptcy in April 1894, a year after preparation of the set was announced.

18. On Twain's involvement with this organization, see Louis J. Budd, "Twain, Howells, and the Boston Nihilists," *New England Quarterly* 32 (Sept. 1959): 357–58. Russia later figured prominently in many of Twain's writings about imperialism, but this was not an anti-imperialist organization. Nor was the American Congo Reform Association that Twain served as vice president in 1905 and 1906. Although formed to protest one of the most brutal colonial regimes in modern history, the Congo Reform Association's goals were limited to ending King Leopold's rule there, and it accepted various other colonial divisions of the Congo that might have followed his regime.

19. "Speech," in Fatout, *Mark Twain Speaking*, 305.

20. "A Word of Encouragement for Our Blushing Exiles," in Albert Bigelow Paine, ed., *Europe and Elsewhere* (New York: Harper & Brothers, 1923), 224; Samuel L. Clemens (hereafter SLC) to Joseph H. Twichell, June 17, 1898, in Albert Bigelow Paine, ed., *Mark Twain's Letters* (New York: Harper & Brothers, 1917), 663.

21. "The Stupendous Joke of the Century," in Jim Zwick, ed., *Mark Twain's Weapons of Satire: Anti-Imperialist Writings on the Philippine-American War* (Syracuse: Syracuse University Press, 1992), 185. This interview also includes one of Twain's few statements criticizing the European conquest of North America. Also see his portrayal of the impact of "civilization" in the American West in "The Dervish and the Offensive Stranger," ibid., 148–49.

22. "The Boston Anti-Imperialist Meeting," in Foner and Winchester, *The Anti-Imperialist Reader*, 275.

23. Anti-Imperialist League, *Address to the People of the United*

States (one-page circular dated Nov. 19, 1898, and signed by Erving Winslow as secretary of the League).

24. Joseph Fels, "Free Trade and the Single Tax vs. Imperialism: A Letter to Andrew Carnegie," http://www.boondocksnet.com/ailtexts/fels1210.html, in Jim Zwick, ed., *Anti-Imperialism in the United States, 1898–1935*, http://www.boondocksnet.com/ail98-35.html (Nov. 18, 2000). Also see Ernest Crosby, "The Real 'White Man's Burden,'" *New York Times* (Feb. 15, 1899), 6. Opposition to imperialism by single taxers is mentioned briefly in Arthur Nichols Young, *The Single Tax Movement in the United States* (Princeton: Princeton University Press, 1916), 242. Their influence in the creation of Anti-Imperialist League branches is discussed in Jim Zwick, "The Anti-Imperialist League and the Origins of Filipino-American Oppositional Solidarity," *Amerasia Journal* 24 (Summer 1998): 67–71. Among other nationally prominent single-taxers who played leading roles in the Anti-Imperialist League were William Lloyd Garrison, Jr., Fiske Warren, Frank Stephens, Samuel Milliken, Jackson H. Ralston, Alice T. and Louis F. Post, Herbert S. Bigelow, S. A. Stockwell, S. W. Sample, and C. E. S. Wood. The idea of unilinear progress was also a focus of debates about imperialism in the 1960s and 1970s. Modernization theories developed in the United States after World War II posited a unilinear path of development from "traditional" to "modern" political, economic, and social systems based on European and American experiences. Scholars working under the rubric of dependency theory countered that the development of the imperial powers *caused* the underdevelopment of their colonies and other areas of the world under their spheres of influence. See, for example, Andre Gunder Frank, "The Development of Underdevelopment," in James D. Cockcroft et al., *Dependence and Underdevelopment: Latin America's Political Economy* (Garden City, N.Y.: Doubleday, 1972), 3–17; and Walter Rodney, *How Europe Underdeveloped Africa* (Washington, D.C.: Howard University Press, 1974).

25. Twain later described Schurz as his political mentor. See "Carl Schurz, Pilot," *Harper's Weekly* 50 (May 26, 1906): 727.

26. Ernest H. Crosby, *Labor and Neighbor* (Chicago: Louis F. Post, 1908), 49.

27. "Platform of the American Anti-Imperialist League," in Carl Schurz, *The Policy of Imperialism*, Liberty Tract No. 4 (Chicago: American Anti-Imperialist League, 1899), inside front cover. In *The*

Social Gospel in Black and White: American Racial Reform, 1885–1912 (Chapel Hill: University of North Carolina Press, 1991), 230, Ralph E. Luker names Bigelow and Spahr among those "who militantly defended the rights of black Americans." Spahr was chair of the executive committee of the Anti-Imperialist League of New York; Bigelow was a vice president of the Cincinnati Anti-Imperialist League and gave the opening prayer at the League's August 1900 National Liberty Congress of Anti-Imperialists. Boutwell was the League's first president, and Storey was its second. Higginson was one of its vice presidents. Among other League officers whose roles in civil rights and related organizations are discussed in Luker's book are Ernest Crosby, Oswald Garrison Villard, Edwin D. Mead, Charles F. Dole, Felix Adler, Jane Addams, Carl Schurz, Andrew Carnegie, and James H. Dillard. Luker's discussions of their various attitudes and organizational involvements provides a better basis for seeing the diversity of views held by the anti-imperialists than early but still frequently quoted studies like Christopher Lasch, "The Anti-Imperialists, the Philippines, and the Inequality of Man," *Journal of Southern History* 24 (Aug. 1958): 319–31, which focused primarily on the response of Southern Democrats to argue that anti-imperialists were as racist as imperialists.

28. A Northampton, Massachusetts, branch formed in 1899 included Smith College professor Mary E. Byrd as secretary and other women among its slate of officers. Along with participating in the predominately white anti-imperialist organizations, African Americans formed the National Negro Anti-Expansion, Anti-Imperialist, Anti-Trust and Anti-Lynching League in 1899 and, primarily through Democratic clubs, campaigned for William Jennings Bryan on anti-imperialist grounds during the 1900 presidential campaign. For an excellent study of the unique situation of African Americans in the debate about imperialism, see Willard B. Gatewood, Jr., *Black Americans and the White Man's Burden, 1898–1903* (Urbana: University of Illinois Press, 1975). For documentation of women's still largely ignored participation, see "Suffrage and Self-Determination: Women in the Debate About Imperialism," http://www.boondocksnet.com/wj/, in Zwick, *Anti-Imperialism in the United States*.

29. "Anti-Imperialist Homecoming" and "The American Flag," in Zwick, *Weapons of Satire*, 4–5, 16. For a good discussion of the divisions within the anti-imperialist movement leading up to the elec-

tion, see chapter 14, "Scylla and Charybdis," in E. Berkeley Tompkins, *Anti-Imperialism in the United States: The Great Debate, 1890–1920* (Philadelphia: University of Pennsylvania Press, 1970), 214–35.

30. *The Public* 3 (Jan. 5, 1901): 610–11; *Springfield Republican* (Feb. 3, 1901), 8.

31. Quoted in James H. Blount, *The American Occupation of the Philippines, 1898–1912* (New York: G. P. Putnam's Sons, 1913), 150.

32. For discussions of Twain's involvement with the Anti-Imperialist League, see the "Introduction" in Zwick, *Weapons of Satire*, xxi–xxix; and Jim Zwick, "'Prodigally Endowed with Sympathy for the Cause': Mark Twain's Involvement with the Anti-Imperialist League," *Mark Twain Journal* 32 (Spring 1994): 3–25.

33. For useful discussions of how the war has been misremembered, see James W. Loewen, *Lies Across America: What Our Historic Sites Get Wrong* (New York: New Press, 1999), 137–43, 377–79. An unintentionally humorous example, because of the title of the book, can be found in G. Kurt Piehler, *Remembering War the American Way* (Washington, D.C.: Smithsonian Institution Press, 1995), 88–89, where the "Philippine Insurrection" is discussed in less than two paragraphs at the conclusion of a chapter on the Civil War. Piehler avoids the thorny issue of imperialism by skipping from the Civil War to World War I, treating the Spanish-American and Philippine-American wars primarily as conflicts that healed sectional wounds within the United States.

34. "Comments on the Moro Massacre," in Zwick, *Weapons of Satire*, 173, 171. Useful discussions of the later warfare can be found in Blount, *The American Occupation of the Philippines*; Orlino A. Ochosa, *"Bandoleros": Outlawed Guerrillas of the Philippine-American War, 1903–1907* (Quezon City, The Philippines: New Day, 1995); and Peter Gordon Gowing, *Mandate in Moroland: The American Government of Muslim Filipinos, 1899–1920* (Quezon City, The Philippines: New Day, 1983).

35. "Saint Joan of Arc," *The $30,000 Bequest and Other Stories* (reprint, New York: Oxford University Press, 1996), 159. For Twain's review-essay, see "Review of Edwin Wildman's Biography of Aguinaldo," in Zwick, *Weapons of Satire*, 86–108.

36. "Passage from 'Outlines of History,'" in Zwick, *Weapons of Satire*, 78.

37. For an example of this argument, see Andrew Hoffman, *In-*

venting Mark Twain: The Lives of Samuel Langhorne Clemens (New York: William Morrow, 1997), 435–37.

38. SLC to J. H. Twichell, Jan. 29, 1901, in Zwick, *Weapons of Satire,* 20.

39. Elizabeth Jordan to SLC, 22 March 1905, and SLC to Dan Beard, 30 March 1905, quoted in Zwick, *Weapons of Satire,* xxvii.

40. SLC to Edmund Dean Morel, April 11, 1905, quoted in Hunt Hawkins, "Mark Twain's Involvement with the Congo Reform Movement: 'A Fury of Generous Indignation,'" *New England Quarterly* 51 (June 1978): 155–56.

41. Zwick, *Weapons of Satire,* 162.

42. A. B. Paine to "Dear Bill," Aug. 1, 1926, quoted in Hamlin Hill, *Mark Twain: God's Fool* (New York: Harper and Row, 1973), 268. Paine's censorship and uses of Twain's writings in later foreign policy debates are discussed more fully in Jim Zwick, "Mark Twain's Anti-Imperialist Writings in the 'American Century,'" in *Vestiges of War: The Philippine-American War and the Aftermath of an Imperial Dream, 1899–1999,* ed. Angel Velasco Shaw and Luis H. Francia (Pasig City: Anvil, forthcoming 2002).

43. "Castro, Elian Father Attend Havana Rally," Reuters (April 3, 2000), http://www.nytimes.com/reuters/international/international-cuba-bo.html (April 4, 2000).

44. Adam Hochschild, *King Leopold's Ghost* (Boston: Houghton Mifflin, 1998), 2.

ILLUSTRATED
CHRONOLOGY

Twain's Life	Historical Events
1835 Samuel Langhorne Clemens born in Florida, Missouri (November 30), to Jane Lampton Clemens and John Marshall Clemens. (Frail and sickly, born two months premature, Sam was the couple's fifth child.)	**1835** Halley's comet reaches perihelion. Steam printing press for newspapers introduced. Andrew Jackson is president. Missouri passes law binding out as apprentices all free negroes and mulattos between ages seven and twenty-one. Missouri legislature also requires all free negroes to obtain licenses from a Missouri county to live in the state. Alexander de Tocqueville publishes *Democracy in America*.
1838 SLC's brother Henry is born.	
1839 SLC's sister Margaret dies. Family moves to Hannibal, Missouri.	
1840 Starts school in Hannibal.	**1837** Martin Van Buren becomes president. Charles Dickens publishes *Oliver Twist*. The telegraph is invented. Victoria becomes Queen of England.
1841 Mother, Jane L. Clemens, and sister Pamela join Presbyterian church; father, John M. Clemens, sends abolitionists to prison as member of circuit court jury in Palmyra.	
	1838 Transatlantic steamship service begins.
1842 SLC's brother Benjamin dies. Brother Orion moves to St. Louis. Family sells slave named Jenny.	**1840** Missouri population of 383,702 includes 57,891 slaves and 1,478 free blacks. James Fenimore Cooper publishes *The Pathfinder*.
1843 Spends first of many summers on the Quarles farm near Florida, Missouri. John Marshall Clemens elected justice of the peace; mother moves children from Methodist to Presbyterian Sunday school.	**1841** William Henry Harrison becomes president and is succeeded by John Tyler when he dies shortly after inauguration. Oberlin College becomes first U.S. institution to award college degrees to women. Ralph Waldo Emerson publishes *Essays: First Series*. James Fenimore Cooper publishes *The Deerslayer*.
1846 Debts force family to move in with local pharmacist, supplying meals in exchange for rent.	

1847 Father, John Marshall Clemens, dies. SLC works at odd jobs in grocery store, bookstore, and pharmacy.

1848 Begins work as apprentice for Joseph Ament's *Missouri Courier.*

1850 Brother Orion buys Hannibal newspaper, the *Western Union.*

1851 Orion buys *Hannibal Journal*; SLC assists in *Journal's* newspaper office, sometimes publishing short sketches.

1852 Publishes "The Dandy Frightening the Squatter" in the *Carpet-Bag;* uses first pen-name, "W. Epaminondas Adrastus Perkins."

1853 Leaves Hannibal to work as journeyman printer in St. Louis, New York, Philadelphia, and other cities, occasionally writing travel letters for brother Orion's newspapers; in New York spends evenings reading in the printers' free library.

1854 Visits Washington, D.C., Philadelphia, and New York; works for Orion's *Muscatine Journal* (Muscatine, Iowa).

1855 Makes first attempt to become a riverboat pilot; lives in St. Louis; visits Hannibal and Keokuk, Iowa.

Interior of jail cell in Palmyra, Missouri, picturing Underground Railroad operatives Alanson Work, James E. Burr, and George Thompson (and other prisoners) convicted of "slave-stealing" by a jury that included Sam Clemens's father, John Marshall Clemens. From Prison Life and Reflections *by George Thompson, Hartford, 1851. From the collection of Shelley Fisher Fishkin.*

1842 Solar eclipse is observed over United States.

1843 The country's first minstrel troupe, the Virginia Minstrels, starts performing.

1844 Samuel F. B. Morse sends first message by electric telegraph. Alexandre Dumas publishes *The Count of Monte Cristo.*

1845 James Polk becomes president. Pneumatic tire invented.

1846 United States declares war on Mexico. Sewing machine invented.

1848 First women's rights convention held in Seneca Falls, N.Y.; discovery of gold in northern California starts Gold Rush; Mexican War ends.

1856 Gives first public speech at printers banquet in Keokuk; writes "Thomas Jefferson Snodgrass" letters for *Keokuk Daily Post.*

1857 Works as a cub pilot on various Mississippi River steamboats.

1858 Brother Henry dies from injuries received during the explosion of the steamboat *Pennsylvania.*

1859 Receives pilot's license and works on the river steadily.

1861 Spends two weeks as an irregular with the Missouri State Guard; goes to Nevada by stagecoach with brother Orion; prospects for silver in Nevada.

Sam Clemens as a riverboat pilot, about 1859–1860. Photo courtesy of the Mark Twain House, Hartford, Connecticut.

1849 Zachary Taylor becomes president; Charles Dickens publishes *David Copperfield.* Henry David Thoreau publishes "Civil Disobedience."

1850 Taylor dies in office and Millard Fillmore succeds him as president. Harsh new Fugitive Slave Act is passed. Nathaniel Hawthorne publishes *The Scarlet Letter.*

1851 Herman Melville publishes *Moby-Dick.* Solar eclipse is observed over the United States.

1852 Harriet Beecher Stowe publishes *Uncle Tom's Cabin.*

1853 Franklin Pierce becomes president. World art and industry exposition opens at New York's Crystal Palace. William Wells Brown publishes *Clotel, or the President's Daughter.*

1854 *People v. Hall* (California Supreme Court) prohibited all nonwhites, including people of Chinese ancestry, from testifying against whites in court in civil and criminal proceedings. Kansas-Nebraska Act opens western territories to slavery. Henry David Thoreau publishes *Walden.*

1855 Walt Whitman publishes *Leaves of Grass.* Fanny Fern publishes *Ruth Hall.* Frederick Douglass publishes *My Bondage and My Freedom.*

1862 Settles in Virginia City, Nevada; works as reporter for *Virginia City Territorial Enterprise.*

1863 Adopts the pen name "Mark Twain."

1864 Leaves Nevada for San Francisco; writes for *San Francisco Morning Call,* as well as for the *Enterprise* back in Nevada, the *New York Mercury,* the *Golden Era,* and the *Californian,* and prospects in Tuolumne and Calaveras counties.

1865 Visits Angel's Camp in Calaveras County, California. Publication of "Jim Smiley and His Jumping Frog" in New York's *Saturday Press* brings him national fame.

1866 Visits Hawaii as *Sacramento Union* correspondent; gives first professional lecture on the Sandwich Islands (in San Francisco); writes travel letters to *Alta California.*

1867 Writes for the *Alta California* and New York papers including the *Sunday Mercury,* the *Evening Express,* and the *Weekly.* Takes *Quaker City* cruise to Europe and the Holy Land. Becomes Washington correspondent for the *Territorial Enterprise, Alta California,* and *New York Tribune.*

1857 James Buchanan becomes president. *Dred Scott v. Sandford* (U.S. Supreme Court) declared that African Americans are not citizens of the United States and that the Missouri Compromise is unconstitutional.

1858 First transatlantic cable completed. Abraham Lincoln and Stephen Douglas debate the issue of slavery in Illinois. Charles Darwin publishes *On the Origin of the Species.*

1859 Nevada's Comstock Lode discovered; abolitionist John Brown raids a federal arsenal in Harper's Ferry to obtain arms for a slave insurrection and is hanged for treason. The last slave ship to bring slaves to the United States (the *Clotilde*) arrives in Mobile Bay, Alabama.

1860 Oliver Winchester introduces the repeating rifle. Internal combustion engine invented. Abraham Lincoln elected president. Receives no vote in ten southern states; South Carolina secedes from the Union.

1861 Abraham Lincoln becomes president. Confederate forces attack Fort Sumter. Start of Civil War. Additional southern states secede. Union proclaims martial law in Missouri.

Publishes first book, *The Celebrated Jumping Frog of Calaveras County, and Other Sketches*; invited to turn travel letters to *Alta California* into a book; meets Olivia Langdon in New York. Lecture on the Sandwich Islands in St. Louis includes discussion of decimation of the Hawaiian population by "civilization and several other diseases."

1868 Courts Olivia Langdon in Elmira. Meets Rev. Joseph Twichell. Embarks on lecture tour.

1869 Lectures through the Midwest and the East. Continues to court Olivia Langdon. Meets Frederick Douglass. Publishes *The Innocents Abroad*. Positive review in the *Atlantic* so pleased SLC that he paid the magazine an unannounced visit recalled fondly by editor William Dean Howells, who became a life-long friend. Buys interest in *Buffalo Express*. Publishes a satirical attack on a Memphis lynching entitled "Only a Nigger" in *The Buffalo Express*.

1870 Marries Olivia Langdon in Elmira. Father-in-law Jervis Langdon dies. First child, Langdon Clemens, born prematurely.

1871 Lectures through the East and Midwest; meets "Sociable Jimmy" in Paris, Illinois. Publishes *Mark Twain's (Burlesque) Autobiography and First Romance*.

1863 Lincoln issues Emancipation Proclamation, freeing slaves in states disloyal to the union.

1864 Grant takes command of all Union troops. Congress passes a bill authorizing equal pay, equipment, arms, and health care for African-American Union troops. Fugitive Slave Law is repealed. David Ross Locke publishes *The Nasby Papers*. Lincoln is reelected president.

1865 Lincoln starts second term. Civil War ends. Lincoln is assassinated. He is succeeded as president by Andrew Johnson. Thirteenth Amendment to the Constitution prohibiting slavery and involuntary servitude ratified. "Black codes" are issued in former Confederate states that severely limit the rights of former slaves. Ku Klux Klan founded in Pulaski, Tennessee.

1866 Reconstruction era begins in the South. Congress overrides President Johnson's veto and passes Civil Rights Act, guaranteeing equal protection under the law to all citizens and nullifying black codes. United States and England are now linked by underwater transatlantic telegraph cable.

1867 Dynamite and typewriter are invented. Congress passes First Reconstruction Act calling for enfranchisement of male former slaves in the South.

Poster used by Mark Twain for Brooklyn lectures, about 1869. Photo courtesy of the Mark Twain House, Hartford, Connecticut.

Olivia Langdon—Mrs. Samuel Clemens, 1873. Photo courtesy of the Mark Twain House, Hartford, Connecticut.

1868 Fourteenth Amendment to U.S. Constitution guaranteeing citizenship to all persons born in the United States is ratified.

1869 Ulysses S. Grant becomes president. Knights of Labor founded. Transcontinental railroad completed. Elizabeth Cady Stanton founds National Women's Suffrage Organization.

1870 Fifteenth Amendment to U.S. Constitution guaranteeing voting rights to all adult males is ratified. Congress passes Enforcement Acts to control Ku Klux Klan and federally guarantee political and civil rights.

1871 William Dean Howells takes over as editor of *The Atlantic.* Congress passes second Ku Klux Klan Act to attempt to restrain Klan violence. Darwin publishes his explosive book, *The Descent of Man.* Fisk University Juibilee Singers begin their first national tour.

1872 William Still publishes *The Underground Railroad.*

1873 Ulysses S. Grant begins second term as president. Severe economic depression (Panic of 1873).

1872 Daughter Susy Clemens born in Elmira. Langdon Clemens dies in Hartford. SLC publishes *Roughing It.*

1873 Patents self-pasting scrapbook; publishes *The Gilded Age* (co-authored with Charles Dudley Warner); visits England; publishes letters about Hawaii in *New York Tribune.*

1874 Moves into unfinished Hartford house designed by architect Edward T. Potter; publishes "A True Story" in the *Atlantic Monthly* and "Sociable Jimmy" in *The New York Times*; daughter Clara Clemens born in Elmira.

1875 Publishes "Old Times on the Mississippi" in the *Atlantic Monthly* and *Sketches, New and Old*; hires George Griffin as family butler.

"Worse than Slavery." Thomas Nast cartoon from Harper's Weekly in *1874, depicting the condition of African Americans in the South. From the collection of Shelley Fisher Fishkin.*

The Clemens family mansion in Hartford designed by Edward T. Potter, where the family lived during Mark Twain's happiest and most productive years, 1874–1891. Photo courtesy of the Mark Twain House, Hartford, Connecticut.

The Billiard Room in Mark Twain's Hartford residence. Photo courtesy of the Mark Twain House, Hartford, Connecticut.

"The Church"—an illustration from The Adventures of Tom Sawyer. From the Oxford Mark Twain edition of the book.

1875 Congress passes Civil Rights Act of 1875, prohibiting racial discrimination in hotels, inns, theaters, transportation, and places of public amusement and providing access to jury duty. Mary Baker Eddy publishes *Science and Health with Key to the Scriptures.*

1876 The telephone is invented. Centennial of Declaration of Independence celebrated across the nation. President Grant sends troops to Hamburg, South Carolina, to restore order after a heavily armed white mob kills several African Americans. National election between Samuel Tilden and Rutherford B. Hayes leaves no clear winner.

1876 Publishes *The Adventures of Tom Sawyer* and begins writing *Adventures of Huckleberry Finn*. Writes "[Date, 1601] Conversation, as It Was by the Social Fireside, in the Time of the Tudors" and presents it orally to male friends.

1877 Visits Bermuda with Rev. Joseph Twichell; speaks at Whittier 70th birthday dinner in Boston; John T. Lewis stops runaway carriage in Elmira.

1878 Visits Europe with family and takes "walking tour" with Rev. Joseph Twichell.

1879 Speaks at Palmer House banquet in Chicago honoring General U.S. Grant.

Reverend Joseph Twichell, Mark Twain's pastor and close friend. Photo courtesy of the Mark Twain House, Hartford, Connecticut.

1877 Rutherford B. Hayes becomes president after crafting of Hayes-Tilden Compromise. Reassigns federal troops left in the South, ending Reconstruction. Phonograph invented. Great Labor Uprising. Nationwide railroad strikes.

1878 First bicycles commercially manufactured.

1879 Henry George publishes *Progress and Poverty*.

1880 Joel Chandler Harris publishes *Uncle Remus: His Songs and Sayings*.

1881 James Garfield becomes president. Frederick Douglass is named Recorder of Deeds for the District of Columbia. Garfield is assassinated and Chester A. Arthur becomes president. Tennessee segregates railroad cars [followed by Florida (1887), Mississippi (1888), Texas (1889), Louisiana (1890), Alabama, Kentucky, Arkansas, and Georgia (1891), South Carolina (1898), North Carolina (1899), Virginia (1900), Maryland (1904), and Oklahoma (1907)].

1882 Standard Oil Trust organized.

1883 Supreme Court Civil Rights cases decision declares Civil Rights Act of 1875 unconstitutional and declares that the Fourteenth Amendment forbids states, but not citizens, from discriminating.

1880 Starts investing in the Paige compositor; publishes *A Tramp Abroad* and (privately) *1601*; daughter Jane Lampton (Jean) born; actively supports Republican presidential nominee James A. Garfield.

1881 Publishes *The Prince and the Pauper*; intercedes with President Garfield to secure political appointment for Frederick Douglass.

1882 Publishes *The Stolen White Elephant, etc.*; travels down Mississippi from St. Louis to New Orleans as part of research to expand 1875 *Atlantic* articles on the Mississippi into a book.

1883 Publishes *Life on the Mississippi*.

1884 Gives lecture tour with George Washington Cable; publishes *Huckleberry Finn* in London and extract from the novel in *Century Magazine*; founds own publishing company, Charles L. Webster & Co., which makes offer for U.S. Grant's memoirs.

1885 Webster & Co. publishes *Adventures of Huckleberry Finn* in the United States; continues lecture tour, visiting Hannibal and Keokuk; undertakes paying board of Warner T. McGuinn, one of the first black law students at Yale, whom he met when he went there to lecture.

Frederick Douglass, distinguished writer, speaker, and national leader whom Twain was proud to call his friend. National Archives photo.

1884 U.S. recognizes Congo regime of King Leopold II of Belgium. Mergenthaler patents linotype machine. Fountain pen is introduced.

1885 Grover Cleveland becomes president. Knights of Labor defeat Jay Gould-owned railroads. Thomas Alva Edison demonstrates electric light bulb. Henry James's *The Bostonians* and William Dean Howells's *The Rise of Silan Lapham* run in *Century Magazine* (along with Twain's *Huckleberry Finn*).

1886 Mergenthaler linotype machine sets type for the *Chicago Tribune*. Haymarket bombing in Chicago. American Federation of Labor is founded.

Olivia Langdon Clemens with daughters Susy, Clara, and Jean in Hartford. Photo courtesy of the Mark Twain House, Hartford, Connecticut.

Mark Twain at fifty. Photo courtesy of the Mark Twain House, Hartford, Connecticut.

1888 Awarded honorary Master of Arts degree from Yale University; visits Thomas Edison at his New Jersey lab.

1889 Publishes *A Connecticut Yankee in King Arthur's Court.*

1890 Mother, Jane Lampton Clemens, dies. Mother-in-law, Olivia L. Langdon, dies. Daughter Jean has first epileptic seizure.

"The Slave Driver." An illustration from Mark Twain's A Connecticut Yankee in King Arthur's Court, *in which illustrator Dan Beard gave the greedy and sadistic Slave Driver the face of financial manipulator Jay Gould. From the Oxford Mark Twain edition of the book.*

George W. Chadwick's "Second Symphony" is published—a classical work which incorporates African-American folk songs.

1887 Charles W. Chesnutt publishes "The Goophered Grapevine" in *The Atlantic Monthly.*

1888 Edward Bellamy publishes *Looking Backward.*

1889 Benjamin Harrison becomes president. Ninety-four African Americans are known to have been lynched this year.

1890 Federal troops massacre two hundred Sioux at Wounded Knee, South Dakota. Mississippi effectively disenfranchises Black voters through literacy and "understanding" tests. [Similar statutes are adopted by South Carolina (1895), Louisiana (1898), North Carolina (1900), Alabama (1901), Virginia (1901), Georgia (1908), and Oklahoma (1910).] White supremacist "Pitchfork Ben" Tillman is elected governor of South Carolina in an election he called "a triumph of . . . white supremacy." Eighty-five African Americans are known to have been lynched this year.

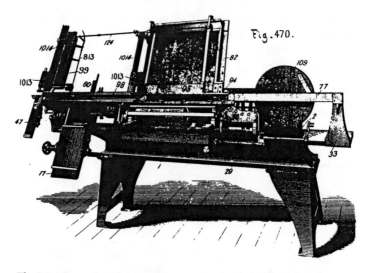

The Paige Compositor, the automatic typesetting machine that bankrupted Mark Twain. Photo courtesy of the Mark Twain House, Hartford, Connecticut.

1891 Closes Hartford house due to financial problems and takes family to Europe. SLC among founding members of the American Friends of Russian Freedom.

1892 Publishes *The American Claimant* and *Merry Tales;* travels to Florence for wife's health.

1893 Publishes *The £1,000,000 Bank-Note and Other New Stories;* Standard Oil Company vice president and director, Henry Huttleston Rogers, agrees to help SLC deal with his financial troubles.

1894 Publishes *Tom Sawyer Abroad* and *The Tragedy of Pudd'nhead Wilson and The Comedy Those Extraordinary Twins.*

1891 Congress adopts International Copyright Act. One hundred thirteen African Americans are known to have been lynched this year. African-American jockey Isaac Murphy becomes the first jockey to win three Kentucky Derbies.

1892 World Columbian Exposition opens in Chicago. Homestead steel strike. Charlotte Perkins Gilman publishes *The Yellow Wall-Paper.* Sisseretta Jones, known as "the Black Patti," is invited to sing at the White House. Paul Laurence Dunbar publishes *Oak and Ivy.*

Standard Oil Company vice president Henry Huttleston Rogers, who helped Clemens deal with his financial troubles. Photo courtesy of the Mark Twain House, Hartford, Connecticut.

1895 Begins world lecture he will record in *Following the Equator*.

1896 Publishes *Personal Recollections of Joan of Arc*; *Tom Sawyer Abroad/Tom Sawyer Detective and Other Stories*; daughter Susy Clemens dies in Hartford.

1897 Publishes *How to Tell a Story and Other Essays* and *Following the Equator*.

1898 Lives with family in Vienna, where he meets numerous artists and intellectuals including Sigmund Freud.

1893 Grover Cleveland begins second term as president. New York Stock Exchange crashes, ushering in Depression. Henry O. Tanner completes his painting *The Banjo Lesson*.

1894 Pullman strike.

1895 W.E.B. Du Bois becomes the first African American to receive a Harvard Ph.D. Cuba starts revolt against Spanish rule. Frederick Douglass dies, marking the end of an era. Atlanta Exposition held, at which Booker T. Washington gives his famous "cast down your bucket where you are" speech. Radio and x-ray machine invented. Ida B. Wells-Barnett publishes *A Red Record*. Paul Laurence Dunbar publishes *Majors and Minors*, and it is reviewed favorably by William Dean Howells in *Harper's Weekly*. There are 112 recorded lynchings.

1896 *Plessy v. Ferguson* finds "separate but equal" principle constitutional (declares that mandating separate railway cars for blacks and whites does not violate equal protection clause of Constitution). Filipinos begin fighting for their country's independence from Spain. Paul Laurence Dunbar publishes *Lyrics of Lowly Life*.

1897 William McKinley becomes president.

"A Salutation Speech from the Nineteenth Century to the Twentieth" by Mark Twain, December 31, 1900. Card published by Albert S. Parsons, chair of the executive committee of the New England Anti-Imperialist League. Library of Congress.

Studying a map of the Philippines in 1898, Uncle Sam exclaims "Guess I'll keep 'em!" in this cartoon from Leslie's Weekly, June 9, 1898. From the Jim Zwick collection.

1900 Lives in London. Returns to New York and declares himself an anti-imperialist. Charles Dudley Warner dies. SLC publishes *The Man That Corrupted Hadleyburg and Other Stories and Essays*, and *English As She Is Taught*. "A Salutation Speech from the Nineteenth Century to the Twentieth" published in *New York Herald*.

1901 Receives honorary Doctor of Letters degree from Yale; publishes "To the Person Sitting in Darkness" and "To My Missionary Critics" in the *North American Review*. Becomes a vice president of the Anti-Imperialist League of New York. Writes "The United States of Lyncherdom."

1902 Visits Hannibal for the last time; receives honorary degree from University of Missouri; publishes *A Double-Barrelled Detective Story*.

1898 United States declares war on Spain. Battle of Manila Bay. Filipinos declare their independence from Spain and government of the Philippine Republic is organized under the leadership of General Emilio Aguinaldo—the first republic formed in Asia through an anti-colonial revolution. First anti-imperialist mass meeting in Boston leads to the formation of the Anti-Imperialist League. Spain and the United States agree on terms of peace to end the Spanish-American War. U.S. troops occupy Manila after mock battle with Spanish forces. Treaty of Paris signed. Charlotte Perkins Gilman publishes *Women and Economics*. Race riot in Wilmington, North Carolina.

American soldiers and dead Filipinos after the battle of Malabon. Underwood & Underwood photo, 1899. From the Jim Zwick collection.

"Mark Twain and His Empire—A Laughing World." An early commentary on Mark Twain's anti-imperialist statements, published in the New York Commercial Advertiser, *December 22, 1900. From the Jim Zwick collection.*

"In Defence of General Funston" published in *North American Review.*

1903 Lives in Riverdale, N.Y. and Florence, Italy; publishes *My Debut as a Literary Person with Other Essays and Stories*; signs contract giving Harper & Brothers the rights to all his books.

1904 Wife, Livy, dies in Florence; daughter Jean has epileptic seizures; daughter Clara enters sanitarium; publishes *A Dog's Tale.*

1899 Philippine-American War begins. Treaty of Paris ratified by U.S. Senate. Boer War begins in South Africa. Charles Chesnutt publishes *The Conjure Woman* and *The Wife of His Youth and Other Stories of the Color Line.* Thorstein Veblen publishes *A Theory of the Leisure Class.*

1900 Sherman Anti-Trust Act passed. International Ladies Garment Workers Union founded. Theodore Dreiser publishes *Sister Carrie.* There are 115 recorded lynchings.

1901 President McKinley starts second term as president. McKinley is assassinated and Theodore Roosevelt becomes president. Roosevelt invites Booker T. Washington to dine at the White House, creating a national furor. Queen Victoria dies. There are 130 recorded lynchings.

Mark Twain in front of his boyhood home in Hannibal in 1902. Photo courtesy of the Mark Twain House, Hartford, Connecticut.

Mark Twain with his friend John Lewis, a farmer in Elmira, New York, 1903. Photo courtesy of the Mark Twain House, Hartford, Connecticut.

1905 Dines at the White House with President Theodore Roosevelt; honored by seventieth birthday banquet at Delmonico's restaurant in New York. "The War Prayer" is rejected by *Harper's Bazaar*. "King Leopold's Soliloquy" is rejected by Harper and Brothers and then published by the American Congo Reform Association. Executive committee of the national Anti-Imperialist League elects Mark Twain as a vice president of the organization.

1906 Autobiographical dictations on the Moro Massacre. Final resignation from American Congo Reform Association. Lives in New York and Dublin, N.H. Publishes *The $30,000 Bequest and Other Stories*, *Eve's Diary*, and *What Is Man?*; starts wearing white suits in public.

1907 Makes last transatlantic trip to England; receives honorary degree from Oxford University; publishes *Christian Science* and *A Horse's Tale*.

1908 Moves into "Stormfield," home built for him in Redding, Connecticut; organizes the "Aquarium," a club of young girls whom he calls his "angelfish."

General Emilio Aguinaldo, first president of the Philippine Republic, frequently portrayed as a "Filipino George Washington," whom Twain compared with Joan of Arc, the liberator of France. National Archives photo. From the Jim Zwick collection.

Theodore Roosevelt, president of the United States, 1901–1909. National Archives photo. From the Jim Zwick collection.

Mark Twain at home, New York City, in 1907. Photo courtesy of the Mark Twain House, Hartford, Connecticut.

1902 Theodore Roosevelt declares that the "Philippine insurrection" is over, but warfare continues.

1903 Airplane invented. W.E.B. Du Bois publishes *The Souls of Black Folk.*

1904 Russo-Japanese War.

1905 Theodore Roosevelt begins second term as president. Tsar's troops fire on strikers in St. Petersburg. Niagara Movement (precursor to NAACP) is organized with help of W.E.B. Du Bois.

1906 Black troops riot in response to an incident involving racial slurs in Brownsville, Texas. President Roosevelt gives dishonorable discharges without a fair trial to three companies of soldiers who were involved. Race riot in Atlanta. United States troops massacre 900 Muslim Filipinos in Moro Province in the Philippines.

1907 "Great White Fleet" sent around the world by President Roosevelt.

1909 Diagnosed with heart disease; publishes *Is Shakespeare Dead* and *Extract from Captain Stormfield's Visit to Heaven*; daughter Clara Clemens marries pianist/conductor Ossip Gabrilowitsch at Stormfield and sails for Europe; daughter Jean Clemens dies at Stormfield.

1910 Visits Bermuda on last trip outside the United States. Dies at Stormfield at sunset on April 21. Buried in Woodlawn Cemetery in Elmira in family plot with his wife, son, and two daughters after funeral service by Rev. Joseph Twichell.

William Dean Howells, a close friend of Mark Twain's, served as editor of The Atlantic *and* Harper's Weekly, *and wrote an affectionate memoir about Twain. Photo courtesy of the Mark Twain House, Hartford, Connecticut.*

1908 Race riot in Springfield, Illinois, after two African Americans lynched and many Black homes destroyed. African-American boxer, Jack Johnson, wins world heavyweight title.

1909 William H. Taft becomes president. National Association for the Advancement of Colored People is founded.

1910 Halley's comet reaches perihelion.

Bibliographical Essay

Shelley Fisher Fishkin

EDITIONS OF MARK TWAIN'S WRITINGS

Mark Twain published journalism, novels, sketches, stories, essays, poems, and travel books during his lifetime and also wrote much that remained unpublished at his death—including extensive notebooks and journals, unfinished imaginative works, and mountains of personal letters. At the dawn of the twenty-first century, new books by Mark Twain continue to be published at a regular clip, making him, perhaps, the country's most prolific dead writer.

The Mark Twain Project at the Bancroft Library, the University of California at Berkeley, has been producing meticulously edited scholarly editions of Mark Twain's private papers and published works since the 1960s. In collaboration with the University of California Press, they have published twenty-three of an estimated seventy volumes in *The Works and Papers of Mark Twain*. Material published to date include more than half of the literary manuscripts in the Mark Twain Papers, letters (in complete form through 1873), early fiction and journalism through 1865, and his notebooks through 1891, along with critically established texts of Twain's fiction and travel books. These critical editions include explanatory and textual notes written by the Mark Twain Project's staff of expert full-time editors under the direction of General Editor Robert H. Hirst.

Publications of the Mark Twain Papers include *Letters to His Publishers 1876–1894*, ed. Hamlin Hill (1967); *Satires & Burlesques*, ed. Franklin R. Rogers (1967); *Which Was the Dream? And Other Symbolic Writings of the Later Years*, ed. John S. Tuckey (1967); *Hannibal, Huck & Tom*, ed. Walter Blair (1969); *Mysterious Stranger Manuscripts*, ed. William M. Gibson (1969); *Correspondence with Henry Huttleston Rogers, 1893–1909*, ed. Lewis Leary (1969); *Fables of Man*, ed. John S. Tuckey (1972); *Notebooks & Journals, Volume 1 (1855–1873)*, ed. Frederick Anderson, Michael B. Frank, and Kenneth M. Sanderson (1975); *Notebooks & Journals, Volume 2 (1877–1883)*, ed. Frederick Anderson, Lin Salamo, and Bernard L. Stein (1975); *Notebooks & Journals, Volume 3 (1883–1891)*, ed. Robert Pack Browning, Michael B. Frank, and Lin Salamo (1979); *Letters, Volume 1: 1853–1866*, ed. Edgar Marquess Branch, Michael B. Frank, and Kenneth Sanderson (1988); *Letters, Volume 2: 1867–1868*, ed. Harriet Elinor Smith and Richard Bucci (1990); *Letters, Volume 3: 1869*, ed. Victor Fischer and Michael B. Frank (1992); *Letters, Volume 4: 1870–1871*, ed. Victor Fischer, Michael B. Frank, and Lin Salamo (1995); and *Letters, Volume 5: 1872–1873*, ed. Lin Salamo and Harriet Elinor Smith (1997).

The Mark Twain Project's textual editions include *Roughing It*, ed. Franklin Rogers and Paul Baender (1972); *What Is Man? And Other Philosophical Writing*, ed. Paul Baender (1973); *A Connecticut Yankee in King Arthur's Court*, ed. Bernard Stein (1979); *The Prince and the Pauper*, ed. Victor Fischer and Lin Salamo (1979); *Early Tales & Sketches, Volume 1 (1851–1864)*, ed. Edgar Marquess Branch and Robert H. Hirst (1979); *The Adventures of Tom Sawyer, Tom Sawyer Abroad & Tom Sawyer, Detective*, ed. John C. Gerber, Paul Baender, and Terry Firkins (1980); *Early Tales & Sketches, Volume 2 (1864–1865)*, ed. Edgar Marquess Branch and Robert H. Hirst (1981); *Adventures of Huckleberry Finn*, ed. Walter Blair and Victor Fischer (1988); *Roughing It*, ed. Harriet Elinor Smith, Edgar Marquess Branch, Lin Salamo, and Robert Pack Browning (1993). The Project also publishes a popular Mark Twain Library edition of these texts that omits the historical and textual records (and also includes *Huck Finn, Tom Sawyer among the Indians, and Other Unfinished Stories*, ed. Dahlia Armon et al. (1989), and *No. 44, The Mysterious Stranger*, ed. John S. Tuckey and William M. Gibson

(1982). Most recently the Mark Twain Project has published a Mark Twain Library edition of *Adventures of Huckleberry Finn*, edited by Victor Fischer and Lin Salamo (2001), that includes insights gleaned from the recently discovered first half of the manuscript of the novel. (The best way to check on new publications of the Mark Twain Project is by consulting their website, http://www.lib.berkeley.edu/BANC/MTP/).

Nearly all the works Twain published in book form in his lifetime appear in the 29-volume *Oxford Mark Twain*, edited by Shelley Fisher Fishkin for Oxford University Press (1996). The edition publishes facsimiles of the first American editions of some thirty-five individual works. Each volume contains an introduction by a contemporary writer and an afterword by a Twain scholar, which sets the work in its historical and cultural context, and each illustrated volume contains interpretive essays on the art work by Beverly David and Ray Sapirstein. The edition includes the following (the authors of the introductions and afterwords respectively follow each title): *The Celebrated Jumping Frog of Calaveras County, and Other Sketches* (Roy Blount, Jr., Richard Bucci); *The Innocents Abroad* (Mordecai Richler, David E. E. Sloane); *Roughing It* (George Plimpton, Henry B. Wonham); *The Gilded Age* (Ward Just, Gregg Camfield); *Sketches, New and Old* (Lee Smith, Sherwood Cummings); *The Adventures of Tom Sawyer* (E. L. Doctorow, Albert E. Stone); *A Tramp Abroad* (Russell Banks, James S. Leonard); *The Prince and the Pauper* (Judith Martin, Everett Emerson); *Life on the Mississippi* (Willie Morris, Lawrence Howe); *Adventures of Huckleberry Finn* (Toni Morrison, Victor A. Doyno); *A Connecticut Yankee in King Arthur's Court* (Kurt Vonnegut, Jr., Louis J. Budd); *Merry Tales* (Anne Bernays, Forrest G. Robinson); *The American Claimant* (Bobbie Ann Mason, Peter Messent); *The £1,000,000 Bank-Note and Other New Stories* (Malcolm Bradbury, James D. Wilson); *Tom Sawyer Abroad* (Nat Hentoff, M. Thomas Inge); *The Tragedy of Pudd'nhead Wilson and the Comedy Those Extraordinary Twins* (Sherley Anne Williams, David Lionel Smith); *Personal Recollections of Joan of Arc* (Justin Kaplan, Susan K. Harris); *The Stolen White Elephant and Other Detective Stories* (Walter Mosley, Lillian S. Robinson); *How to Tell a Story and Other Essays* (David Bradley, Pascal Covici, Jr.); *Following the Equator and Anti-imperialist Essays* (Gore Vidal, Fred Kaplan); *The Man That Corrupted Hadleyburg and Other Stories and Essays* (Cynthia Ozick, Jeffrey Rubin-Dorsky); *The Diaries of Adam and Eve* (Ursula K. Le Guin, Laura E. Skandera-Trombley); *What Is Man?* (Charles Johnson, Linda Wagner-Martin); *The $30,000 Bequest and Other Stories* (Frederick Busch, Judith Yaross Lee); *Christian Science* (Garry Wills, Hamlin Hill); *Chapters from My Autobiography* (Arthur Miller, Michael J. Kiskis); *1601, and Is Shakespeare Dead?* (Erica Jong, Leslie A. Fiedler); *Extract from Captain Stormfield's Visit to Heaven* (Frederik Pohl, James A. Miller); *Speeches* (Hal Holbrook, David Barrow).

Twain's most popular books are also widely available in paperback editions. In addition to the Mark Twain Library editions noted above, for example, there are paperback editions of works like *Adventures of Huckleberry Finn* and *A Connecticut Yankee in King Arthur's Court* in the Oxford World Classics series, with excellent prefaces, respectively, by Emory Elliott and M. Thomas Inge. There are also several editions of *Huckleberry Finn* designed for the classroom that include excerpts from scholarly criticism— including one edited by Susan Harris (Riverside/Houghton Mifflin, 2000), one by Thomas Cooley (W.W. Norton, 1998), and one by Gerald Graff and James Phelan (Bedford Books, 1995). In 1996, Random House published an edition of *Huckleberry Finn*, which inserts into the text material that appears in the recently recovered original manuscript of the novel, but which Twain cut before he published the book. Twain's historical novels and Mississippi writings are also available in annotated Library of America editions edited, respectively, by Susan Harris and Guy Cardwell. Michael Patrick Hearn's *The Annotated Huckleberry Finn* (W.W. Norton, 2001) pulls much useful information together in one place. One edition of *Huckleberry Finn* to be avoided in the 1985 Doubleday edition edited by Charles Neider, in which the final section of the novel is abridged, reflecting the editor's preferences, but clearly not Mark Twain's.

Many of Mark Twain's books are also available online as e-texts. The best source for locating e-texts (as well as myriad other Mark Twain resources on the world wide web) is Jim Zwick's extraordinary website at http://boondocksnet.com./

twainwww/. Another useful source of e-texts (as well as contemporary reviews, articles, and related historical documents) is Stephen Railton's "Mark Twain in His Times" at the University of Virginia (http://etext.virginia.edu/railton/index2.html).

While scholars await the Mark Twain Project's definitive annotated editions of more of Twain's journalism, sketches, speeches, and letters, several other collections remain extremely useful. The richest compendium of Twain's short pieces is the Library of America's two-volume set, *Mark Twain: The Collected Tales, Sketches, Speeches, and Essays*, ed. Louis J. Budd (1992). Volume one covers the period 1852–1890 and volume two covers 1891–1910. Also useful are *Mark Twain at the Buffalo Express: Articles and Sketches by America's Favorite Humorist*, ed. Joseph B. McCullough and Janice McIntire-Strasburg (DeKalb: Northern Illinois University Press, 1999); *Mark Twain of the Enterprise: Newspaper Articles & Other Documents, 1862–1864*, ed. Henry Nash Smith and Frederick Anderson (Berkeley: University of California Press, 1957); *Contributions to the Galaxy, 1868–1871, by Mark Twain*, ed. Bruce R. McElderry, Jr. (Gainesville, Fla.: Scholar's Facsimiles and Reprints, 1961); *Mark Twain: Life as I Find It*, ed. Charles Neider (Garden City, N.Y.: Hanover House, 1961); *Letters from the Earth*, ed. Bernard DeVoto (New York: Harper, 1962); *Mark Twain's San Francisco*, ed. Bernard Taper (New York: McGraw-Hill, 1963); *Mark Twain's Letters from Hawaii*, ed. A. Grove Day (New York: Appleton-Century, 1966); and *Clemens of the Call: Mark Twain in San Francisco*, ed. Edgar M. Branch (Berkeley: University of California Press, 1969). An excellent online source of Twain's contributions to newspapers is a site operated by Barb Schmidt (http://www.twainquotes.com) that directs readers to full text versions of pieces by (and about) Twain in the *Virginia City Territorial Enterprise*, the *San Francisco Daily Morning Call*, the *Sacramento Daily Union*, the *Daily Hawaiian Herald*, the *San Francisco Alta California*, the *Galaxy*, the *New York Times*, and other publications. Twain's published and unpublished short pieces attacking imperialism have been elegantly collected by Jim Zwick in *Mark Twain's Weapons of Satire: Anti-Imperialist Writings on the Philippine-American War* (Syracuse, N.Y.: Syracuse University Press, 1995).

The key collections of Mark Twain's speeches (in addition to the 1910 volume reproduced in the *Oxford Mark Twain*) are *Mark Twain's Speeches*, ed. A. B. Paine (New York: Harper Brothers, 1923) and *Mark Twain Speaking*, ed. Paul Fatout (Iowa City: University of Iowa Press, 1976).

Collections of Twain's letters, beyond those published by the Mark Twain Project, include *Mark Twain's Letters*, ed. Albert Bigelow Paine, 2 vols. (New York: Harper, 1910); *Mark Twain's Letters from the Sandwich Islands*, ed. G. Ezra Dane (Palo Alto, Calif.: Stanford University Press, 1937); *Mark Twain's Travels with Mr. Brown*, ed. Franklin Walker and G. Ezra Dane (New York: Knopf, 1940); *The Love Letters of Mark Twain*, ed. Dixon Wecter (New York: Harper, 1949); *Mark Twain to Mrs. Fairbanks*, ed. Dixon Wecter (San Marino, Calif.: Huntington Library, 1949); *Mark Twain-Howells Letters: The Correspondence of Samuel L. Clemens and William D. Howells, 1872–1910*, ed. Henry Nash Smith and William M. Gibson (Cambridge, Mass.: Harvard University Press, 1960); and *Mark Twain's Aquarium: The Samuel Clemens Angelfish Correspondence, 1905–1910*, ed. John Cooley (Athens: University of Georgia Press, 1991). The Mark Twain Project has also published catalogs of letters which Clemens wrote and received (*The Union Catalog of Clemens Letters*, edited by Paul Machlis. Printed text and microfiche supplement, 1986; *Union Catalog of Letters to Clemens*, edited by Paul Machlis, with the assistance of Deborah Ann Turner. Printed text and microfiche supplement, 1992). Both are searchable in an online database created by the Mark Twain Project (http://library.berkeley.edu/BANC/MTP/database/).

With the exception of the portions he published in the *North American Review*, Mark Twain left most of his dictated autobiography in unsequenced, unpublished fragments at his death. The key editions of it that have appeared to date are *Mark Twain's Autobiography*, ed. Albert Bigelow Paine (New York: Harper & Brothers, 1924); *Mark Twain in Eruption: Hitherto Unpublished Pages about Men and Events*, ed. Bernard DeVoto (New York: Capricorn Books, 1940); *The Autobiography of Mark Twain*, ed. Charles Neider (New York: Harper, 1959); *and Mark Twain's Own Autobiography: The Chapters from the North American Review*, ed. Michael Kiskis (Madison: University of Wisconsin Press, 1990). As his thesis project in American Studies at the University of Virginia, Hal L. Waller charted these different versions of Twain's life in hypertext, allowing readers to compare the various editors' decisions and also to view the material in the order of composition. Until the Mark Twain Project publishes the authoritative version of Twain's autobiographical dictations, readers will need to rely on the incomplete, edited autobiographies that have appeared in print. Hal Waller's website (http://xroads.virginia.edu/~MA98/waller/TwainAuto_Site/) helps make it easier to access and interpret that material.

The main bibliography for identifying Mark Twain's first editions remains Merle Johnson's *A Bibliography of the Works of Mark Twain: A List of First Editions in Book Form and of First Printings in Periodicals and Occasional Publications* (New York: Harper & Brothers, 1935). For translations and international editions of Twain's works, the essential source is Robert M. Rodney's *Mark Twain International: A Bibliography and Interpretation of His Worldwide Populartity* (Westport, Conn.: Greenwood Press, 1982). Sources useful for identifying quotes by Mark Twain are R. Kent Rasmussen's *The Quotable Mark Twain: His Essential Aphorisms, Witicisms and Concise Opinions* (Chicago: Contemporary Books, 1998); Brian Collins's, *When In Doubt, Tell The Truth: And Other Quotations From Mark Twain* (New York: Columbia University Press, 1996); and Caroline Thomas Harnsberger's *Mark Twain at Your Fingertips* (New York: Beechhurst Press, 1948). Engaging and often inspired popular collections of primary material by Mark Twain appear frequently, focused on a particular theme—such as Mark Dawidziak's *Mark My Words: Mark Twain on Writing* (New York: St. Martin's Press, 1996), R. Kent Rasmussen's *Mark Twain's Book for Bad Boys and Girls* (Chicago: Contemporary Publishers, 1995), and Howard G. Baetzhold and Joseph B. McCullough, eds. *The Bible According to Mark Twain: Writings on Heaven, Eden, and the Flood* (Athens: University of Georgia Press, 1995).

GENERAL REFERENCE WORKS AND BIBLIOGRAPHIES OF CRITICISM

An excellent starting place for scholars and general readers interested in Mark Twain is R. Kent Rasmussen's magisterial *Mark*

Twain A to Z: The Essential Reference to His Life and Writings (New York: Oxford University Press, 1996). Also very helpful is *The Mark Twain Encyclopedia*, ed. J. R. LeMaster and James D. Wilson (New York: Garland, 1993). Alan Gribben's *Mark Twain's Library: A Reconstruction*, 2 vols. (Boston: G.K. Hall, 1980) is indispensable for researching Twain's reading habits. Other useful reference books are *A Reader's Guide to the Short Stories of Mark Twain* by James D. Wilson (Boston: G.K. Hall, 1987), *The New Mark Twain Handbook* by E. Hudson Long and J. R. LeMaster (New York: Garland, 1985), and *Mark Twain: A Descriptive Guide to Biographical Sources* by Jason Gary Horn (Lanham, Md.: Scarecrow Press, 1999).

Thomas Asa Tenney's *Mark Twain: A Reference Guide* (Boston: G.K. Hall, 1977) will direct readers to the most important Twain criticism published before 1977, and the annual supplements from 1977–1983 of the journal *American Literary Realism* pick up where Tenney leaves off, as do periodic bibliographic listings in the *Mark Twain Circular*, the publication of the Mark Twain Circle of America. Readers interested in gauging the state of Twain criticism any given year should consult the annual *American Literary Scholarship* (Durham, N.C.: Duke University Press, 1963 to the present).

COLLECTIONS OF ESSAYS

Anderson, Frederick, and Kenneth M. Sanderson, eds. *Mark Twain: The Critical Heritage*. London: Routledge and Kegan Paul, 1971.

Bloom, Harold, ed. *Mark Twain*. New York: Chelsea House, 1986.

Budd, Louis J. *Mark Twain: The Contemporary Reviews*. Cambridge: Cambridge University Press, 1999.

———, ed. *Critical Essays on Mark Twain, 1867–1910*. Boston: G.K. Hall, 1982.

———, ed. *Critical Essays on Mark Twain, 1910–1980*. Boston: G.K. Hall, 1983.

———, ed. *New Essays on "Adventures of Huckleberry Finn."* Cambridge: Cambridge University Press, 1985.

———, and Edwin H. Cady, eds. *On Mark Twain: The Best from American Literature*. Durham: Duke University Press, 1987.

Champion, Laurie, ed. *The Critical Response to Mark Twain's "Huckleberry Finn."* Westport, Conn.: Greenwood Press, 1991.

Davis, Sara deSaussure, and Philip D. Beidler, eds. *The Mythologizing of Mark Twain.* Tuscaloosa: University of Alabama Press, 1984.

Gillman, Susan, and Forrest G. Robinson. *Mark Twain's "Pudd'nhead Wilson": Race, Conflict, and Culture.* Durham, N.C.: Duke University Press, 1990.

Hutchinson, Stuart, ed. *Mark Twain: Critical Assessments.* 4 vols. Robertsbridge, East Sussex, UK: Helm Information Ltd., 1993.

Inge, M. Thomas, ed. *Huck Finn Among the Critics: A Centennial Selection.* Frederick, Md.: University Publications of America, 1985.

Leonard, James S., ed. *Making Mark Twain Work in the Classroom.* Durham, N.C.: Duke University Press, 1999.

Leonard, James S., Thomas A. Tenney, and Thadious M. Davis. *Satire or Evasion? Black Perspectives on "Huckleberry Finn."* Durham, N.C.: Duke University Press, 1991.

Robinson, Forrest, ed. *The Cambridge Companion to Mark Twain.* Cambridge: Cambridge University Press, 1995.

Sattelmeyer, Robert, and J. Donald Crowley. *One Hundred Years of "Huckleberry Finn": The Boy, His Book and American Culture.* Columbia: University of Missouri Press, 1985.

Scharnhorst, Gary, ed. *Critical Essays on The Adventures of Tom Sawyer.* New York: G.K. Hall, 1993.

Simpson, Claude M., ed. *Twentieth Century Interpretations of Adventures of Huckleberry Finn: A Collection Of Critical Essays.* Englewood Cliffs, N.J.: Prentice-Hall, 1968.

Sloane, David E.E., ed. *Mark Twain's Humor: Critical Essays.* New York: Garland, 1993.

Smith, Henry Nash, ed. *Mark Twain: A Collection of Critical Essays.* Englewood Cliffs, N.J.: Prentice-Hall, 1963.

Sundquist, Eric J., ed. *Mark Twain: A Collection of Critical Essays.* Englewood Cliffs, N.J.: Prentice-Hall, 1994.

BIOGRAPHICAL AND CRITICAL SECONDARY WORKS

Andrews, Kenneth R. *Nook Farm: Mark Twain's Hartford Circle.* Cambridge, Mass.: Harvard University Press, 1950.

Baetzhold, Howard G. *Mark Twain and John Bull: The British Connection.* Bloomington: Indiana University Press, 1970.

Beaver, Harold. *Huckleberry Finn.* London: Unwin Hyman, 1988.

Berret, Anthony J. *Mark Twain and Shakespeare: A Cultural Legacy.* Lanham, Md.: University Press of America, 1993.

Blair, Walter. *Mark Twain & Huck Finn.* Berkeley: University of California Press, 1960.

Branch, Edgar. *The Literary Apprenticeship of Mark Twain.* Iowa City: University Press of Iowa, 1950.

Bridgman, Richard. *Traveling in Mark Twain.* Berkeley: University of California Press, 1987.

Budd, Louis J. *Mark Twain, Social Philosopher.* Bloomington: Indiana University Press, 1962.

———. *Our Mark Twain: The Making of His Public Personality.* Philadelphia: University of Pennsylvania Press, 1983.

Camfield, Gregg. *Sentimental Twain: Samuel Clemens in the Maze of Moral Philosophy.* Philadelphia: University of Pennsylvania Press, 1994.

Cardwell, Guy. *The Man Who Was Mark Twain: Images and Ideologies.* New Haven: Yale University Press, 1991.

———. *Twins of Genius.* East Lansing: Michigan State College Press, 1953.

Chadwick-Joshua, Jocelyn. *The Jim Dilemma: Reading Race in Huckleberry Finn.* Jackson: University Press of Mississippi, 1998.

Clemens, Clara. *My Father Mark Twain.* New York: Harper & Bros., 1931.

Clemens, Susy. *Papa: An Intimate Biography of Mark Twain,* ed. Charles Neider. Garden City, N.Y.: Doubleday, 1985.

Covici, Pascal Jr. *Humor and Revolution in American Literature: The Puritan Connection.* Columbia: University of Missouri Press, 1997.

———. *Mark Twain's Humor: The Image of a World.* Dallas: Southern Methodist University Press, 1962.

Cox, James M. *Mark Twain: The Fate of Humor.* Princeton, N.J.: Princeton University Press, 1966.

Cummings, Sherwood. *Mark Twain and Science: Adventures of a Mind.* Baton Rouge: Louisiana State University Press, 1988.

David, Beverly R. *Mark Twain and His Illustrators, vol. 1 (1869–1875).* Troy, N.Y.: Whitson, 1986.

DeVoto, Bernard. *Mark Twain's America.* Boston: Little, Brown, 1932.

———. *Mark Twain at Work.* Cambridge, Mass.: Harvard University Press, 1942.

Dolmetsch, Carl. *"Our Famous Guest": Mark Twain in Vienna.* Athens: University of Georgia Press, 1992.

Doyno, Victor A. *Writing "Huck Finn": Mark Twain's Creative Process.* Philadelphia: University of Pennsylvania Press, 1992.

Duckett, Margaret. *Mark Twain and Bret Harte.* Norman: University of Oklahoma Press, 1964.

Eble, Kenneth E. *Old Clemens and W.D.H.: The Story of a Remarkable Friendship.* Baton Rouge: Louisiana State University Press, 1985.

Ellison, Ralph. *Shadow and Act.* New York: Random House, 1953.

Ensor, Allison. *Mark Twain and the Bible.* Lexington: University of Kentucky Press, 1969.

Emerson, Everett. *Mark Twain: A Literary Life.* Philadelphia: University of Pennsylvania Press, 1999.

Fatout, Paul. *Mark Twain on the Lecture Circuit.* Bloomington: University of Indiana Press, 1960.

———. *Mark Twain in Virginia City.* Bloomington: Indiana University Press, 1964.

Fishkin, Shelley Fisher. *From Fact to Fiction: Journalism and Imaginative Writing in America.* Baltimore: Johns Hopkins University Press, 1985 (Oxford University Press, 1987).

———. *Lighting Out for the Territory: Reflections on Mark Twain and American Culture.* New York: Oxford University Press, 1997.

———. *Was Huck Black? Mark Twain and African-American Voices.* New York: Oxford University Press, 1993.

Florence, Don. *Persona and Humor in Mark Twain's Early Writings.* Columbia: University of Missouri Press, 1995.

Foner, Philip S. *Mark Twain Social Critic.* New York: International Publishers, 1958.

French, Bryant Morey. *Mark Twain and "The Gilded Age": The Book That Named an Era.* Dallas: Southern Methodist University Press, 1965.

Fulton, Joe B. *Mark Twain's Ethical Realism: The Aesthetics of Race, Class, and Gender.* Columbia: University of Missouri Press, 1997.

Ganzel, Dewey. *Mark Twain Abroad: The Cruise of the "Quaker City."* Chicago, Ill.: University of Chicago Press, 1968.

Geismar, Maxwell. *Mark Twain: An American Prophet.* New York: Houghton Mifflin, 1970.

Gerber, John C. *Mark Twain*. New York: Twayne, 1988.

Gibson, William M. *The Art of Mark Twain*. New York: Oxford University Press, 1976.

Gillman, Susan. *Dark Twins: Imposture and Identity in Mark Twain's America*. Chicago, Ill.: University of Chicago Press, 1989.

Gribben, Alan, Nick Karanovich et al., eds. *Overland with Mark Twain: James B. Pond's Photographs and Journal of the North American Lecture Tour of 1895*. Elmira, N.Y.: Center for Mark Twain Studies at Quarry Farm; Elmira College, 1992.

Griffith, Clark. *Achilles and the Tortoise: Mark Twain's Fictions*. Tuscaloosa: University of Alabama Press, 1998.

Harris, Susan K. *The Courtship of Olivia Langdon and Mark Twain*. Cambridge: Cambridge University Press, 1996.

———. *Mark Twain's Escape From Time: A Study Of Patterns And Images*. Columbia: University of Missouri Press, 1982.

Hays, John Q. *Mark Twain and Religion: A Mirror of American Eclecticism*. New York: Peter Lang, 1989.

Hill, Hamlin. *Mark Twain and Elisha Bliss*. Columbia: University of Missouri Press, 1964.

———. *Mark Twain/God's Fool*. New York: Harper & Row, 1973.

Hoffman, Andrew. *Inventing Mark Twain: The Lives of Samuel Langhorne Clemens*. New York: William Morrow, 1997.

Horn, Jason Gary. *Mark Twain and William James: Crafting a Free Self*. Columbia: University of Missouri Press, 1996.

Howe, Lawrence. *Mark Twain and the Novel: The Double-Cross of Authority*. Cambridge: Cambridge University Press, 1998.

Howells, William Dean. *My Mark Twain: Reminiscences and Criticisms*. New York: Harper & Brothers, 1910.

Janows, Jill. Executive Producer. *Born to Trouble: Adventures of Huckleberry Finn*. [Television documentary] Boston: WGBH, 2000.

Jerome, Robert D., and Herbert A. Wisbey, eds. *Mark Twain in Elmira*. Elmira, N.Y.: Mark Twain Society, 1977.

Kahn, Sholom J. *Mark Twain's Mysterious Stranger: A Study of the Manuscript Texts*. Columbia: University of Missouri Press, 1978.

Kaplan, Justin. *Mr. Clemens and Mark Twain*. New York: Simon & Schuster, 1966.

Knoper, Randall. *Acting Naturally: Mark Twain in the Culture of Performance*. Berkeley and Los Angeles: University of California Press, 1995.

Krause, Sydney. *Mark Twain as Critic*. Baltimore, Md.: Johns Hopkins University Press, 1967.

Krauth, Leland. *Proper Mark Twain*. Athens: University of Georgia Press, 1999.

Kruse, Horst H. *Mark Twain and "Life on the Mississippi."* Amherst: University of Massachusetts Press, 1981.

Ladd, Barbara. *Nationalism and the Color Line in George Cable, Mark Twain, and William Faulkner*. Baton Rouge: Louisiana State University Press, 1996.

Lauber, John. *The Making of Mark Twain: A Biography*. New York: Noonday Press/Farrar, Straus & Giroux, 1985.

———. *The Inventions of Mark Twain*. New York: Hill & Wang, 1990.

Lawton, Mary. *A Lifetime with Mark Twain: The Memories of Katy Leary, for Thirty Years His Faithful and Devoted Servant*. New York: Harcourt, Brace & Co., 1925.

Leon, Philip W. *Mark Twain and West Point*. Toronto, Ont.: ECW Press, 1996.

Lorch, Fred W. *The Trouble Begins at Eight*. Mark Twain's Lecture Tours. Ames: Iowa State University Press, 1968.

Lowry, Richard S. *"Littery Man": Mark Twain and Modern Authorship*. New York: Oxford University Press, 1996.

Lynn, Kenneth S. *Mark Twain and Southwestern Humor*. Boston, Mass.: Little, Brown, 1959.

Macnaughton, William R. *Mark Twain's Last Years as a Writer*. Columbia: University of Missouri Press, 1979.

McWilliams, Jim, ed. *Mark Twain in the St. Louis Post-Dispatch, 1874–1891* (Troy, N.Y. : Whitston, 1997).

Marotti, Maria Ornella. *The Duplicating Imagination: Twain and the Twain Papers*. University Park: Pennsylvania State University Press, 1990.

Marx, Leo. *The Machine in the Garden*. New York: Oxford University Press, 1964.

———. *The Pilot and the Passenger*. New York: Oxford University Press, 1988.

Meltzer, Milton. *Mark Twain Himself*. New York: Thomas Y. Crowell, 1960.

Mensh, Elaine, and Harry Mensh. *Black, White, and Huckleberry Finn: Re-Imagining the American Dream*. Tuscaloosa: University of Alabama Press, 2000.

Messent, Peter B. *Mark Twain.* Houndmills, Basingstoke, Hampshire (Eng.): Macmillan, 1997.

———. *New Readings of the American Novel: Narrative Theory and Its Application.* Houndmills, Basingstoke, Hampshire (Eng.): Macmillan, 1990.

———. *The Short Works of Mark Twain: A Critical Study.* Phildelphia: University of Pennsylvania Press, 2001.

Michelson, Bruce. *Mark Twain on the Loose: A Comic Writer and the American Self.* Amherst: University of Massachusetts Press, 1995.

Miller, Robert Keith. *Mark Twain.* New York: F. Ungar, 1983.

Moreland, Kim Ileen. *The Medievalist Impulse in American Literature: Twain, Adams, Fitzgerald, and Hemingway.* Charlottesville: University Press of Virginia, 1996.

Norton, Charles A. *Writing Tom Sawyer: The Adventures of a Classic.* Jefferson, N.C.: MacFarland, 1983.

Obenzinger, Hilton. *American Palestine: Melville, Twain, and the Holy Land Mania.* Princeton, N.J.: Princeton University Press, 1999.

Paine, Albert Bigelow. *Mark Twain: A Biography: The Personal and Literary Life of Samuel Langhorne Clemens.* 4 vols. New York: Harper & Brothers, 1912.

Pettit, Arthur G. *Mark Twain and the South.* Lexington: University of Kentucky Press, 1974.

Powers, Ron. *Dangerous Water: A Biography of the Man Who Became Mark Twain.* New York: Basic Books, 1999.

Quick, Dorothy. *Enchantment: A Little Girl's Friendship with Mark Twain.* Norman: University of Oklahoma Press, 1961.

Quirk, Tom. *Coming to Grips with Huckleberry Finn.* Columbia: University of Missouri Press, 1993.

———. *Mark Twain: A Study of the Short Fiction.* New York: Twayne Publishers. London: Prentice-Hall International, 1997.

Robinson, Forrest G. *In Bad Faith: The Dynamics of Deception in Mark Twain's America.* Cambridge, Mass.: Harvard University Press, 1986.

Rodney, Robert M. *Mark Twain Overseas: A Biographical Account of His Voyages, Travels, and Reception in Foreign Lands, 1866–1910.* Washington, D.C.: Three Continents Press, 1993.

Rowe, John Carlos. *Literary Culture and U.S. Imperialism.* New York: Oxford University Press, 2000.

Sanborn, Margaret. *Mark Twain: The Bachelor Years.* New York: Doubleday, 1990.

Sanderlin, George. *Mark Twain as Others Saw Him.* New York: Coward, McCann & Geoghegan, 1978.

Sewell, David R. *Mark Twain's Languages: Discourse, Dialogue and Linguistic Variety.* Berkeley: University of California Press, 1987.

Shillingsburg, Miriam Jones. *At Home Abroad: Mark Twain in Australasia.* Jackson: University Press of Mississippi, 1988.

Skandera-Trombley, Laura. *Mark Twain in the Company of Women.* Philadelphia: University of Pennsylvania Press, 1994.

Sloane, David E. E. *Adventures of Huckleberry Finn: American Comic Vision.* Boston: Twayne Publishers, 1988.

———. *Mark Twain as a Literary Comedian.* Baton Rouge: Louisiana State University Press, 1979.

Smith, Henry Nash. *Mark Twain: The Development of a Writer.* Cambridge, Mass.: Harvard University Press, 1962.

———. *Mark Twain's Fable of Progress: Political and Economic Ideas in "A Connecticut Yankee."* New Brunswick, N.J.: Rutgers University Press, 1964.

Stahl, H. D. *Mark Twain, Culture and Gender: Envisioning America through Europe.* Athens: University of Georgia Press, 1994.

Steinbrink, Jeffrey. *Getting to Be Mark Twain.* Berkeley: University of California Press, 1991.

Stone, Albert E., Jr. *The Innocent Eye: Childhood in Mark Twain's Imagination.* New Haven, Conn.: Yale University Press, 1961.

Stoneley, Peter Nicholas. *Mark Twain and the Feminine Aesthetic.* Cambridge: Cambridge University Press, 1992.

Strong, Leah. *Joseph Hopkins Twichell: Mark Twain's Friend and Pastor.* Athens: University of Georgia Press, 1966.

Sumida, Stephen H. *And the View from the Shore: Literary Traditions of Hawai'i.* Seattle: University of Washington Press, 1991.

Sundquist, Eric J. *To Wake the Nations: Race in the Making of American Literature.* Cambridge, Mass.: Belknap Press of Harvard University Press, 1993.

Tanner, Tony. *The Reign of Wonder: Naivete and Reality in American Literature.* Cambridge: Cambridge University Press, 1965.

Taper, Bernard. *Mark Twain's San Francisco.* New York: McGraw-Hill, 1963.

Tuckey, John S. *Mark Twain and Little Satan: The Writing of "The Mys-*

terious Stranger." West Lafayette, Ind.: Purdue University Press, 1963.

Vaidhanathan, Siva. *Copyrights and Copywrongs: The Rise of Intellectual Property and How It Stifles Creativity.* New York: New York University Press, 2001.

Webster, Samuel Charles. *Mark Twain, Business Man.* Boston, Mass.: Little, Brown, 1946.

Wecter, Dixon. *Sam Clemens of Hannibal.* Boston, Mass.: Houghton Mifflin, 1952.

Welland, Dennis. *Mark Twain in England.* London: Chatto & Windus, 1978.

———. *The Life and Times of Mark Twain.* New York: Crescent Books, 1991.

Wieck, Carl F. *Refiguring Huckleberry Finn.* Athens: University of Georgia Press, 2000.

Willis, Resa. *Mark and Livy: The Love Story of Mark Twain and the Woman Who Almost Tamed Him.* New York: Atheneum, 1992.

Wilson, James D. *A Reader's Guide to the Short Stories of Mark Twain.* Boston: G. K. Hall, 1987.

Wonham, Henry B. *Mark Twain and the Art of the Tall Tale.* New York: Oxford University Press, 1993.

HISTORICAL CONTEXTS

Bederman, Gail. *Manliness and Civilization: Gender and Race in the United States, 1880–1917.* Chicago: University of Chicago Press, 1995.

Blight, David. *Race and Reunion: The Civil War in American Memory.* Cambridge, Mass.: Harvard University Press, 2001.

Blumin, Stuart. *The Emergence of the Middle Class: Social Experience in the American City, 1760–1900.* Cambridge: Cambridge University Press, 1989.

Bruchey, Stuart. *Enterprise: The Dynamic Economy of a Free People.* Cambridge: Harvard University Press, 1990.

Burke, Martin. *The Conundrum of Class: Public Discourse on the Social Order in America.* Chicago, Ill.: University of Chicago Press, 1995.

Bush, Harold K., Jr. *American Declarations: Rebellion and Repentance in American Cultural History.* Urbana: University of Illinois Press, 1999.

Carter, Paul. *The Spiritual Crisis of the Gilded Age.* DeKalb: Northern Illinois University Press, 1971.

Crunden, Robert M. *A Brief History of American Culture.* Armonk, N.Y.: Paragon Books/M.E. Sharpe, 1996.

D'Emilio, John, and Estelle B. Freedman. *Intimate Matters: A History of Sexuality in America.* New York: Harper & Row, 1988.

Douglas, Ann. *The Feminization of American Culture.* New York: Knopf, 1977.

Elliott, Emory et al., eds. *The Columbia Literary History of the United States.* New York: Columbia University Press, 1988.

Erenberg, Lewis. *Steppin' Out: New York Nightlife and the Transformation of American Culture, 1890–1930.* Westport, Conn.: Greenwood Press, 1981.

Foner, Philp S., and Richard C. Winchester, eds. *The Anti-Imperialist Reader: A Documentary History of Anti-Imperialism in the United States, vol. 1, From the Mexican War to the Election of 1900.* New York: Holmes & Meier, 1984.

Franchot, Jenny. *Roads to Rome: The Antebellum Protestant Encounter with Catholicism.* Berkeley: University of California Press, 1994.

Franklin, John Hope. *Race and History: Selected Essays, 1938–1988.* Baton Rouge: Louisiana State University Press, 1989.

Fredrickson, George. *The Black Image in the White Mind: The Debate on Afro-American Character and Destiny, 1817–1914.* Middletown, Conn.: Wesleyan University Press, 1971.

———. *White Supremacy: A Comparative Study in American and South African History.* New York: Oxford University Press, 1981.

Glenn, Myra C. *Thomas K. Beecher: Minister to a Changing America, 1824–1900.* Westport, Conn.: Greenwood Press, 1996.

Gossett, Thomas. *Race: The History of an Idea in America.* 2nd ed. New York: Oxford University Press, 1997.

Gould, Stephen Jay. *The Mismeasure of Man.* New York: W.W. Norton, 1996.

Greene, Lorenzo J., Gary R. Kremer, and Antonio F. Holland. *Mis-*

souri's Black Heritage. Rev. ed. Columbia: University of Missouri Press, 1980.

Hagood, J. Hurley, and Roberta Hagood. *Hannibal, Too: Historical Sketches of Hannibal and Its Neighbor*. Marceline, Mo.: Walworth, 1986.

Hall, Donald, ed. *Muscular Christianity: Embodying the Victorian Age*. New York: Cambridge University Press, 1994.

Halttunen, Karen. *Confidence Men and Painted Women: A Study of Middle-Class Culture in America, 1830–1870*. New Haven, Conn.: Yale University Press, 1982.

Hilkey, Judy. *Character Is Capital: Success Manuals and Manhood in Gilded Age America*. Chapel Hill: University of North Carolina Press, 1997.

Hochchild, Adam. *King Leopold's Ghost*. Boston: Houghton Mifflin, 1998.

Holcombe, R. I. *History of Marion County Missouri 1884*. Reprint, Marion County Historical Society, Hannibal, Mo., 1979.

Hunter, James Davison. *American Evangelicalism: Conservative Religion and the Quandary of Modernity*. New Brunswick, N.J.: Rutgers University Press, 1983.

Jones, Gavin Roger. *Strange Talk: The Politics of Dialect Literature in Gilded Age America*. Berkeley, Calif.: University of California Press, 1999.

Keita, Maghan. *Race and the Writing of History: Riddling the Sphinx*. New York: Oxford University Press, 2000.

Kerr, Howard. *Mediums, Spirit-Rappers, and Roaring Radicals: Spiritualism in American Literature, 1850–1900*. Urbana: University of Illinois Press, 1972.

Kete, Mary Louise. *Sentimental Collaborations: Mourning and Middle-Class Identity in Nineteenth-Century America*. Durham, N.C.: Duke University Press, 1999.

Kimmel, Michael. *Manhood in America: A Cultural History*. New York: Free Press, 1996.

Klinkner, Philip A., and Rogers Smith. *The Unsteady March: The Rise and Decline of Racial Equality in America*. Chicago: University of Chicago Press, 1999.

Laurie, Bruce. *Artisans into Workers: Labor in Nineteenth-Century America*. Urbana: University of Illinois Press, 1989.

Levine, Lawrence. *Highbrow/Lowbrow: The Emergence of Cultural Hi-*

erarchy in America. Cambridge, Mass.: Harvard University Press, 1988.

Licht, Walter. *Industrializing America.* Baltimore, Md.: Johns Hopkins University Press, 1995.

Logan, Rayford W. *The Betrayal of the Negro from Rutherford B. Hayes to Woodrow Wilson.* [1965] Intro. by Eric Foner. New York: Da Capo Press, 1997.

Lott, Eric. *Love and Theft: Blackface Minstrelsy and the American Working Class.* New York: Oxford University Press, 1993.

Luker, Ralph E. *The Social Gospel in Black and White: American Racial Reform, 1885–1912.* Chapel Hill: University of North Carolina Press, 1991.

Magdoff, Harry. *Imperialism: From the Colonial Age to the Present.* New York: Monthly Review Press, 1978.

Marty, Martin. *The Infidel: Freethought and American Religion.* Cleveland, Ohio: World, 1961.

Montgomery, David. *The Fall of the House of Labor: The Workplace, the State and American Labor Activism, 1865–1925.* Cambridge: Cambridge University Press, 1989.

Noll, Mark. *The Scandal of the Evangelical Mind.* Grand Rapids, Mich.: Eerdmans, 1994.

O'Connor, Leo F. *Religion in the American Novel: The Search for Belief, 1860–1920.* Lanham, Md.: University Press of America, 1984.

Rotundo, E. Anthony. *American Manhood: Transformations in Masculinity from the Revolution to the Modern Era.* New York: Basic Books, 1993.

Showalter, Elaine. *Speaking of Gender.* New York : Routledge, 1989.

Smith-Rosenberg, Carroll. *Disorderly Conduct: Visions of Gender in Victorian America.* New York: Oxford University Press, 1985.

Sokolow, Jayme A. *Eros and Modernization: Sylvester Graham, Health Reform, and the Origins of Victorian Sexuality in America.* Rutherford, N.J.: Fairleigh Dickinson University Press, 1983.

Szasz, Ferene Morton. *The Divided Mind of Protestant America, 1880–1930.* Tuscaloosa: University of Alabama Press, 1982.

Tompkins, E. Berkeley. *Ani-Imperialism in the United States: The Great Debate, 1890–1920.* Philadelphia: University of Pennsylvania Press, 1970.

Trachtenberg, Alan. *The Incorporation of America: Culture and Society in the Gilded Age.* New York: Hill and Wang, 1982.

Trexler, Harrison Anthony. *Slavery in Missouri, 1804–1865*. Baltimore: Johns Hopkins University Press, 1914.

Ward, Andrew. *Dark Midnight When I Rise: The Story of the Jubilee Singers Who Introduced the World to the Music of Black America*. New York: Farrar, Straus and Giroux, 2000.

Weir, Robert. *Beyond Labor's Veil: The Culture of the Knights of Labor*. University Park: Pennsylvania State University Press, 1996.

Wyatt-Brown, Bertram. *Southern Honor: Ethics and Behavior in the Old South*. New York: Oxford University Press, 1982.

CONTRIBUTORS

HAROLD K. BUSH, JR. teaches American literature and culture at Saint Louis University in Saint Louis, Missouri. His book, *American Declarations: Rebellion and Repentence in American Cultural History*, was published by the University of Illinois Press in 1999. Currently he is working on a volume titled *Mark Twain's Pastor*, which will historicize Twain's involvement in nineteenth-century American Christianity, and in particular his long friendship with Joe Twichell, and will publish for the first time Twichell's compelling correspondence with Twain.

GREGG CAMFIELD is currently writing *The Oxford Reader's Companion to Mark Twain* and is helping to edit Twain's dispatches from Hawaii for the Mark Twain Project's complete edition of Mark Twain's works. He has published *Sentimental Twain: Samuel Clemens in the Maze of Moral Philosophy* (University of Pennsylvania Press, 1994) and *Necessary Madness: The Humor of Domesticity in Nineteenth-Century American Literature* (Oxford University Press, 1997). He is a professor of American literature at the University of the Pacific.

SHELLEY FISHER FISHKIN is the author of the award-winning books *Was Huck Black? Mark Twain and African-American Voices*

(Oxford University Press, 1993) and *From Fact to Fiction: Journalism and Imaginative Writing in America* (Johns Hopkins University Press, 1985). Her most recent book is *Lighting Out for the Territory: Reflections on Mark Twain and American Culture* (Oxford University Press, 1997). A professor of American studies and English and Chair of the Department of American Studies at the University of Texas at Austin, she is the editor of the twenty-nine-volume *Oxford Mark Twain* (Oxford University Press, 1996), past president of the Mark Twain Circle of America, and co-editor of the *Encyclopedia of Civil Rights in America* (M.E. Sharpe, 1997), *People of the Book: Thirty Scholars Reflect on Their Jewish Identity* (University of Wisconsin Press, 1996), *Listening to Silences: New Essays in Feminist Criticism* (Oxford University Press, 1994), and Oxford's "Race and American Culture" book series. She has served on the editorial board of *American Quarterly* and on advisory boards for *The Oxford Reader's Companion to Mark Twain* and Ken Burns's "Mark Twain."

SUSAN K. HARRIS is professor of American literature at Penn State University. She is the author of *Annie Adams Fields, Mary Gladstone Drew, and the Work of the Late 19th-Century Hostess* (Palgrave/St. Martin's, 2002), *The Courtship of Olivia Langdon and Mark Twain* (Cambridge University Press, 1996), *19th-Century American Women's Novels: Interpretive Strategies* (Cambridge University Press, 1990), and *Mark Twain's Escape from Time: A Study of Patterns and Images* (University of Missouri Press, 1982). She has edited Mark Twain's *Adventures of Huckleberry Finn* (Houghton Mifflin, 2000), Harriet Beecher Stowe's *The Minister's Wooing* (Penguin, 1999), and *Mark Twain: Historical Romances* (Library of America, 1994). Her essays have appeared in collections published by Oxford, Johns Hopkins, and Rutgers University presses and in journals such as *American Literature*, *New England Quarterly*, and *Studies in the Novel*. She has edited *Legacy: A Journal of American Women's Writing* and has served on advisory boards for *Leviathan: The Melville Society Journal*, *The Oxford Reader's Companion to Mark Twain*, and the Mark Twain Museum in Hannibal, Missouri.

FORREST G. ROBINSON is professor of American studies at the University of California, Santa Cruz. His writings on Mark

Twain include *In Bad Faith: The Dynamics of Deception in Mark Twain's America* (Harvard University Press, 1986), and two edited volumes, *The Cambridge Companion to Mark Twain* (Cambridge University Press, 1995) and (with Susan Gillman) *Mark Twain's Puddn'head Wilson: Race, Conflict, and Culture* (Duke University Press, 1990). He is presently at work on a biographical study of his favorite American humorist.

ROBERT WEIR is the author of *Beyond Labor's Veil: The Culture of the Knights of Labor* (Penn State University Press, 1996), *Knights Unhorsed: Internal Conflict in a Gilded Age Social Movement* (Wayne State University Press, 2000), and numerous articles and reviews for *Labor History*. He has a Ph.D. in ninenteenth-century social and labor history from the University of Massachusetts, Amherst. An associate professor of liberal studies at Bay Path College, Longmeadow, Massachusetts, he is currently a Senior Fulbright Research Fellow in New Zealand.

JIM ZWICK is the editor of *Mark Twain's Weapons of Satire: Anti-Imperialist Writings on the Philippine-American War* (Syracuse University Press, 1992) and has published numerous articles about the Anti-Imperialist League and Mark Twain's anti-imperialist writings. He is also the creator of the *Mark Twain, Anti-Imperialism in the United States, 1898-1935*, and other sites at BoondocksNet.com.

Index